# Rethinking
# Shiloh

# Rethinking Shiloh

## Myth and Memory

Timothy B. Smith

The University of Tennessee Press / Knoxville

First Edition.

The paper in this book meets the requirements of American National Standards Institute / National Information Standards Organization specification Z39.48-1992 (Permanence of Paper). It contains 30 percent post-consumer waste and is certified by the Forest Stewardship Council.

Library of Congress Cataloging-in-Publication Data

Smith, Timothy B., 1974–
Rethinking Shiloh: myth and memory / Timothy B. Smith. — 1st ed.
p. cm.
Includes bibliographical references and index.
ISBN 978-1-57233-941-5 (alk. paper) — ISBN 1-57233-941-1 (alk. paper)
1. Shiloh, Battle of, Tenn., 1862.
2. Shiloh, Battle of, Tenn., 1862—Historiography.
3. Shiloh National Military Park (Tenn. and Miss.)—History.
I. Title.

E473.54.S63 2013
973.7'31—dc23
2012032039

*To*

*Bennie and Barbara*

# Contents

# Illustrations

## Figures



## Maps

# Preface

Ulysses S. Grant was no doubt in a nostalgic mood as he wrote about his wartime experiences late in life, but he was more than brutally honest when he remarked that the Battle of Shiloh "has been perhaps less understood, or, to state the case more accurately, more persistently misunderstood, than any other engagement . . . during the entire rebellion." The former general and president kept abreast of his treatment in the most current literature and thus reacted in the 1880s to several emerging historical trends regarding Shiloh, some of which put Grant in a less-than-stellar light. There is more than a tinge of reprisal in his words regarding how the history of the battle had been distorted by some, perhaps purposefully, and his warning is illustrative if nothing else of the need to examine myth, memory, and historiography as it concerns Shiloh. But another potential area of concern not enumerated by Grant, except perhaps in his description of the battle being "less understood," is how much of the story has never been told.[1]

Given the almost monthly treatment of Gettysburg, it is incredible that, to date, there have been only four major, modern, academic volumes published on Shiloh. And three of those were written in the 1960s and 1970s. Obviously, as good as those four books are—and each has its own strengths—there are still major portions of the story that have never been told or fully analyzed. In an effort to close some of those gaps, I wrote about several less-than-fully treated topics in a collection of essays, most of them previously published, titled *The Untold Story of Shiloh*. In that volume, I looked at several neglected topics, such as the battle's historiography, several myths that have grown since the battle, the navy's role in the campaign, and the attending action near Corinth after the battle, as well as several postbattle topics such as the creation of the Shiloh National Cemetery and biographical essays about figures crucial to Shiloh's preservation and memory. After publication, however, I continued to write articles on other neglected topics, the sum of which has resulted in this second volume, *Rethinking Shiloh*.[2]

Although this second effort differs in many ways from the previous book, it nevertheless is tied to the first volume. The first book contained an essay examining ten of the greatest myths about Shiloh. After completing that somewhat generic essay, I began to look deeper at several of those myths and to write full articles on many of them, and they appear herein. Thus, while somewhat akin to the first book, this second volume differs in its scope and theme. While the first volume carried the subtitle *The Battle and the Battlefield* and examined general aspects of the history of the engagement at Shiloh and the resulting commemoration and preservation, the present volume, carrying the subtitle *Myth and Memory,* aims to delve further into the story of Shiloh and examine in detail how the battle has been treated in historiography and public opinion. Thus many of the articles analyze myth, as generated in the essay on myths in the first volume, and a corresponding examination of why that myth gained traction and became so prevalent.

As a manner of introduction, the first essay, "'Difficult and Broken Ground': The Terrain Factor at Shiloh," delves into the untold story by examining what I have come to believe is the foremost factor that determined why the battle turned out the way it did. Leadership, weaponry, ability, and many other factors all had an impact at Shiloh, but the single greatest advantage the North had in winning the battle was terrain. Originally published in the *Tennessee Historical Quarterly* in 2011, this essay provides an overview of the action during the battle with an emphasis on how the lay of the land influenced the fighting.[3]

One of the articles that resulted from the earlier myths article deals with Albert Sidney Johnston's actions at Shiloh. "To Conquer or Perish: The Last Hours of Albert Sidney Johnston" was originally published in volume 3 of *Confederate Generals in the Western Theater* (University of Tennessee Press, 2011). This piece examines several myths surrounding Johnston's death, including the death site, its effect, and his state of mind.[4]

The third essay, "Anatomy of an Icon: Shiloh's Hornet's Nest in Civil War Memory," delves into the memory of the battle. Appearing in Steve Woodworth's edited volume *The Shiloh Campaign* (2009), this article examines the Hornet's Nest both in the actual combat on the first day of battle and in the postwar historiographical and memory realms. I argue that the Hornet's Nest is overemphasized in popular memory due to the claims of the battle's veterans, which in itself is not unexpected. No doubt every man on the field thought the action he was involved in was the most important at Shiloh. But in comparison to the historic record, the icon that is the Hornet's Nest is inflated.[5]

The fourth essay is a case in point, and continues to reflect the expansion of the original myth analysis found in the first volume. "A Case Study in Civil War Memory: Benjamin M. Prentiss as the Hero of Shiloh" looks at Prentiss's role in building the Hornet's Nest's popularity. Although initially published in a much abbreviated form in *Civil War Times* in 2008, along with some purposefully added controversial editorial statements comparing Prentiss with false Vietnam veterans, this larger essay seeks to examine Prentiss's role in creating the collective memory of Shiloh and particularly the Hornet's Nest.[6]

One of the more persistent myths of Shiloh is that Lew Wallace was lost. To analyze the true story, I set out to find and travel Wallace's actual route. "Rewriting History: Locating Lew Wallace's Route of March to Shiloh," which also appeared in abbreviated form in *Civil War Times* in 2008, examines his march, his route, and his mindset using modern technology and research. Wallace, as I explain in the essay, knew where he was going and got there pretty fast, which will hopefully do away with the myth and some of the criticism leveled at him.[7]

The sixth article, "Secession at Shiloh: Mississippi's Convention Delegates and Their State's Defense," is a short piece that originally appeared for Shiloh's 150th anniversary in 2012 in the Civil War Trust's magazine *Hallowed Ground*. Taking a somewhat different view of Shiloh, this article examines the members of the Mississippi secession convention who fought there. Couched in the context of Shiloh being those members' first real effort to defend their state, the realization emerges that those who signed the ordinance of secession, in some cases, were literally signing their death warrants, and Shiloh was a significant episode in that process.[8]

The seventh essay seeks to correct some of the myths of the civilian ownership of the Shiloh battlefield and the hatred of a government that supposedly took the land to make it a park. In "The Forgotten Inhabitants of Shiloh: A Case Study in a Civilian-Government Relationship," which appeared in the *Tennessee Historical Quarterly* in 2008, I seek to explain the local inhabitants' important role in the story of Shiloh.[9]

In "A Case Study in Change: The New Deal's Effect on Shiloh National Military Park," I examine some of the changes that came to Shiloh during the major reconstruction era of the New Deal. Much of what we see today at the park dates back to the government's response to the Great Depression, including the concrete roads, the visitor center, and even some of the aesthetic attributes such as rock walls and trails. Published in the *Tennessee Historical Quarterly* in 2007, this essay points to the fact that the battlefield (and the story) has gone through a lot of change over the years, and it is almost as necessary to understand the postwar change as it is to understand the original events when studying Shiloh.[10]

The final essay is a case in point about understanding the changing nature of Shiloh's battlefield, historiography, and memory. There has been no greater influence regarding Shiloh on the general public than the park's introductory film, *Shiloh: Portrait of a Battle.* In "History in the Making: *Shiloh: Portrait of a Battle* Fifty Years Later," which appeared also in the *Tennessee Historical Quarterly* in 2006, I seek to explain how influential the film has been in swaying popular opinion toward the importance of the Hornet's Nest. The fact that the film ran for more than fifty-five years is testament to the fact that it has introduced literally millions of people to the battle. In an almost bittersweet change, the venerable old film was finally retired on the 150th anniversary of the battle in 2012, fifty-six years exactly after its first showing.[11]

These nine essays, most working off the earlier examination of myth, each add in some way or another to our understanding of the historiographical and popular memory of Shiloh. I am convinced that we cannot truly understand Shiloh or any other battle, no matter how many facts we know, unless we understand the postbattle historiography and memory developments that affect how we view the engagement. It is hoped that these essays will shed more light on the battle after the battle and will broaden our thinking about the aspects that are still part of the untold story of Shiloh.

* * *

Numerous people have aided me in the research and publication of the various essays and this book. The editors of the books and journals in which they originally appeared were kind, enthusiastic, and professional. Steve Woodworth, Larry Hewitt, and the late Art Bergeron edited books in which two of the essays appeared. Dana Shoaf and Chris Howland at *Civil War Times,* Mary Koik at *Hallowed Ground,* and Van West, Kris Ray, and Ann Toplovich at the *Tennessee Historical Quarterly* shepherded the articles in those journals and magazines.

Several friends read these essays, including John F. Marszalek, who read them all. Gail Stephens, Lew Wallace's biographer, read the Wallace essay. Jeff Gentsch read the terrain piece. The various readers for the different journals also added helpful suggestions, as did James Lee McDonough and Gary R. Matthews, who read the manuscript for the University of Tennessee Press.

My family, as always, has been a constant source of help and encouragement, including my wife, Kelly, and my girls, Mary Kate and Leah Grace. My parents, George and Miriam Smith, continue to be unequaled supporters. I have dedicated this book to my in-laws, Bennie and Barbara Castleman, who are totally supportive as well. God has richly blessed me, and I am thankful to be part of such a wonderful family.

Timothy B. Smith
Adamsville, Tennessee

# 1

# "Difficult and Broken Ground": The Terrain Factor at Shiloh

Braxton Bragg was unnerved, to say the least, about fighting a battle on ground that he did not know well. As the Confederate army moved northward in early April 1862 to attack the Federals near Shiloh Church and Pittsburg Landing, Tennessee, "the commanders of divisions and brigades were assembled at night, the order of battle was read to them, and the topography of the enemy's position was explained, as far as understood by us," Bragg remembered. That hint of doubt about the lack of knowledge of Shiloh's terrain was more than verified during the battle. Bragg filled his postbattle report of Shiloh with statements about the effect terrain had had on the Confederate effort. The front line, he wrote, was "necessarily broken by the nature of the ground." He also included such phrases as "in the broken country occupied by us" and "in moving over the difficult and broken ground," the latter case resulting in a whole brigade losing contact with the main line. Back in Corinth later in April, Bragg summed up the battle in his report, saying, "Such was the nature of the ground over which we had fought, and the heavy resistance we had met, that the commands of the whole army were very much shattered." Obviously, the enemy's resistance will always be a major part of battles, but to Bragg, the terrain at Shiloh was a major factor as well.[1]

To be sure, the environment plays a significant role in shaping military events, but other factors, such as weaponry, leadership, timing, and political, economic, and social aspects, can help us understand those events on a deeper level. And in some cases, terrain played less of a role than would be expected. At Champion Hill, for instance, the Confederates held a strong position atop high ground yet still took a thumping at the hands of Ulysses S. Grant. Thus environmental history is only one aspect that needs explanation in order to understand military history. And even the field of environmental history casts a wide net. It can include the obvious terrain study or the lay of the land, which was so important at Shiloh. But it also includes other factors, such as weather (precipitation and temperature), river stages, vegetation, soil composition and ground conditions, sound travel, and even human cultural developments. Thus a wide-ranging effort is needed to explain and understand any particular event such as a Civil War battle. But while all aspects of military, social, political, economic, and environmental history played themselves out in the calamity that was Shiloh, one of the most dominant variables was the terrain on the battlefield. At Shiloh, terrain was the key feature among many others that turned the tide toward Union victory on the Tennessee. Examining the natural and manmade terrain at Shiloh in an exercise in the subfield of landscape history can offer many clues about how the battle was fought and why commanders did what they did. It can also help us understand more fully not only the parameters and significance of the battle but also that it is quite possible the Confederates never actually had a chance to win at Shiloh.[2]

Braxton Bragg certainly understood that Shiloh's terrain had more to do with how that battle was fought, who won, and who lost than any other factor. Yet simply saying Shiloh's terrain affected the outcome of the battle is inadequate. Most Shiloh enthusiasts can reel off the fact that the Confederate plan was to turn the Union left flank and that the large ravines in that area caused the battle to be fought in an exactly opposite fashion. While true, there is much more to the battlefield's terrain than just those ravines, and that terrain had much more of an impact than that one set of ravines. Shiloh's terrain contained numerous layers, both natural and manmade, that had a tremendous impact on both how the battle was fought and the outcome. When examined separately as individual items and then as layers constructed atop one another comprehensively, the idea emerges that the physical framework on which the Battle of Shiloh was fought had enormous implications on the outcome.

Civil War historiography has been severely lacking in the field of terrain studies, perhaps better labeled geographic or landscape history. In fact, most Civil War publications dealing with battlefield terrain have been in the form of maps. Numerous published atlases attest to the desire of readers and scholars alike to learn more about mapping and to view events as they unfolded on paper. Unfortunately, the primary emphasis of recent atlases has been to convey troop movements rather than to study the actual ground. To be sure, extremely large and detailed maps are necessary, but because of cost they do not lend themselves well to publication in books. As a result, there are few such maps today and readers generally have to go back to the veterans' work of the 1890s and early 1900s for large, terrain-rich maps. Veterans were keenly aware of the need to study (and preserve) the ground at battlefields and thus produced a large number of very good maps, generally of the fold-out type. Fortunately, there has been some recent modern success in this field with the series of battlefield maps produced by Trailhead Graphics Company in

Colorado. In addition, there have been a few environmental/geographical–based studies, such as Warren Grabau's *Ninety-Eight Days: A Geographer's View of the Vicksburg Campaign* (2000) and John Keegan's *Military Geography of the American Civil War* (1997). A very useful recent publication, *Civil War Weather in Virginia* (2007) by Robert Krick, deals with that aspect of the war in Virginia. But as a general rule, what gains that have been made in this geographical field are small and in great need of expansion.[3]

It is perhaps not surprising, then, that so little attention has been given to Shiloh's terrain. Historians writing on the battle have attempted to describe the area, but providing a detailed analysis of the battleground has not been a major emphasis of these books. Each of the four major writers on the battle, Edward Cunningham, Wiley Sword, James Lee McDonough, and Larry Daniel, spent about one page on the terrain features as an introduction to the battle, although they also covered more of the specifics in detailing the battle's ebb and flow. Even the foremost Shiloh historian, David W. Reed, spent less than a page on terrain description, although he and early park engineer Atwell Thompson collaborated to create several large, highly valuable, and accurate terrain maps of the field. The only major study of Shiloh's terrain and geography, and how it affected the battle, is a too-little-known master's thesis by Jeff Gentsch. Thus a firm knowledge of Shiloh's terrain is essential to understanding, and advancing, our collective knowledge of the cataclysmic events that took place on the banks of the Tennessee River in April 1862.[4]

## The Terrain

By far, the dominant terrain feature at Shiloh was the Tennessee River. Flowing south to north through Hardin County, Tennessee, the river was a major transportation route for West Tennessee in peacetime and a major avenue of invasion during wartime. A primarily Unionist area early in the war, Hardin County nevertheless saw the wrath of conflict as the Federal Army of the Tennessee used the river as a highway to invade deep into the Confederate heartland after the impressive victories at Forts Henry and Donelson in February 1862. By mid-March, thousands of Federal troops were encamped around Savannah and several landings to the south, including Crump's, Hagy's, Brown's, and, particularly, Pittsburg Landing. The Federals all came south on the river, and although encamped and thus somewhat idle, they used the river as their lifeline for supply, transportation, and communication.[5]

Consequently, the Tennessee River played a vital role in the battle. At some three to four hundred yards wide, the river was far too broad to ford in the rainy springtime, but it became much smaller during the dry summer months. Although wider today because of the work of the Tennessee Valley Authority and its dams, the river was nevertheless a major terrain feature that caused problems for anyone without a boat. As such, it formed the wide and impassable eastern boundary of the Shiloh battlefield.[6]

Although the river was the entire reason the Federals were even in Hardin County, and although it formed the eastern boundary of the battlefield, lesser water systems flowing into the river actually played a far greater role in shaping the battle and the battlefield. These lesser streams can be further divided into primary and secondary creeks that literally transected the battlefield and shaped the fighting in major ways.[7]

Two primary watercourses flowed into the Tennessee River and set the basic parameters of the battlefield itself. Snake Creek flowed into the Tennes-

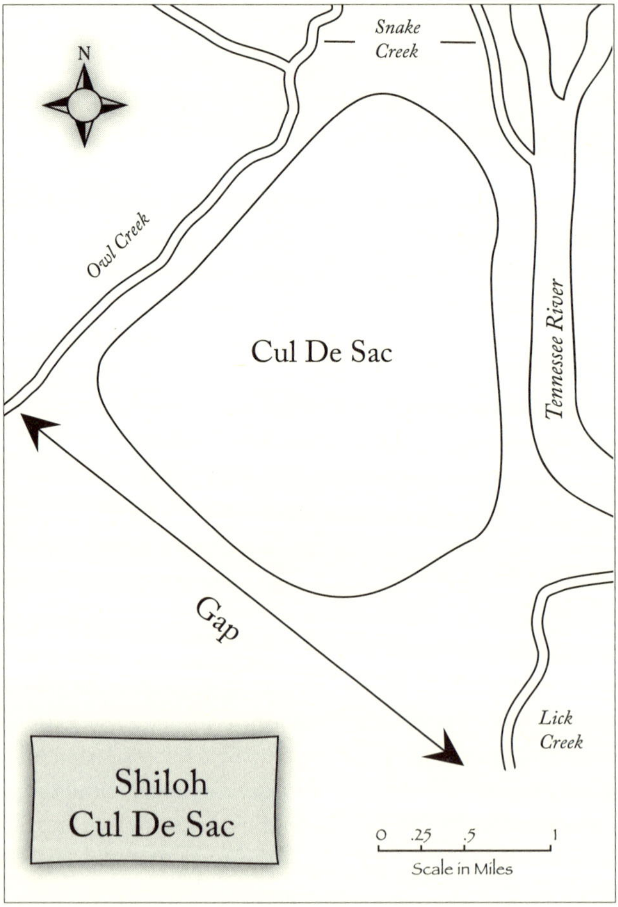

see River about half a mile north of Pittsburg Landing. This major waterway was wide and deep, with steep banks for much of its path contiguous with the battlefield. Especially in the wet spring, the creek was a major impediment and could only be crossed at bridges, and sometimes not even there. The creek had its headwaters far to the northwest but flowed into the Shiloh area in a southwest-to-northeast fashion at the very northern end of the battlefield before making a wide loop and then running relatively southward, parallel with the river, before flowing into the Tennessee between Pittsburg Landing and Diamond Island.[8]

While Snake Creek thus formed the northern and northeastern boundaries of the battlefield, another primary creek that flowed into Snake Creek actually had more of an effect on the boundaries of the battlefield. Owl Creek had its headwaters southwest of Pittsburg Landing and flowed in a meandering southwest-to-northeast direction until it met Snake Creek coming in from the northwest. Owl Creek was also a substantial stream that could not be forded just anywhere. Although smaller than Snake Creek due to its being farther up the watershed from the river, Owl Creek was still a major terrain factor and thus required bridging to cross. Particularly in the wet winter and spring, when the flooded river backed up into the creeks, these two primary watersheds effectively formed the northern and western boundaries of the Shiloh battlefield.[9]

Forming the southeastern boundary was Lick Creek, which flowed into the Tennessee River about two miles south of Pittsburg Landing. This deep and wide creek had its headwaters south of the battlefield and, like Owl Creek, generally flowed from southwest to northeast. Like the other major creeks that could be overflowed by a backup of river water at high stages, Lick Creek could not easily be forded and had to be bridged.[10]

Thus with the Tennessee River and Snake, Owl, and Lick creeks, the basic parameters of the Shiloh battlefield were laid out. What emerged was a cul-de-sac of high ground tucked into the narrow gap between the parallel-flowing Owl and Lick creeks, with the Tennessee River and Snake Creek capping the cul-de-sac at the north and east. The areas immediately surrounding the creeks and many parts of the river were very low and thus swampy, muddy, and overgrown with briars and trees. Little agriculture or habitation could be performed there, so most of these areas were left to grow wild. The habitation, as well as the fighting, took place mostly on the high ground inside the cul-de-sac.[11]

With the exception of three bridges across the creeks, there was only one way by land into the cul-de-sac and one way out, particularly during high water. In times of highest water, even some of those bridges were impassable, making the gap between Owl and Lick creeks the only consistent and efficient way to enter the area. Ulysses S. Grant himself spoke of the creeks being "very high at the time, and contribut[ing] to protect our flanks." Understanding the layout of the various watersheds also makes Albert Sidney Johnston's prebattle rhetoric make sense. Most Shiloh connoisseurs are familiar with his famous words: "I would fight them if they were a million." Lesser known are the words that immediately followed. Johnston further remarked, "They can present no greater front between these two creeks [Owl and Lick] than we can; and the more men they crowd in there, the worse we can make it for them."[12]

The high ground inside the cul-de-sac has been illustrated in many ways, with most participants and historians describing it as a triangle. Taking that description, it is best to look at the triangle with the base being the gap of land between Lick and Owl creeks. One side of the triangle is formed by Lick Creek and the Tennessee River, while the other is formed by Owl and Snake creeks. The apex of the triangle is the great loop of Snake Creek, near where it empties into the river. As Johnston realized, the only sure way in and out of the triangle for large numbers of troops was at the base, in the gap between Owl and Lick creeks. The only other ways were by boat on the river or the three bridges across the three creeks, one on each. Neither boat nor bridge, however, offered a quick and feasible entry or exit for large numbers of troops under battle conditions. Thus Johnston and his Confederates hoped to plug the gap at the base of the triangle and trap the enemy army between them and the overflowed river and creeks, ultimately driving the enemy northwest, away from the river (and any reinforcements) and into the swamps of Owl and Snake creeks.[13]

By no means, however, were the river and the three primary creeks the only water courses on the Shiloh battlefield. In fact, a series of secondary creeks, running mostly into the primary creeks and then into the river itself, actually had more of an effect on how the battle was fought than the primary creeks or the river. If the Tennessee River and Snake, Owl, and Lick creeks defined the parameters of the battlefield, these secondary creeks, with their marshy bottoms soiled by recent heavy rains, defined *how* the battle was fought.[14]

Two sets of roughly parallel creeks flowed on each side of the battlefield. On the western side, Shiloh and Tilghman branches ran basically parallel to each other a mile and a half apart, flowing southeast to northwest into Owl Creek from headwaters on the high ground in the center of the battlefield. In an almost mirror image on the eastern side, two more watercourses, Dill and

Locust Grove branches, also ran parallel, at the same distance, from headwaters in the center of the battlefield, but this time running west to east and emptying into Lick Creek and the Tennessee River. The headwaters of each pair of creeks lay near each other, but the creeks flowed away from each other in opposite directions. The rise of so many watersheds within the center of the battlefield is attributable to the many natural springs that appear in the area.[15]

The southernmost set of creeks, Shiloh Branch and Locust Grove Branch, each had their headwaters on the high ground at the extreme southern end of

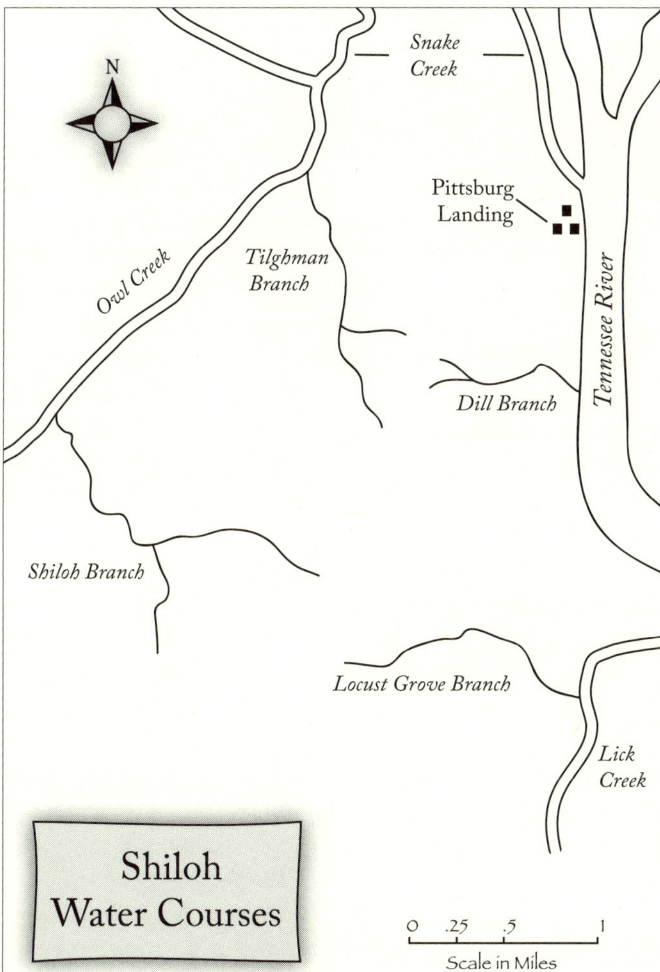

While the Tennessee River and the larger Owl, Snake, and Lick creeks formed the parameters of the battlefield of Shiloh, the smaller creeks that drained the area actually had more of an impact on the tactical fighting. Here is a view of the Shiloh Branch watershed, looking from the Confederate position as denoted by the early park troop position tablets. The Confederates had to cross this low land and attack the Federal line on the ridge in the distance. (Courtesy of Shiloh National Military Park.)

the battlefield. General Don Carlos Buell, in fact, remarked that these headwaters were "interlocking." Each flowed in opposite directions from that high ground, with Locust Grove running almost due east into Lick Creek. Shiloh Branch actually began as several branches, which ran together as they flowed basically northwestward into Owl Creek. As a result, the base of the triangle was almost totally covered across its east-west width with watersheds; the only gap between the creeks was the high ground between the contiguous headwaters. Thus it was behind (north of) these two creeks that the Federals formed their southernmost camps, situated on the ridgeline to the north. Of course, when the battle began and units began taking their initial positions, they were in the perfect position to repel attacks—on high ground overlooking muddy and tangled creek bottoms through which the enemy had to assault. Moreover, such a deployment immediately fostered a line of battle along almost the entire width of the gap.[16]

Roughly a mile and a half to the north, the second set of secondary creeks had similar headwaters on the high ground in the center of the battlefield and also flowed in opposite directions. Tilghman, the larger of the two, had several tributaries but became substantial the farther it ran northwestward toward its confluence with Owl Creek. Dill Branch was smaller but had a deeper ravine, flowing as it did due eastward through the high bluffs along the Tennessee River, into which it emptied less than half a mile south of Pittsburg Landing. It was behind these northernmost secondary watersheds that the tired and bloodied Federal units retired and formed their last line of defense late in the first day's action. Like the southernmost set of creeks, Tilghman and Dill branches provided great protection for the Union infantry and artillery on the high ground overlooking them almost all the way across the triangle, forcing the enemy to move through the swampy and steep ravines. In between each set of creeks, of course, were other, smaller feeder branches, the most notable being those that ran into the Tennessee River through the semilarge ravines on the eastern side of the battlefield, the same broken area that hindered the Confederate attempt to turn the Union left flank.[17]

The lay of the land thus created a slope on each side of the battlefield, falling off toward the major watersheds to the east and west. In the center of the battlefield lay what one geographer and historian has termed an "interfluvial" ridge, something similar to a continental divide but much smaller. Ulysses S. Grant himself remarked on "the ridge which divided the waters of Snake and Lick creeks." This "Shiloh divide" ran from the center of the triangle base northeast to Pittsburg Landing. It was within the hollows of this Shiloh divide that natural springs fostered the headwaters of Shiloh, Tilghman, Locust Grove, and Dill branches, with the headwaters sitting on each creek's respective side of the divide. This divide varied in width as it ran southwest to northeast, depending on the tributaries of the various secondary creeks, but it generally grew wider as it left the headwaters of Shiloh and Locust Grove branches and the higher elevations of the south end of the battlefield at the base of the triangle. It became much wider as it reached the center of the battlefield but then constricted again as the headwaters of Dill and Tilghman branches ate away at the tableland. After constricting through those headwaters, the divide widened again somewhat before ending on the bluffs near Pittsburg Landing overlooking the Tennessee River and Snake Creek; General Buell described the ridge coming up "boldly to the river at the landing." It formed the steep bluffs overlooking the landing and the initial stretches of Snake Creek. Buell remarked that Tilghman and Dill branches "divide[d] the table-land into two main ridges." Thus the Shiloh divide took somewhat of an hourglass form as it moved from southwest to northeast, with the northern half of the glass much smaller than the southern half. It was on this southern half that the majority of the Battle of Shiloh raged.[18]

Shiloh, Locust Grove, Tilghman, and Dill branches, running as they did perpendicular to the advancing attackers, were major obstacles through which the Confederate army had to pass just to attack the Federals on the high ground on the north side of each. While none of them was so large that they could not be forded, they were nevertheless boggy, swampy, and choked with underbrush, which delayed and disfigured the Confederate line of battle even before it encountered Union resistance. In addition, some banks were very steep, with Confederate general P. G. T. Beauregard describing them as "deep, with abrupt sides." The Federals definitely used these secondary creeks to their advantage. The battle tended to widen and become more

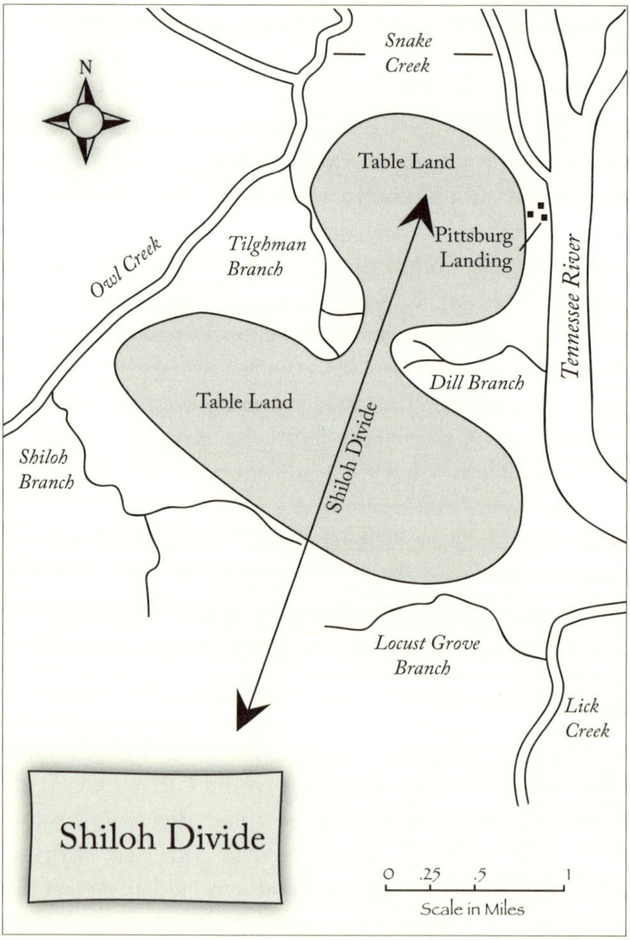

even handed, however, on the wider tableland of the divide in the center of the battlefield. That is where the famous areas such as the Crossroads, Hornet's Nest, and Peach Orchard stood. Even there, however, along the Shiloh divide itself, numerous small feeder branches of these major streams created numerous hollows, ravines, and undulations that were used by both attacker and defender. Grant stated that "the ground on which the battle was fought was undulating," while Buell described it as "undulating table-land, quite broken in places, elevated a hundred feet or thereabout above the river."[19]

Although setting the boundaries of the battlefield and in most ways even determining how the battle was fought, these watersheds and divides were by no means the only terrain features on the Shiloh battlefield. The terrain's cover had a major impact on operations. The vast majority of the battlefield was covered with timber, most of it hard wood, such as oak, hickory, elm, poplar, sweetgum, and dogwood. There were patches of undergrowth in creek bottoms and elsewhere, with some of the tableland's undergrowth cleared by the roaming animals let loose by the inhabitants in an open range policy. Ulysses S. Grant described the battlefield as "heavily timbered, with scattered clearings, the woods giving some protection to the troops on both sides. There was also considerable underbrush."[20]

The most notable manmade layers which affected the battle were the roads, which formed a confusing system of connecting thoroughfares ranging from major roads to trails through small farms. These proved very important for defense, movement, and communication during the battle.[21]

There were five major roads in the area, although none were modernized or macadamized. By far, the most important was the Corinth Road, which ran from Pittsburg Landing on the river basically southwestward to Corinth, Mississippi, some twenty-two miles distant. This road meandered out on the Shiloh divide to the wide tableland in the center of the battlefield but then took a westerly jog and crossed some of the branches of Shiloh Branch on the south end of the battlefield. The road itself crossed two of the major channels of the creek, which required bridges for wheeled vehicles, although the creek could be crossed on foot.[22]

Most likely because the path of the main Corinth Road led across the branches of Shiloh Branch, which could be boggy and wet in the winter and spring, an alternative thoroughfare developed farther to the east. Known as the Eastern Corinth Road, this alternative left the main Corinth Road (sometimes referred to as the Western Corinth Road) in the wide tableland between the two pairs of secondary creeks and continued up the Shiloh divide, passing over the tableland between the headwaters of Shiloh and Locust Grove

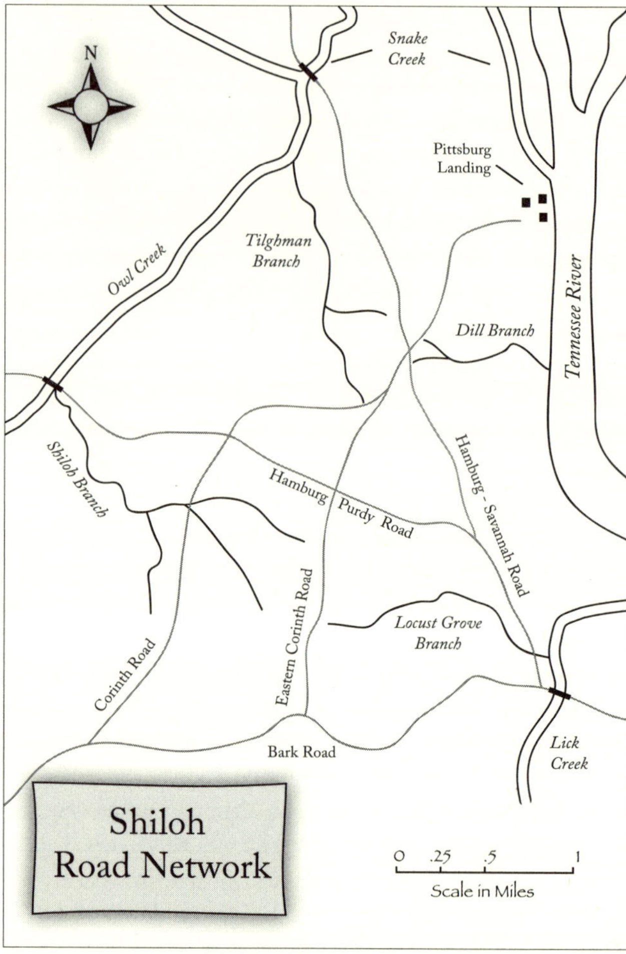


branches. After reaching the high ground south of those creeks, the Eastern Corinth Road joined the Bark Road, which led to the main Corinth Road once it emerged from the defiles of Shiloh Branch.[23]

The Bark Road was not a major factor in the battle, although there was some movement on it during the conflict. It ran basically east and west along the elevated base line of the triangle, south of Locust Grove and Shiloh branches. Buell described these hills as "two hundred feet or more in height, and sloping gradually toward the battle-field." As a result, the Bark Road was outside the Federal camping and defense area, and it was mainly used by the Confederates to position and reposition troops.[24]

Another primarily north and south major road was the Hamburg-Savannah Road, also known as the River Road. This thoroughfare ran from Hamburg, which was four miles south of Pittsburg Landing on the Tennessee River, to a crossing of Lick Creek. Here apparently was found a bridge across the creek. After meeting the Bark Road just west of Lick Creek, the River Road continued across Locust Grove Branch and then up the slope to the high ground of the Shiloh battlefield. From there, it ran northward across the eastern portion of the battlefield tableland, crossing the Corinth Road in the process atop the Shiloh divide between Tilghman and Dill branches. It eventually ran off the high ground and crossed Snake Creek on a bridge at the extreme north end of the battlefield. From there, it ran to Crump's Landing and Savannah.[25]

The only major east-west road on the battlefield proper was the Hamburg-Purdy Road, which left the River Road, once it topped the high ground, and ran westward crossing both the Eastern and main Corinth roads. On the western edge of the battlefield the road ran down the slope into the valley of Owl Creek, which it crossed on a bridge, and continued to Purdy.[26]

Other, smaller roads had an impact on the battle as well, such as the famous Sunken Road, which was primarily a localized farm path. These roads provided ample opportunity, especially the outgoing roads from Pittsburg Landing, for the Federals to send out reinforcements to beleaguered frontline divisions. They also made front to rear communication possible, although the existence of only one major east-west road made lateral communication more difficult.[27]

Despite the myth that the Federals were totally unprepared for assault, frontline Union division commanders did have each of these roads covered. There were four avenues of entrance to the Federal camping area, not counting the Snake Creek bridge where the River Road crossed; that route was presumably covered by a Union division at Pittsburg Landing as well as a detached division at Crump's Landing, along with high water, it being far down the watershed of Snake Creek. Confederates could approach the Union camps via the Hamburg-Purdy Road across Owl Creek, along the main Corinth Road across Shiloh Branch, down the Eastern Corinth Road along the Shiloh divide, or on the River Road across Lick Creek. William T. Sherman's division covered three of those crossings. One brigade sat atop the high ground at the Owl Creek bridge, two brigades straddled the main Corinth Road on the high ground north of Shiloh Branch, and one brigade camped on the road on the high ground north of the Lick Creek bridge. Another division, commanded by Benjamin Prentiss, straddled the Eastern Corinth Road. Thus strong Federal units sat at the entrance of all four major roads into the Federal campsite, all of them on high ground ready to deploy. With so few entrances to such a large area, no wonder William T. Sherman stated the tableland "admits of easy defense by a small command, and yet affords admirable camping ground for a hundred thousand men."[28]

Other human creations sat interspersed throughout the battlefield along this intricate road system. White Americans and their few slaves had begun to move into the area in the 1830s and 1840s and began clearing fields and setting up homesteads. By the time of the battle, around forty fields existed, most small in nature and growing everything from cotton to corn. As the Federal army squatted on the land in mid-March, however, there was little planting taking place, and what was planted was soon tramped underfoot by the training Union soldiers. There are numerous recorded instances during the battle when Federal officers placed their line so that the enemy would have to cross an open field, thus allowing the defenders a greater field of fire and a warning of incoming threats. In fact, fields played a major role in the Union defense of the central tableland, where no watercourses provided aid. The Hornet's Nest, Peach Orchard, and operations around the Crossroads and Jones Field were all affected more by open fields to allow better firing zones and reorganization areas than by watersheds.[29]

Within those fields, of course, there were normally cabins and other outbuildings, such as barns, henhouses, smokehouses, outhouses, fences, and well houses. The typical family lived in a crude log cabin, steady enough buildings, but they rarely stood the effects of battle. Many of these structures saw action as a cover for advancing or defending units.[30]

Interspersed among these homesteads and fields were other manmade creations, such as cemeteries, churches, orchards, and stores. The most famous church was the Shiloh Church, which sat on the Corinth Road just north of Shiloh Branch, but there were others in the area as well. A store sat for years at Pittsburg Landing itself, which was named for the operator, Pitts Tucker. Many farmers in the area had orchards, which were in bloom at the time of the battle. Likewise, many families had their own cemeteries located near their homes, while the largest was the church cemetery at Shiloh Church. All these manmade terrain objects also became caught up in the battle.[31]

One important manmade terrain feature that was not found at Shiloh, however, was earthworks. Those that still exist today were created during or after the battle. Despite orders to entrench the position, Federal commanders chose not to do so, spending their time and effort on drilling and training instead of digging. As a result, there were no earthworks to secure the Federal campsite.[32]

## The Battle

Within such a physical framework, the Battle of Shiloh developed along logical lines on the first day, melding to the major terrain features within the heart of the fighting area. Three distinct phases of fighting on that first day were linked to those three major terrain features. The first phase was tied to the southernmost pair of watersheds, Shiloh and Locust Grove branches. The second phase occurred on the wide tableland devoid of watercourses. The third, in the continual progression of northeastward movement, was tied to the second set of watercourses, Tilghman and Dill branches. In all three phases, the Federals on the defense used the terrain to their advantage, and what Southern success there was came when the attacking Confederates used terrain features as well.

The initial contact in the Battle of Shiloh, at Fraley Field where a skittish Federal brigade commander's early morning patrol located and skirmished with the Confederate army, took place well south of the Federal encampment, nearly a mile south of Shiloh Church. There were no Union encampments that far out. The nearest Federal camps were primarily back on the ridges north of Shiloh Branch and continuing eastward onto the Shiloh divide and out onto the ridge north of Locust Grove Branch. When the patrol maneuvering south of the creeks engaged the enemy and alerted the Federal camps, those camping units immediately formed a line of battle, most of them on the high ground in front (south) of their camps but north of the creeks. Thus they were in a strong position looking out over the valleys below, through which any attacking Confederate force had to advance. One Confederate described the enemy army in retrospect as "flanked by Owl and Lick creeks, with their marshy margins, and with his front protected by a swampy valley."[33]

The first major fighting came as the Confederate left engaged Sherman's division near Shiloh Church. As the Confederate right was somewhat south rather than east due to forming the army perpendicular to the Corinth Road, which at that point led northeast rather than north, the left engaged before the right did, causing the action to gradually pick up as the Confederate line of battle conformed to the southward-facing Federal lines arrayed along the ridges north of the creeks. By 8:00 a.m., the Confederate right had made contact as well, with Prentiss on the Eastern Corinth Road.[34]

The Confederates found it very difficult to cross Shiloh Branch. The creeks, bogs, and undergrowth effectively stalled their advance, with the morass of Shiloh Branch south of the church literally splitting the brigade commanded by Confederate general Patrick Cleburne. The general described "an almost impassable morass, jutting out from the foot of the height on which

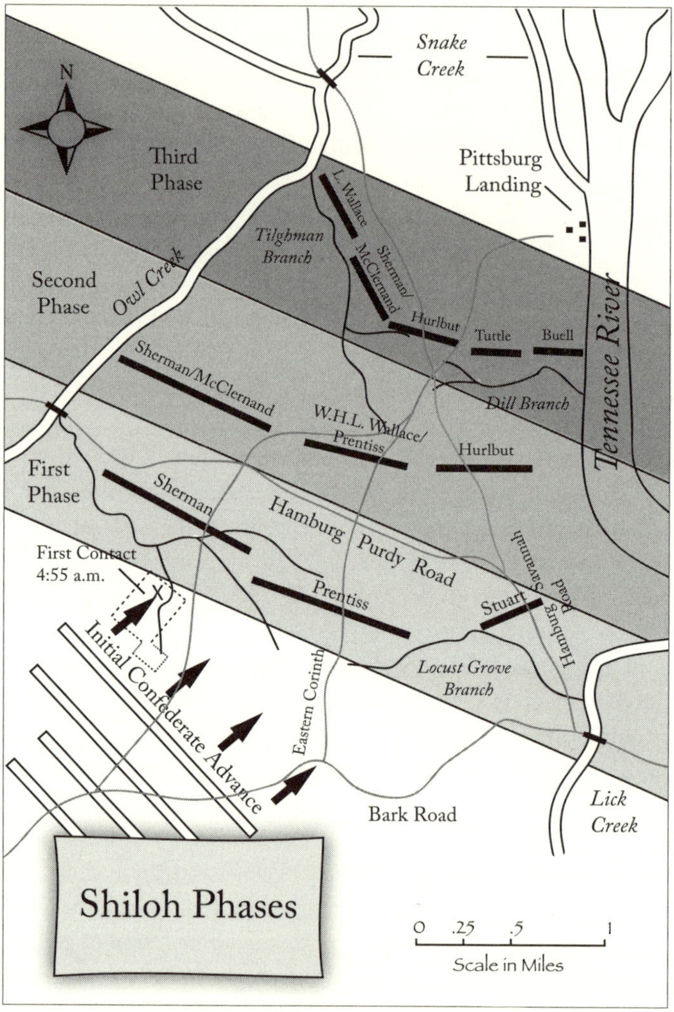


the enemy's tents stood." Add Union small arms and artillery fire, and the valley of Shiloh Branch became very deadly, especially as Confederate brigade after brigade stacked up behind the frontline units who could not dislodge Sherman from his commanding position atop the ridge. In fact, Sherman's lines overlooking Shiloh Branch were never taken by frontal assault. They were that strong.[35]

The Confederate success in the first phase came where the terrain aided their advance or at least did not hinder it. Unlike the fighting at Shiloh Branch,

Confederate brigades smashed through the Union line of Prentiss's division, which lay along the Eastern Corinth Road atop the Shiloh divide. There, on tableland, there was no major defensive terrain to help the Federals stop the Confederate surge. When the Southerners smashed Prentiss's position, punching a large hole in this initial Union line of six brigades arrayed roughly west to east behind Shiloh and Locust Grove branches, some Southern units turned westward and outflanked Sherman's position atop the Shiloh Branch ridge. Thus Sherman had to fall back, not because his front line was taken but because a less defensible area along the battle line had allowed the enemy to flank him.[36]

Still within this first phase, Confederate commanders realized that they had not yet located and turned the Union left flank, which was the plan all along. They began to send reserve units farther to the right to extend the line. Unfortunately for them, the valley of Locust Grove Branch was too difficult for maneuvering, so they chose to send units out the Bark Road to come up the River Road across Locust Grove Branch. This movement resulted in Confederate brigades fighting their way across Locust Grove Branch during the midmorning hours. The advance was successful, despite what one commander called "a very steep and perfectly abrupt hill." The Confederate success here was not the result of favorable terrain but because only one small and badly frightened Union brigade held this portion of the line. Had the Federals placed more men on the ridges north of Locust Grove Branch, they probably could have held as easily as Sherman had at Shiloh Branch.[37]

By the end of the first phase of fighting along Shiloh and Locust Grove branches around 10:30 or 11:00 a.m., the Confederates had taken the initial line of Federal camps and made lodgments on the tableland between Shiloh and Locust Grove branches to the south and Tilghman and Dill branches to the north. But it had cost them dearly. They had planned to attack the enemy in their camps at sunrise, but due to the broken ground and heavy fighting, most notably at Shiloh Branch, the Confederates were not able to take these camps and effect a beachhead on the high ground until between 10:00 and 11:00 a.m. Moreover, it had required nearly the entire Confederate army to do so. A large percentage of the sixteen Confederate brigades were on line. In fact, only two brigades could be specifically classified as in reserve. Contrast that to the Federal army, which had no more than seven of fifteen brigades in major action by 10:00 or 10:30 a.m. Nearly the entire Union army was deployed, but some eight Federal brigades had scarcely fired a shot, and most of those were at long ranges against the enemy's extreme forward skirmishers, who had crept forward at the end of the major fighting of the first phase. And those Federal units not yet in major action were veterans. The Confederates

While the various creeks funneled the Confederate attack into a certain area and the smaller branches delayed the advance, the majority of the battle at Shiloh took place on high, relatively flat and dry tableland. This view shows some of the level ground around the famous Crossroads in the defensive line held by John A. McClernand's division. (Courtesy of Shiloh National Military Park.)

had hit the two greenest divisions in the Federal army and it had taken five or six hours to sweep them aside, in large part due to the terrain they held.[38]

Once the tide of battle drifted up onto the wide tableland boxed between the river and the six creeks, the second phase of the battle began and events slowed down considerably. There were no major watersheds to aid the Federal defense, but there were other factors that slowed the battle. One was the full engagement of both armies. By midday, both sides had just about all available troops engaged. Thus, although the Confederates had growing firepower, they continually assailed an increasingly strong defender. And many Confederates units that had been in action all day driving against the Union lines in the first phase were bloody, leaderless, tired, and out of ammunition, thus causing a reduction in striking potential.[39]

Terrain also played a major role in this second phase, however. The units on the western third of the battlefield fought one another on the tableland, which was cut up frequently by smaller feeder branches that fed both Shiloh and Tilghman branches as well as those that flowed directly into Owl Creek. While presenting nothing remotely close to the major watersheds in terms of defensibility, these depressions nevertheless factored into the ebb and flow of the battle. More significant for this western third of the tableland were man-made features such as fields. The Confederate attack ran into a strongly posted line of John A. McClernand's division, aided by the remnants of Sherman's troops. Fighting in this sector developed into horrendous close-quarter fighting, and the Federals gradually fell back through open spaces, holding several successive lines of defense. Finally stabilizing a major line in Jones Field, the Federal commanders reorganized their commands on the open ground and launched a counterattack that completely caught the Confederates off guard. The Federals retook most of their lost ground, driving the enemy back across those same fields fought over before. But then the last Confederate reserves engaged, in turn driving the Federals back toward Jones Field once more. A large portion of both armies thus fought back and forth on the meandering tableland, neither side gaining a distinct advantage from the neutral terrain.[40]

The eastern third of the tableland was much different. Confederates who had fought their way across Locust Grove Branch were doomed to fight the remainder of the day in extremely deep ravines stacked up one after another along and flowing into the Tennessee River. Because the Confederates chose to move westward to more easily traversed terrain, the action was not as fluid as it had been on the western side. In fact, many of the Confederate troops would ultimately maneuver on the tableland above the ravines rather than try to go through them. The result was a major bloodbath at the famous Peach Orchard, where numerous Confederate charges attempted to cross the open spaces in an effort to break the formidable Union line. Because of clear fields of fire and plenty of open space, Federal commanders under Stephen A. Hurlbut were able to hold their positions throughout much of the day instead of yielding large chunks of territory and then taking it back, as Sherman and McClernand had done on the Union right. Thus the fighting on the eastern side of the battlefield, although much less spectacular and not as dramatic because of the terrain aid to the Federals, was nevertheless extremely important in helping the Union hold its critical left flank.[41]

The center of this second phase, which has come to be known in history as the focal point of the battle, contained the important area of the Hornet's Nest. The famous Sunken Road, though not a major factor, aided in the defense of this area, but it was actually other more important terrain features that specifically provided the Union with very defensible territory. One of the major factors was the wide-open Duncan Field, which covered a large portion of the Hornet's Nest line, about half of it in fact. Corresponding to Duncan Field on the right of the Union center was what Confederates described as "an almost impenetrable thicket" in front of the left of the Hornet's Nest. Braxton Bragg commented on the enemy in the Hornet's Nest "being strongly posted, with infantry and artillery, on an eminence immediately behind a dense thicket." Thus any Confederate attempt to break the center would either have to go across the wide-open Duncan Field or through the almost impassable thicket. Because the Confederate lines there were not nearly as crowded as the two flanks, Confederate commanders in the center had the fluidity and option of sending their units toward the Federal lines at different points. Most obviously chose to shun the open field and attack through the thickets. That in itself, while providing some cover, nevertheless offered its own major problems, most notably in keeping alignment and organization, on which Civil War tactical cohesion rested. As might be expected with the terrain aids to the Federals of W. H. L. Wallace's and Benjamin Prentiss's divisions, Confederate attempt after attempt swept toward the Hornet's Nest but failed to dislodge the enemy in its strong position.[42]

In all, the battle crept forward for some seven hours in this second phase on the tableland in the center of the battlefield. Most of the Federals on the two flanks ultimately fell back behind Dill and Tilghman branches, but the last remnants of this phase's defenders left the line as prisoners of war when the famous Hornet's Nest surrendered between 5:30 and 6:00 p.m. The Confederates had broken through the major Federal lines of the day, but it had taken several hours to advance only a short distance. And worse, the vast majority of those second phase Union defenders had retreated intact to a new line behind Dill and Tilghman branches, ready to hold yet another successive line of defense.[43]

By midafternoon, Union commander Grant had seen that yet another line to the rear was needed. He began to set up a line of defense north of the Tilghman and Dill branch watersheds, taking special concern for the tableland portion where the Shiloh divide (and several roads) ran between the two. As retreating units from the battlefield filed rearward, they took position in this line, which recreated the early morning action of the first phase all over again, only with an even stronger position this time. Situated on the high ground north of the creeks, this line could better handle the advancing Confederates, who had to negotiate the muddy and tangled creek bottoms. And these watersheds were steeper than the earlier bottoms; some ravine slopes were almost vertical. The Federals studded this line with artillery, especially on the tableland where the Shiloh divide narrowed in the middle of the hourglass. Also present were masses of infantry from the battlefield, reserve siege guns intended to be used at Corinth, and the two gunboats in the river. It was a very strong line.[44]

The bloodied and tired Confederate army had neither the daylight nor the strength to mount an effective attack against this impressive last line.

Confederate commanders variously described the Tilghman Branch defile as "a deep ravine" and "the gorge below," illustrating their respect for it. They soon learned even more to respect it and the defense it provided the enemy. A few Confederate units, most notably Colonel Preston Pond's brigade and a few horse soldiers, tramped across Tilghman Branch to attack the enemy. The Louisianans of Pond's Brigade were able to use a defile of a feeder branch that led into Tilghman Branch to cover their approach toward the Union line, but as soon as they cleared the defile, Sherman's and McClernand's divisions, with massed artillery and infantry, easily turned them back with horrendous casualties. Thereafter, the Confederates were satisfied with watching the enemy with a worn-out brigade and lobbing a few shells across the ravine from an artillery battery.[45]

The major attack on this third Federal line came across Dill Branch to the east when elements of four Confederate brigades crossed the creek, with only one actually attempting to assault the Union line. That brigade commander, James Chalmers, described the Dill Branch declivity, stating that "our men struggled vainly to ascend the hill, which was very steep." Another officer described the ground as "a deep and precipitous ravine." Chalmers's Mississippians found the going extremely difficult as they topped the ridge on which the Union line sat. Hit by a barrage of infantry, artillery, and gunboat fire, the Mississippians quickly realized how futile their task was. It did not help that some of the firing then directed at them was coming from some of Buell's fresh troops even then disembarking in increasing numbers at the landing. The Confederate high command soon opted to hold what they had in the increasing darkness and try to finish off the enemy the next morning. The third phase of the first day's battle thus ended with darkness.[46]

Although night fell on the first day of battle, another day was to be fought. And the Confederates thought they could simply mop up what they had left undone the night before. As might be expected with all the reinforcements, however, the resurgent Federals held their line the next morning, and more. Heavily reinforced with Buell's Army of the Ohio and Lew Wallace's missing division, Grant counterattacked and began driving the Confederates southward. On this second day, the battle developed exactly the same way it had on the day before, only in reverse. The Federal units first made contact with Confederate skirmishes as they made their way up and out of the first set of creeks they had to traverse, Tilghman and Dill branches. As the tired Confederate army slowly reacted, the battle again slowed in the center tableland, with the same sunken roads and open fields witnessing the majority of the fighting, just as they had the day before. Then, as the Confederate army later retreated, they used Shiloh Branch, much like the Federals had used Dill and

Tilghman branches the day before, as a final defensive line to hold back the enemy. Artillery and infantry units positioned south of Shiloh Branch helped hold back driving Federal units until the bulk of the Confederate army could move southward along the Corinth Road in retreat.[47]

Terrain thus played a major role in the Battle of Shiloh. It not only determined the extent and parameters of the battlefield itself but also dictated where the heaviest fighting took place and who was victorious. In an effort to trade space for time on the first day, Grant realized he could fall back gradually but incrementally, eating up the daylight hours until nightfall, at which time he would receive massive reinforcements and have the battle practically won. Shiloh's terrain helped him do just that.

## Historiography

Terrain has sometimes been shunted off to the side when explaining victory and defeat on the first day at Shiloh. For instance, major Shiloh historians have often leaned toward certain factors or events as the keys to the battle, but in each case the terrain factors can be at least partially included as reasons for that proposed key's importance. For example, historian Wiley Sword makes a strong case in *Shiloh: Bloody April* that Confederate commander Albert Sidney Johnston's death was the key blow at Shiloh. Historian and Johnston biographer Charles Roland has made the same argument. The terrain's role in causing Johnston's death is rarely evidenced, however, probably because of its obviousness, but it did play a significant function. The whole reason Johnston was personally leading the attack that proved fatal to him was because of terrain issues. He felt it necessary to lead yet another of the multiple attacks across Sarah Bell's cotton field toward the Peach Orchard because earlier attacks had not been successful. Realizing his chances of victory hinged on turning that Union left flank, he personally oversaw operations in that area and led the fatal charge. Because of the open nature of the terrain, however, prior Confederate assaults had failed, prompting Johnston to lead and thus be mortally wounded. The larger effect of the huge ravines to the east had also forced Confederate brigades to stuff themselves into the small area on the Confederate right to avoid the deep watersheds. Thus, unlike the action in the center where Confederate commands were not nearly so numerous, commanders on the east side could not pick and choose where to attack. Someone had to go across those open fields, and most of those attacks were doomed to failure because of the open terrain. Obviously, that Johnston was operating out in the open also acted as a factor in his wounding.[48]

One of Larry Daniel's arguments in *Shiloh: The Battle that Changed the Civil War* is a failure of leadership on the Confederate side. Obviously, command and control broke down very early in the battle, and it was due to several factors, such as the lack of unity of command, failure to mass, lack of simplicity, and other major noncompliance factors with the famous principles of war. But terrain also played a major role in the breakup of command and control among the Confederate officer corps. As the initial Confederate charges went forward, corps and even division commanders found it exceedingly difficult to maintain communication with their units not only because of distance but also because of the heavily wooded terrain and frequent watersheds that broke up organization. Even brigade and some regimental commanders had a hard time keeping all of their men on the same page. Because of the undulating nature of the ground, thick vegetation in some areas, and heavily wooded topography, Confederate command and control broke down very quickly. At one point, Confederate corps commanders scrapped their initial organizations and in an on-the-spot decision divided up sectors of the line. The apparent problematical command issues attending such an action can well be understood, from getting word out to all subordinates of the change to even physically recognizing new subordinates with whom they had not served in the only recently gathered-together army.[49]

The most dominant theme of Shiloh historiography revolves around the Hornet's Nest and its effect on the battle. There is no doubt that the defenders of that area fought long and hard and ultimately sacrificed themselves to help delay the Confederate advance. Often overlooked, however, in the works of historians who emphasize the Hornet's Nest are the terrain features that helped the Federals hold that position. The dominant characteristics of Duncan Field and the impenetrable thicket have already been discussed. They were such important factors, along with the Union defense, that the Confederates were never able to take the position by frontal assault. The position was doomed because the flanks fell, and those failures also partially rested upon terrain factors. The Confederates, therefore, were able to surround the Hornet's Nest and take the remaining defenders as prisoners.[50]

Other factors that historians have attributed both success and failure at Shiloh to also rest on a terrain foundation. Some argue Buell's arrival sealed the fate of the Confederate attacks on the first day. Whether one agrees with this argument or not, the terrain aspects are clear cut. Buell's men entered the Union line on extremely defensible terrain and helped hold that position. Some argue Lew Wallace's arrival earlier in the day would have had a major effect, but the terrain features, especially the road layout, attending his march and countermarch are obvious. Larry Daniel even takes a much wider approach in *Shiloh: The Battle that Changed the Civil War*, arguing that the lack of sixteen thousand reserves lost at Fort Donelson made a major difference in Confederate ability on the first day. Naturally, these men were in prison and did not participate in the battle, but terrain can conceivably be assigned some, but certainly not all (leadership comes to mind first and foremost), of the blame there as well. Had they not been bottled up in a surrendering fort, they in all probability would have been available to make a difference at Shiloh. Terrain was thus a factor strategically, operationally, and, most important, tactically on the first day at Shiloh, and the same case can be made on the second day as well.[51]

## The Effects

In examining Shiloh's terrain, however, larger lessons are available; using Shiloh as a case study can reap rewards for many interested readers. Certainly, Confederate as well as Union military officers learned major lessons at Shiloh, which they no doubt put into use later in the war. Even today, modern military officers can still learn the lessons of Shiloh. While today's modern military has many advantages that Braxton Bragg did not have in April 1862, including aerial and satellite images, modern military officers still place large stock in knowing a battlefield's terrain. In fact, Shiloh National Military Park routinely hosts army, marine, and even navy "staff rides," where officers learn the lessons of Shiloh. While weaponry, tactics, and styles have changed over time, other factors have not, including the famous and timeless "principles of war" and, of course, terrain awareness.[52]

Historians and preservationists can also use Shiloh as an example of what can be gleaned from a landscape or geographical study. Preservationists can hail the success with which Shiloh was preserved more than a hundred years ago, thus providing a nearly pristine battlefield for study today. The existing ground is normally the most important primary source for the study of any given battle, if it is preserved to at least some degree, and Shiloh is an example of what preservationists can do and how historians can use a battlefield.[53]

In addition, modern computerization can also have a broad effect on the study of individual sites. Programs such as geographic information system (GIS), which is currently used at the national park at Shiloh, can provide a layered approach to understanding Shiloh's history. The benefits are enormous, such as realizing the chronological development of the site, analyzing the changes in the terrain over time, and even plotting the movements of troops on the battlefield. Historians have been somewhat slow in developing and using modern software for understanding Civil War battles, often relying simply on fixed maps. But the GIS software and even other programs, such as animated maps, are the wave of the future. The Civil War Trust (CWT; formerly the Civil War Preservation Trust) is one of the leaders in this new technology.[54]

By looking at how terrain affected the battle, Shiloh historians can thus glean a deeper and more realistic view of how and why the battle was fought the way it was. Given the lack of environmental emphasis in modern Civil War tactical studies, and any other war's battles for that matter, perhaps historians need to make a more concerted effort to let the ground speak, like it does at Shiloh.

2

# To Conquer or Perish: The Last Hours of Albert Sidney Johnston

A somewhat surprised Albert Sidney Johnston stood and listened to his second in command call for a withdrawal. General P. G. T. Beauregard, second in command of the Confederate Army of the Mississippi, argued that the delays in marching northward from Corinth and the army's lack of stealth had alerted the enemy army that lay nearby. All chance for a surprise was gone, the Creole argued, and the enemy would be "intrenched to the eyes." Johnston could not fathom Beauregard's sudden loss of will. The army had marched nearly twenty miles through difficult terrain and worse weather and sat poised for an attack that would alter the course of the war. To withdraw was ludicrous, Johnston no doubt thought to himself. With several other high-ranking generals around a small campfire, Johnston took firm control of the situation and spoke forcefully: "Gentlemen, we shall attack at daylight tomorrow." Later, he added, "I would fight them if they were a million. They can present no greater front between these two creeks than we can, and the more men they crowd in there, the worse we can make it for them." With those words, all knew that the attack would go forward at daylight the next morning, April 6, 1862, toward a small and insignificant log church named Shiloh. And with those words, Albert Sidney Johnston issued his own death sentence. Within twenty-four hours, he would be dead.[1]

It is arguable that Johnston knew he would die, or at least thought it possible he would not live through the battle that would begin in just hours. He had to win if the South had any chance of stemming the vast blue tide that was even then surging into the heartland of the Confederacy. This was the line he had drawn; Shiloh had to be a victory. And Johnston was perfectly willing to die gaining that victory, if that was the cost. In a statement given out to the troops upon their march to Shiloh, Johnston had written that they were fighting "for all worth living or dying for." Even a cursory look at Johnston's rhetoric on the evening of April 5 and even during the battle itself shows that Johnston's mind was on one thing: victory or death. He would give his own life's blood to win it if he had to. Johnston's own son later remembered his dad in years past had often confided to him that he preferred a soldier's death. Now, Johnston's mind seemed to be on that very possibility. His remark that he would fight the enemy if they numbered a million does not show bluster and conceit, as in the case of some younger Civil War generals, such as John Pope and Joseph Hooker, but shows Johnston's desperation, a chance he would have to take even when the odds greatly outweighed him. Johnston made a similar comment when he spoke of rolling the "iron dice of battle," which betrayed his view that this attack was a major gamble but had to be done. Similarly, he told his son's best college friend, brigade commander Randall Gibson, that he hoped the young man would come through the battle intact, but then added significantly, "but we must win a victory." As heart rending as it would be to sacrifice his son's best friend, Johnston saw the situation demanded it if needed. Perhaps most telling, Johnston remarked to Colonel John S. Marmaduke, "We must this day conquer or perish." Johnston had to win this gamble, even if it took himself entering the fight on the front lines and dying. If he did not win, he would die trying.[2]

Johnston's earlier command decisions had placed him in this position. Although a highly exalted leader at the beginning of the war, his star had only fallen through the turbulent months between his ascension to command of Department Number Two in September 1861 and his do-or-die gamble in April 1862. He had come eastward from California and his post as commander of the U.S. Army's Department of the Pacific in late 1861, upon the secession of his adopted state of Texas, and offered his services to the Confederacy. With that, he was hailed as the savior of the South. To be sure, nothing in his life prior to this left any doubt about his abilities. Although a native Kentuckian, he had, like his friend Jefferson Davis, left his native state to attend the United States Military Academy. He later adopted Texas as his home, serving in that territory's fight for independence and becoming the new nation's secretary of war. Later, as a high-ranking officer back in the United States Army, Johnston served continually higher billets and ultimately resigned as a brigadier general. When he threw his lot with the Confederacy, his old friend Jefferson Davis did him a favor and made him a full general; Davis did him no favor, however, when he appointed him to a hopeless task.[3]

Johnston had far too much territory to defend and far too few men with which to defend it. Making matters worse, Johnston faced the enemy's most able general, although no one knew it at the time. Ulysses S. Grant would pierce Johnston's makeshift defense line across the northern border of the western Confederacy, capture an entire fort's garrison (some fourteen thou-

Albert Sidney Johnston led his Army of the Mississippi to a death struggle at Shiloh, their attitude "conquer or perish." Shiloh was do or die for the Confederate army as well as Johnston, who died instead of winning the victory he so desperately needed to reverse his major losses in the Western Theater in the spring of 1862. Johnston was the highest ranking officer killed in the war and remains the highest ranking officer to die in combat in all of American military history. (Library of Congress.)

sand men), and open broad avenues of invasion into the Confederate heartland. Even worse, Grant and the Federals were now using those avenues of invasion. By the end of March 1862, the Federal Army of the Tennessee, Grant commanding, lay at Pittsburg Landing, just over twenty short miles from Corinth, Mississippi, and the crossroads of the western Confederacy's two most important railroads. If Grant took Corinth, Johnston's logistical network would be in shambles and the infrastructural base needed for a counteroffensive would be captured. Making the situation worse, the Federals were concentrating their armies, with Don Carlos Buell's Army of the Ohio marching even then overland from Nashville to join Grant. Once the two combined, Johnston knew the game was up.

Thus it was that Johnston deemed early April as the time to attack. It had to be done then, before Buell arrived and joined Grant, making the enemy numbers far superior to Johnston's roughly forty-five thousand men. If he could destroy Grant's army before Buell arrived, the odds would be more even. It was a gamble indeed, but the lesser of two evils.

But Johnston had more than just arithmetic to think about. Nothing had gone right since his heartwarming arrival in the Confederacy just a few short months earlier. Johnston had lost portions of Kentucky, Nashville's major logistical center, all of Middle Tennessee, much of West Tennessee, and some fifteen thousand irreplaceable troops. And now the enemy was knocking on the door of the lower Mississippi Valley. Suddenly, those cheers at his arrival had turned to calls for removal. All but one of the Tennessee delegation in the Confederate Congress had called for his resignation. And now, Johnston had a curious second in command who it seemed could do nothing wrong on the battlefield. Beauregard had been the hero of Fort Sumter and had earned much glory at First Manassas. No wonder Johnston offered Beauregard tactical command of the army while retaining strategic command of the department.[4]

Even though stung by the calls for removal and taunts thrown in his direction, Johnston was not shaken to the core. He expressed a reality of the situation when he told Colonel E. W. Munford, "With the people there is but one test of merit in my profession, that of success. It is a hard rule, but I think it right." And he still had the one solid supporter who mattered most: Jefferson Davis. Asked about a replacement for Johnston because he was no general, a Tennessee congressmen said, Davis replied, "If *he* is not a general, we had better give up the war, for we have no general." Obviously, with Grant breathing down his neck and Buell about to join him, with many Southerners out of patience with him, and with Jefferson Davis still backing him but obviously, privately, wanting something done to turn the foreboding events around, Johnston had to come up with a victory. He had to act now, even with that action being so large a gamble. It was now or never. Johnston had to lead his troops to victory if he was to turn the tables, if he was to defend the Mississippi Valley, if he was to quell the desperate calls of the public, if he was to make his friend Davis glad he had supported him. Johnston had to win, now, and he was even willing to die to bring that about.[5]

Johnston spent the night of April 5, his last, at his headquarters near the rear of the deployed army. He would continue the conversations about the need for battle with his officers and staff for a while, but he ultimately lay down in an ambulance for a few hours' sleep. Even the next morning, however, Beauregard was back advising a retreat. Beauregard had declined Johnston's offer of tactical command but apparently thought the offer entitled him to make some of the decisions. In fact, Johnston had curiously allowed him to plan the attack at Shiloh, which diverged from Johnston's original plan to use his corps in linear fashion, one beside the other, to sweep around the enemy left flank and drive them into the swamps to the northwest. Beauregard, rather, devised an unwieldy plan to use the corps in column. While the generals talked near daylight, however, the sounds of shots came from the front. Johnston again declared the army would move forward: "The battle has opened gentlemen; it is too late to change our dispositions." As the confident general mounted his horse Fire Eater to ride to the front, he alerted his staff: "To-night, we will water our horses in the Tennessee River." He would never make it.[6]

With the obvious sounds of battle to the front, Johnston rode forward with his staff, leaving Beauregard in the rear to oversee the entire effort. As the general reached the front, the battle began to pick up all along the initial line of William J. Hardee's corps. Hardee had not yet met the stiffest resistance at the camps but was battling a fair number of skirmishers and pickets, augmented by reinforcements sent out to delay the Confederates. This small band of Federals did their job well, falling back from position to position but offering at least a semblance of resistance. The effect among the green Confederates was stark. New to battle, the soldiers of Hardee's front line stopped and started, delaying to dress ranks. The same thing happened on the brigade level. These Confederates were not used to operating in such large numbers together. What later in the war would have been a whirlwind movement against minimal resistance was rather a major delay for the Confederates in the early hours of Shiloh.

Johnston followed the slowly progressing lines of his extreme right flank, moving up behind Adley Gladden's and Robert Shaver's brigades. A few casualties resulted from the fighting, but the green Confederates were more confused than bloodied. When he heard that a portion of the line had broken, Johnston himself galloped to the area and rallied a portion of Shaver's brigade that had come unglued at the first shock of battle. One of Johnston's aides, his brother-in-law William Preston, remembered that Johnston dove into the fight and reformed his lines. "There were many dead and wounded, and some stragglers breaking ranks," Preston remembered, "whom General Johnston rallied in person." A member of Johnston's escort company verified this. "Instantly he quickened to a gallop, with the staff and escort following, and right into the *melee* we plunged." A staff member cautioned him about exposing himself, but the general smiled and moved on toward the front. Obviously chagrined at the confusion already appearing and the resulting lack of momentum, all caused by what could only be described as light Federal resistance, Johnston chose to take no chances. He sent Preston to the rear to bring up his second line, Braxton Bragg's corps of about ten thousand bayonets. Surely, Johnston no doubt thought, Bragg's weight in numbers would take care of whatever was in front.[7]

While Bragg moved forward and entered the battle, Johnston rode to the west to observe the battle in that sector. There, the general watched as Patrick Cleburne's brigade engaged the Federals near Shiloh Church. Johnston sat near two cabins that stood on the eastern side of the Corinth–Pittsburg Landing

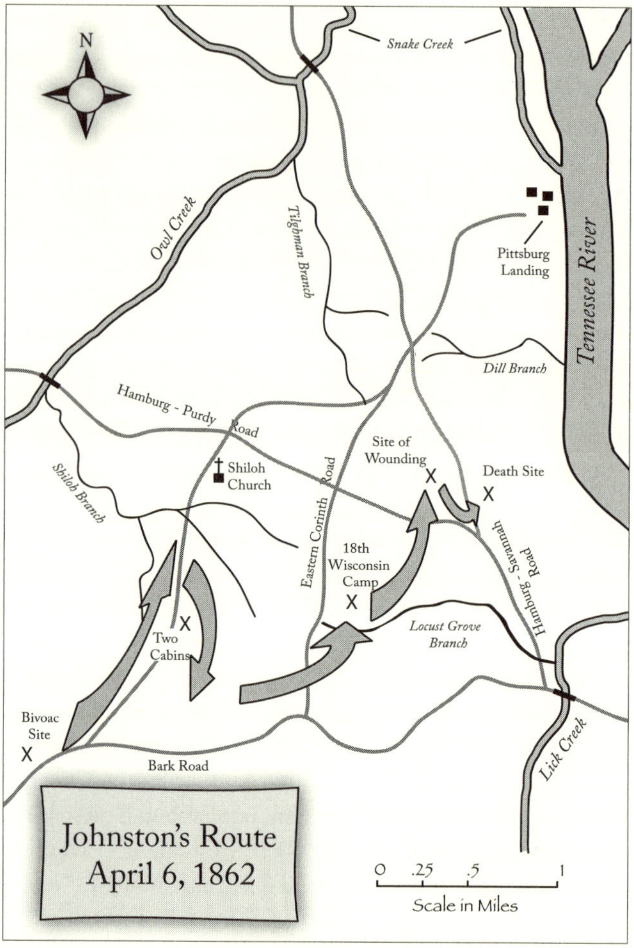


Road and watched the action across Rhea Field. One eyewitness described the scene: "Through this field General Cleburne's brigade moved in fine order, with loud and inspiring cheers, to attack the camp." Unfortunately, Cleburne was not successful, and neither would the next two lines be able to break the Shiloh Church position held by William T. Sherman. The ground was extremely good for the defense, and the Confederate brigades made charge after futile charge up the ridge, only to come bounding back down in defeat.[8]

To make matters worse, the line in this area seemed to be outflanked on the left, which caused Johnston to call on Beauregard for reinforcements for that sector. Colonel Jacob Thompson, a former secretary of the interior and now an aide to Beauregard, had ridden forward and found Johnston squarely amid the battle. He described the scene: "The battle was then raging furiously. General Johnston was sitting on his horse where the bullets were flying like hail-stones. I galloped up to him amid the fire, and found him cool, collected, self-possessed, but still animated and in fine spirits." Johnston was obviously bothered by the report he had just received that the enemy was "sending forward strong re-enforcements to our left." This report probably described the convoluted antics of John McDowell's Federal brigade; there were no Federal reinforcements heading to the extreme Confederate left. Still, Johnston acted decisively and ordered Thompson to make his way to Beauregard and report the situation. "Say to General Beauregard," Johnston barked, "we are sweeping the field before us, and in less than half an hour we shall be in possession of their camps, and I think we shall press them to the river. Say, also, I have just learned from a scout, or messenger, that the enemy is moving up in force on our left, and that General [John] Breckinridge had better move to our left to meet him." Thompson later remembered that as he turned his horse to gallop away, Johnston stopped him: "Do not say to General Beauregard that this is an order, but he must act on what additional information he may receive. The reports to him are more to be relied on than to me." Obviously, Johnston was amid the thick of the raging battle and could not see a comprehensive view of the happenings. He had left Beauregard in the rear for that exact purpose. Beauregard actually started Breckinridge to the left, but when news arrived that Sherman had withdrawn, the Creole later called Breckinridge back and sent him to the right, where he deemed the biggest need to be.[9]

After taking care of the perceived threat to the left, Johnston started to ride back to the right of his line, where new threats were emerging. Johnston had apparently always been concerned about his right flank, with which he hoped to turn the enemy and drive them into the swamps and destruction. Spying Colonel George Maney with five companies of the 1st Tennessee Infantry, Johnston ordered him to move across Lick Creek and watch that flank for any Federal movement from the direction of Hamburg. Maney remembered with apparent satisfaction, "General Johnston, commanding in person, directed me to change my course." The most pressing problem Johnston was getting word of, however, was not a perceived threat like the one from Hamburg but an all out Federal defense on his right flank. By this time, Shaver's and Gladden's brigades had run into Prentiss's division line at his camps. The Federals, at least for the moment, were offering stiff resistance. Gladden's brigade was particularly hit hard, and Gladden himself was down with a nasty shoulder wound that would eventually take his life. Bragg's second-line brigades had to move forward to help break this line. Most notably, James

Chalmers's Mississippi brigade was fighting in the large ravines that bordered Locust Grove Branch. With foreboding reports from that sector, Johnston saw the need for additional weight on this wing as well.[10]

Breckinridge, Johnston thought, was moving to the left, which left Leonidas Polk's Corps, the third in line, to move to the right. Obviously having been apprised of the resistance on the right, Johnston rode about behind his temporarily stalled lines, finding Polk himself near the two cabins on the Corinth Road. Polk was impressed with what he saw: "It was observed that he entered upon his work with the ardor and energy of the true soldier, and the vigor with which he pressed forward his troops gave assurance that his persistent determination would close the day with a glorious victory." Johnston ordered Polk to send a brigade to the right. Polk ordered his head division commander Charles Clark, who was apparently with Polk, to send the brigade. Johnston then personally ordered Clark to send A. P. Stewart's Brigade to the right. Clark sent the orders, and, going that way anyway, Johnston personally led Stewart toward the right.[11]

Stewart had led his brigade forward but then was no doubt awe inspired when he saw who would guide him into position. None other than General Johnston himself would lead Stewart and his Tennesseans and Arkansans into the battle. "We continued to advance," Stewart later remembered, "until General A. S. Johnston came up and directed me to move my brigade to the right, to support of General Bragg." But just as quickly, Johnston was gone. Stewart moved through open woods, a field, and up to an abandoned enemy camp, but then, Stewart reported, "General Johnston having gone to some other part of the field, and finding no one to give me directions, after halting a few minutes I moved the brigade forward." Stewart would never see Johnston again, but his few minutes with the army commander had made a lasting impression on him. "No one who saw him on the field of battle on that fateful morning of April sixth could fail to be struck by his bearing. His whole mien was singularly noble and soldierly, characterized by a calm dignity that was inspired by a consciousness of power and confidence."[12]

But Johnston had not ridden far, just over the hill to the camp of the 18th Wisconsin, which sat on some of the highest ground on the battlefield. From there, Johnston would direct the battle for several hours. By this time, around 9:30 a.m., Johnston was beginning to get his bearings. He had admittedly spent most of the morning riding back and forth behind his lines in a very reactionary posture. A member of his escort company later remembered, "Always at a gallop, we traversed a great part of the field. [But] he seemed cool and collected all the time." Indeed, he at times outran his escort. Far worse, however, the initial attack had ground down to a slow trudge at best, with heavy resistance developing the closer the Confederates came to the initial Federal camp line. By this time, at least two shot-up brigades, Cleburne's and Gladden's, were all but out of the action for several hours. Others units, particularly those in the first wave of attack, had been hit hard as well. Johnston had sped from one troubled spot to the next, often issuing reactionary orders to send or bring units to meet a threat that was not there. Such was the case with sending Breckinridge to the left and Stewart to the right. Beauregard later called Breckinridge back and sent him with two-thirds of his command to the right, while Stewart, with no one to direct him, later moved back to the left. It seems the entire Confederate army, Johnston included, spent much of the morning getting their bearings and jabbing at phantom Federals.[13]

By about 9:30 a.m., however, Johnston seemed to have gathered his wits and began to direct the battle with initiative and verve. To be sure, he had not lacked confidence throughout the morning, and his ability to inspire his men had never left him. One must only look at the comments of Thompson, Polk, and Stewart to see the inspiration that was Johnston on the field of Shiloh. And even in the midst of the floundering in the confusion of the opening actions, Johnston' Confederates had managed to drive Prentiss's entire division from the field and were preparing to outflank the tremendously heavy resistance Sherman was offering at Shiloh Church. Temporarily confused and staggered in the early morning hours, Johnston would now use his dogged attitude, his do-or-die mentality, to take control of the situation.

By 9:30 a.m., Johnston was beginning to see a clearer picture. Always intending to hook around the enemy's left flank, he spent much of his time in that area. Witnessing the hard fighting near Spain Field, which had cost him Gladden and many soldiers of lower rank, Johnston realized that his right far outflanked the enemy left in this area. In fact, the sounds of battle could be heard far to the west, all the way to and past Shiloh Church. But absolutely nothing was heard to the east. Johnston thus decided he had located the enemy flank, and according to his plan, he began to turn it.

From the high ground around the 18th Wisconsin camp, the general directed a large-scale movement that shifted a large portion of his army from a northward posture to a northwestward slant, hoping to push Grant's army into the swamps of Owl and Snake creeks to the northwest of Pittsburg Landing. Colonel Edward W. Munford, one of Johnston's staff officers, remembered Johnston "was in the act of swinging his troops round on his left as a pivot," and commented that "the completion of this movement faced the troops at an angle of about 45° toward the left, when the forward movement became uniform." Hardee was also there, and the two senior officers and their staffs rode forward to reconnoiter a second line of camps in the distance, perhaps eight hundred yards to the front. The large assemblage of mounted officers of course caught the enemy's eye, and Federal batteries soon opened up on the group. Shells from the gunboat *Tyler* in the Tennessee River also fell nearby, although these could not have been fired in response to Johnston's presence. Despite the danger, Johnston was apparently very much hands on in moving troops in this sector. Hardee later reported that he was satisfied that Johnston was "in person directing the battle" in this sector, and he moved off to the left in response to a large cannonade that had developed there. Although taking some refuge from the cannonade (William Preston later remembered, "General Johnston rode down the hill to escape the shells"), Johnston nevertheless continued to direct events on the right, putting himself in danger at times in order to do what had to be done.[14]

Unfortunately, Johnston had made a severe misjudgment. The silence Johnston had heard to the east was not because there were no more Federals in that direction. There were indeed no Federals for half a mile to the east, which was only as far as Chalmers's right extended. Farther down the line, however, was the brigade of Colonel David Stuart. A gap half a mile wide existed, which was to be plugged by Prentiss's third brigade, which had not yet been formed. So, much of Chalmers's brigade hit empty space, prompting Johnston to think he had located the enemy flank. In reality, the flank was actually on Lick Creek, another mile to the east.

Johnston soon received word of this force to the east from an engineer sent out early that morning to scout the Federal left. Samuel Lockett returned with word that an entire Federal division was farther to the east. Unbeknown to the general, it was in actuality only a badly scared brigade of just three regiments, but obviously Johnston was taken aback by this bit of news. Preston remembered the general "pondering [the situation] a little while." Soon Johnston made up his mind; something had to be done to counter this new threat, this new flank. It was too late to call back the majority of the troops he had sent bounding off to the northwest to drive the enemy army into the swamps. He could, however, recall two of the far right brigades. Chalmers had proceeded northward toward the Peach Orchard and was even then trading some long-range fire with Stephen Hurlbut's brigades, which added even another Union division to the eastern sector of the battlefield. John K. Jackson's Alabamians were also nearby, having begun their move to the northwest. Both of these brigades were in Jones Withers's division, and Johnston ordered Withers to call these two brigades back, send them on a flanking march along the

Bark Road to the rear, and have them redeploy on the new enemy flank on the River Road. Withers remembered, "General A.S. Johnston, who was present, immediately ordered the division to move to the right." Chalmers remembered, "We were about to engage them again, when we were ordered by General Johnston to fall back, which was done." To take Withers's place in line, Johnston called on Beauregard to send two of Breckinridge's reserve brigades to fill the resulting gap in the line. Obviously Johnston had gotten word that they had not been sent into action on the left and were still available. The general sent William Preston and Captain Nathaniel Wickliffe to guide John Bowen's and Winfield Statham's brigades into line. Johnston was playing musical chairs with his brigades, shifting two farther to the right and filling the empty space with reserve units.[15]

Watching Chalmers's brigade, the far right unit in the army, move forward, Johnston was obviously happy with this move. He had basically unfolded a new right wing of the Confederate army, and he was perfectly confident that these four brigades could handle this new threat, turn it, and join in on the effort to drive the Federals into the swamps to the northwest. Johnston was so confident, in fact, that he expressed to Colonel Munford that this was the key stroke of the battle. Munford remembered: "We sat on our horses, side by side, watching that brigade [Chalmers] as it swept over the ridge; and, as the colors dipped out of sight, the general said to me, 'That checkmates them.' I told him I was glad to hear him announce 'checkmate,' but that 'he must excuse so poor a player for saying he could not see it.' He laughed, and said, 'Yes, sir, that mates them.'"[16]

Feeling the victory, Johnston continued directing the battle from the vicinity of the 18th Wisconsin camp for roughly two hours, until about noon. While there, he witnessed what was becoming a problem in the Confederate army all over the battlefield: soldiers breaking ranks and looting the enemy's camps. A Confederate officer burst from a captured Union tent holding several valuable items. Spying the general, the guilty officer held the items up in victory. Johnston was not amused. "None of that, sir; we are not here for plunder!" Perhaps feeling he had overreacted, Johnston then took a single tin cup between his fingers and remarked, "Let this be my share of the spoils to-day."[17]

It was also in the 18th Wisconsin camp that Johnston made a fateful decision that would affect him dearly. Seeing a number of wounded of both sides from the earlier action, Johnston ordered his personal surgeon, D. W. Yandell, to set up a hospital and care for them. Johnston told his doctor, "These men were our enemies a moment ago, they are prisoners now; take care of them."

Yandell tried to make the point that he should stay with his general, but Johnston was adamant and later left the scene without telling Yandell. The surgeon would be of no more use to him that day.[18]

While Johnston tarried near the Federal camp, the battle went on. By noon or a little before, Breckinridge's two reserve brigades were arriving on the scene and Johnston personally helped to place them in position. In fact, Johnston seems to have moved forward over the gullies and ravines with the soldiers, moving up directly in rear of Bowen's brigade. There, just on the high ground overlooking a tributary of Locust Grove Branch, Johnston found more high ground from which he could direct the movements of his right wing. Governor Isham G. Harris, who had temporarily attached himself to Johnston's staff for the battle, remembered Johnston's activities at this place. Visiting the spot years later, in 1896, Harris remembered, "Here, within ten steps of the place where I am, General Johnston sat on his horse for over an hour and a half or two hours from about noon on Sunday, putting his Reserve in position. Everything is perfectly natural just as I remember it. There is the stream where our orderlies went for water and where soldiers were filling their canteens, over there was the camp that we passed through in coming here."[19]

From his high-ground position, Johnston watched as his reserve brigades tried in vain to push the enemy line out of the Peach Orchard. Fierce fighting took place as the Confederate brigades tried to push the Federal line back, thus turning the all-important enemy left flank. But the terrain was playing havoc with Johnston's plan; the big ravines near the river were funneling all the Confederate brigades into a smaller space that allowed the Federals to use the open fields to their advantage. Finally, seeing his units were not making progress, Johnston made his fatal decision. His troops were not currently able, under the present leadership of Breckinridge and Withers, to drive on to victory. And there were no more reserves to call forward as he had done on several occasions earlier in the day. The only option left was to wade into the melee himself and inspire his troops to greater efforts. Certainly, the army commander's place was not on the front line, but this was the critical point in Johnston's critical gamble. It all came down to this effort at turning the enemy flank. Johnston had to lead. If it cost him his life to win the victory, then so be it. Conquer of perish.

Positioned well behind Bowen's brigade, Johnston rode forward through the rear areas of the fight around 1:00 p.m., coming under fire as he did so. Taking refuge with his men in a small hollow in which sat a "mule lot," Johnston continued to direct the battle from there. Colonel Munford remembered Johnston sitting in "a depression about thirty yards behind our front line, where the bullets passed over our heads; but he could see more than half of his line, and, if an emergency arose, could meet it promptly." Munford also related how "the general passed his eye from the right of the line to his extreme point of vision in the direction of the left, and slowly back again." Johnston sent various staff officers on errands to position certain brigades and batteries and at times rode up and down the line itself. He did not remain in the sheltered ravine the entire time. Governor Harris remembered, "Here the firing was kept up with great energy by both armies for, perhaps, an hour, during the whole of which time the general remained upon the line, more exposed to the fire of the enemy than any soldier in the line. After the firing had been thus continued for near an hour, the general said to me: 'They are offering stubborn resistance here. I shall have to put the bayonet to them.'" Johnston was going to lead the charge.[20]

When Breckinridge received word of the pending assault, he rode to Johnston and told him he could not get his men to charge. Johnston replied, "Oh, yes, general; I think you can." When Breckinridge responded that he had tried and failed, Johnston calmly replied, "Then, I will help you. . . . We can get them to make the charge." Harris remembered that the Confederate line at this time "slightly wavered with a backward tendency." Johnston told Harris, "I will go to the front, order, and lead the charge." Harris later remembered, "Just as he was in the act of passing through the line to the front, he said to me, 'Go to the extreme right and lead the Tennessee regiment stationed there." The general began to ride his line, whipping up the emotions of his men in prelude to the bayonet charge. To the infantry of Bowen's brigade, Johnston "told us a few more charges and the day was ours." Riding along the line of soldiers with fixed bayonets, Johnston tapped each bayonet with the tin cup taken from some anonymous Wisconsin soldier. "These must do the work," he implored. "Men! They are stubborn; we must use the bayonet."[21]

At the climax of emotions, for both general and soldiers, Johnston yelled, "I will lead you!" He wheeled Fire Eater around and moved forward, followed immediately by the Confederates of Bowen's battle line that was "thrilling and trembling with that tremendous and irresistible ardor." The soldiers nearest him moved forward with him, one soldier declared, "as if drawn to him by some overmastering magnetic force." All along the line, the rest of the Confederate units joined the advance while Johnston led the wildly cheering Confederates in an attack across Sarah Bell's cotton field. One of the colonels in Bowen's brigade, John D. Martin, reported that Johnston "halted in 200 or 300 yards, and told us to charge ahead; the enemy were before us."[22]

Johnston's attack was successful, due in most part to his personal leadership. He could get his men to do what other officers could not. In addition to the responses already chronicled, a vast number of officers and soldiers later

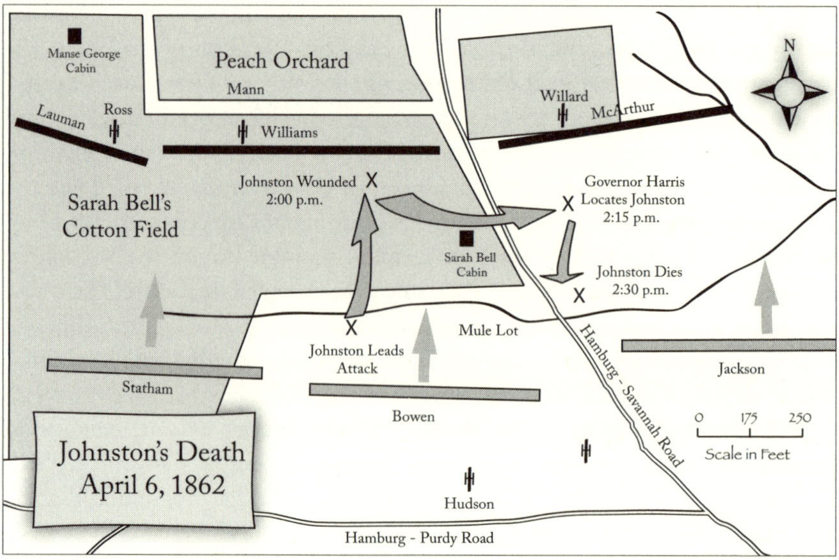


remembered how majestic and knightly Johnston had appeared that day. One of his brigade commanders, probably Randall Gibson, remembered Johnston "looked like a hero of the antique type, and his very appearance on the field was a tower of more than kingly strength." Braxton Bragg remembered being "inspired by his coolness, confidence, and determination. Few men have equaled him in the possession and display at the proper time of these great qualities of the soldier." Johnston's personal leadership, even in great danger, is illustrated by the episode in which he convinced Breckinridge's men to attack even when the former vice president and senator could not.[23]

Hurlbut's Federals withdrew under the pressure to another line of defense, which Johnston soon began to press by repositioning his units and sending them onward. He had ridden back a short distance behind the Confederate line to use the heights of a small knoll to get the best view possible. There, Harris found him. "I had never, in my life, seen him looking more bright, joyous, and happy, than he looked at the moment that I approached him. The charge he had led was heroic. It had been successful, and his face expressed a soldier's joy and a patriot's hope." Apparently, Johnston was also in a playful mood. Colonel Thomas M. Jack remembered the general "slapping his thigh and smiling, upon a spent ball which had struck and stung him." Showing Governor Harris a cut in his boot caused by enemy fire, he remarked, "Governor, they came very near putting me *hors de combat* in that charge." A frightened Harris asked if he was wounded, but Johnston replied in the negative.[24]

As the fighting raged on and the two sat on the knoll talking, a Federal battery opened up on the new Confederate line. Governor Harris remembered, "He paused in the middle of a sentence to say, 'Order Colonel Statham to wheel his regiment to the left, charge, and take that battery.'" The governor rode the two hundred yards, delivered the order, and made his way back to Johnston. As he reported the order delivered and the troops in motion, Harris sadly remembered, "The General sank down in his saddle, leaning over to the left." The startled governor remembered it was "in a manner that indicated he was falling from his horse." Harris grabbed Johnston by the collar and held him on the horse. He bent forward and looked Johnston in the face: "General, are you wounded?" With what Harris described as "a very deliberate and emphatic tone," Johnston answered, "Yes, and I fear seriously."[25]

A horrified Harris yelled to nearby Captain W. L. Wickam of Johnston's staff to ultimately find Yandell, but to send the first surgeon he saw on the way. Just in that short amount of time, the general was obviously getting worse. Harris remembered, "The general's hold upon his reigns relaxed, and it dropped from his hand." Taking Johnston's reigns with his own in one hand and supporting the general with the other, Harris and the not-yet-departed Wickam guided the horses into a small ravine behind the lines and out of the line of fire. Harris slipped off his horse and pulled Johnston "over upon me, and eased him to the ground as gently as I could." Wickam then galloped away to find a doctor. Harris spied a nearby soldier and sent him to locate any staff officer and bring them quickly. By this time, Johnston was hardly conscious, and a horrified Governor Harris, now with Johnston's head in his lap, was alone with his dying general. "With eager anxiety I asked many questions about his wounds," Harris sadly remembered, "to which he gave no answer, not even a look of intelligence."[26]

As Harris unloosed Johnston's cravat and searched for a torso wound, other staff officers arrived, including Johnston's brother-in-law, William Preston. Although the staff would later find out that he had been hit as many as four times, only one bullet penetrated the skin. No other wound could be found aside from a liberally bleeding wound in his right leg. Johnston had been hit in the popliteal artery, and he was dying from a loss of blood. Yandell could have treated the wound successfully with a tourniquet, but Johnston had ridden forward without him earlier in the battle. Harris tried to pour brandy into his mouth, the governor remembered, "but he made no effort to swallow; it gurgled in his throat in his effort to breathe, and I turned his head so as to relieve him." A grieving Preston, kneeling beside his brother-in-law, cried, "Johnston, do you know me?" Some thought they saw only a faint smile. Then it happened. "In a few moments he ceased to breathe," Harris reported. "He died calmly, and, to all appearances, free from pain—indeed so calmly, that the only evidence I had that he had passed from life was the fact that he ceased to breathe, and the heart ceased to throb. There was not the slightest struggle, nor the contortion of a muscle; his features were as calm and as natural as at any time in life and health." It was around 2:30 p.m., April 6, 1862.[27]

Preston requested that Governor Harris go inform Beauregard he now commanded the army. Harris's horse had run off, so he mounted Fire Eater. Harris remembered that he "found him so badly crippled that I dismounted

Johnston's death site has produced some controversy, but most historians accept the site marked in the Shiloh National Military Park as the actual place. Isham G. Harris, governor of Tennessee and a volunteer aide to Johnston at Shiloh, returned in 1896 as a U.S. senator and marked the spot. (Courtesy of Shiloh National Military Park.)

and examined him, and found upon examination that he was wounded in three legs by musket balls." Harris rode him to the rear where Johnston had left an orderly and fresh horses. Harris mounted one of the fresh horses and made his way to Beauregard. Meanwhile, Preston and Johnston's staff took the body by ambulance to his headquarters site of the night before. The staff served Beauregard the rest of the day, but the Creole allowed them to carry Johnston's body to Corinth that night. There, Johnston's body was cleaned and sent to New Orleans, where it was buried until 1867, when he was removed to Austin Texas, his adopted state. Johnston had once remarked to William Preston, "When I die, I want a handful of Texas earth on my breast." That is exactly what he got.[28]

Albert Sidney Johnston had entered the Battle of Shiloh a desperate man. Reeling from defeat and calls for his removal and facing a combination of enemy armies on his front, he had to win a victory on April 6. It was the last gamble. If this attempt failed, then Corinth and probably the entire Mississippi Valley was doomed, and with it the Confederacy. Johnston had to win a victory, and he was determined to do whatever was in his power to win that victory. But at 2:00 p.m. on April 6, 1862, Johnston was out of options. He had sent in his last reserves, and they were stalled. His only option left was to wade into the battle himself and hopefully inspire his men to greater efforts. It was do or die. Johnston did so, and it cost him his life. Perhaps mercifully, however, he died at the height of his success. He was wounded in the successful charge, and saw nothing other than his legions sweeping the field.

That success, however, was only temporary, and his army would not win the victory at Shiloh, his successors would not defend the Mississippi Valley, and his nation would not win its independence. Perhaps he died for nothing, but Albert Sidney Johnston probably would not have looked at it that way. He had done everything he humanly could have, even giving the ultimate sacrifice. His declaration was conquer or perish. He did the latter.

# 3

# Anatomy of an Icon: Shiloh's Hornet's Nest in Civil War Memory

The sweat-lathered soldier, caked with black powder and grime, peered through lengthening shadows to see if they were coming again. Along with neighboring units, his regiment, the 12th Iowa Infantry, had for some six hours repelled at least seven or eight attacks on their position. Those Rebels in butternut and gray had attacked over and over again, fresh unit after unit, only to be turned away by the thunder-like volleys from their Enfields and those of the regiments on either flank. But the enemy just kept coming back, finally with heavy artillery support that caused the Iowa boys to lie down and hug the earth as close as possible. Just when it seemed the situation could get no worse, news came that the enemy was now in their rear. Orders came to fall back, but the enemy seemed to have every avenue of escape blocked. In one area the crossfire was especially dangerous, causing the soldiers to term the place "Hell's Hollow." Soon, white flags began to appear. But this young soldier was spared from surrender because of a worse fate: a Confederate bullet slammed into his thigh and he went down. He spent a miserable night watching as his comrades surrendered and were carted off as prisoners of war, bleeding from his wound, and ultimately suffering on the battlefield through the long, rainy night.[1]

Forty years later, almost to the day, that same soldier stood on that same historic ground and must have felt extreme pride as he pondered what had happened all those years before. The man was David W. Reed, and although he did not know it at the time, he and his comrades had defended the famous Hornet's Nest at Shiloh on April 6, 1862. Making him even more proud, Reed had by 1902 become the one man who wielded more power on how the Hornet's Nest would be remembered than anyone else. Of the nearly 110,000 men who had struggled at Shiloh, Reed had become the authority on the battle. He was the historian on the commission charged with establishing Shiloh National Military Park, and his pen literally wrote volumes about what was important at Shiloh. In 1902, forty years after his miserable experience on the battlefield in 1862, Reed issued his history of the clash: *The Battle of Shiloh and the Organizations Engaged.* The Hornet's Nest, his fight, played the starring role.[2]

Today, in large part because of Reed's historical efforts, historians view the Hornet's Nest as the focal point in the Battle of Shiloh. It is Shiloh's Pickett's Charge; it is Shiloh's Bloody Lane. It is the area that most visitors want to see. Telling evidence in the Shiloh National Military Park's visitor center shows just how much of an American icon the Hornet's Nest has become. On the large wall map (with battle lines located by David W. Reed, no doubt), so many visitors have pointed to the famous spots at Shiloh that at certain places the print is wearing thin. Thousands upon thousands of fingers have pointed to Pittsburg Landing, Shiloh Church, and Bloody Pond, causing small globes of wear on the map. In the Hornet's Nest, however, the entire Union line is worn from one end to the other. It is as if visitors make their point that this place was crucial by emphasizing their touch all up and down the line there.

But was the Hornet's Nest really that important? If so, the attention is justified. If not, then the question of why it has become such an icon must be asked. Was the Hornet's Nest really the focal point of the battle, or are we the benefactors of a collective and selective memory of Shiloh veterans?

In actuality, the Hornet's Nest's iconic status is a result of a few veterans' interpretation of the facts, and that interpretation has been growing in reputation ever since. An examination of those early veterans and their efforts in singling out the Hornet's Nest, as well as later National Park Service historians in continuing that thesis, can offer many answers regarding the battle. When taken as a case study of Civil War memory, the Hornet's Nest at Shiloh can not only provide a better understanding of the battle but also point to the need for further research into the historiography of other battles, examining how they were treated by veterans and historians years later. In many cases, and certainly at Shiloh, the treatment of the events after the fact has had more to do with how we view the battles today than how they were actually fought.

## The Hornet's Nest—April 6, 1862

So what really happened at the Hornet's Nest on that bright spring day, and how did it fit into the battle as a whole? The Federal line in the Hornet's Nest was the result of the meeting between withdrawing frontline divisions and advancing reserve divisions of the Federal army. The two first divisions the Confederates attacked were those of Brigadier General William T. Sherman and Brigadier General Benjamin M. Prentiss, and they began to fall back from their initial lines of defense around midmorning. As these two units began to fall back, they met advancing divisions from the rear. Brigadier General Stephen A. Hurlbut moved his men forward on the Union left into the Peach Orchard sector, while Major General John A. McClernand moved his brigades up on the Federal right to support the Shiloh Church line. In the center, Brigadier General W. H. L. Wallace led his troops forward into what would become the Hornet's Nest, the center of the line. As the shattered divisions of Sherman and Prentiss encountered the advancing reserves, they reformed and joined the developing line, thus creating a Federal line of battle that stretched almost three miles from Owl Creek on the west to the Tennessee River on the east. The Confederates would literally pound their way through most of this line, but not at the Hornet's Nest.[3]

The reason the Hornet's Nest never broke under repeated Confederate assaults was not because of the strength of the Federal line but rather a result of what was occurring on other parts of the battlefield, leaving the center of the line the least fought over portion of the battlefield. Earlier in the day, long before any Confederates reached the Hornet's Nest area, Confederate commander General Albert Sidney Johnston had put into motion his plan of driving the enemy into the swamps of Snake and Owl creeks northwest of Pittsburg Landing. Inherent in the plan, of course, was hooking the left flank of the Federal army and then driving it. Johnston personally witnessed the fighting near Peter Spain's field as his brigades dealt Prentiss's division a cruel morning greeting. He heard the sounds of heavy firing all along the line but realized that it stopped just inside the woods east of the field. Logically thinking that where he heard no fighting there was no enemy presence, Johnston thought he had found the Federal left flank and could begin his turning and driving movement. In actuality, the fighting had fallen off east of Spain's field, but not because it was the enemy left flank. There was a gap between Prentiss's division and the next unit in line to the east, Colonel David Stuart's brigade of Sherman's division. Johnston had found that gap and perceived it to be the left flank of the Federal army. The damage was done when Johnston sent his hard-charging brigades surging to the northwest to drive into the swamps the Federals he had flanked.[4]

The result of Johnston's predetermined plan was that almost all the Confederate Army of the Mississippi moved off to the northwest to drive the Federals in one mass attack into the swamps. The eventual contact between this Confederate surge and the advancing units of McClernand's division was the bloody and brutal fighting between 10:30 and 11:00 a.m. around what is today known as the Crossroads. Most of the assaulting Confederates, in this move, went well west of the Hornet's Nest, thus placing as many as nine Confederate brigades on that western third of the battlefield.[5]

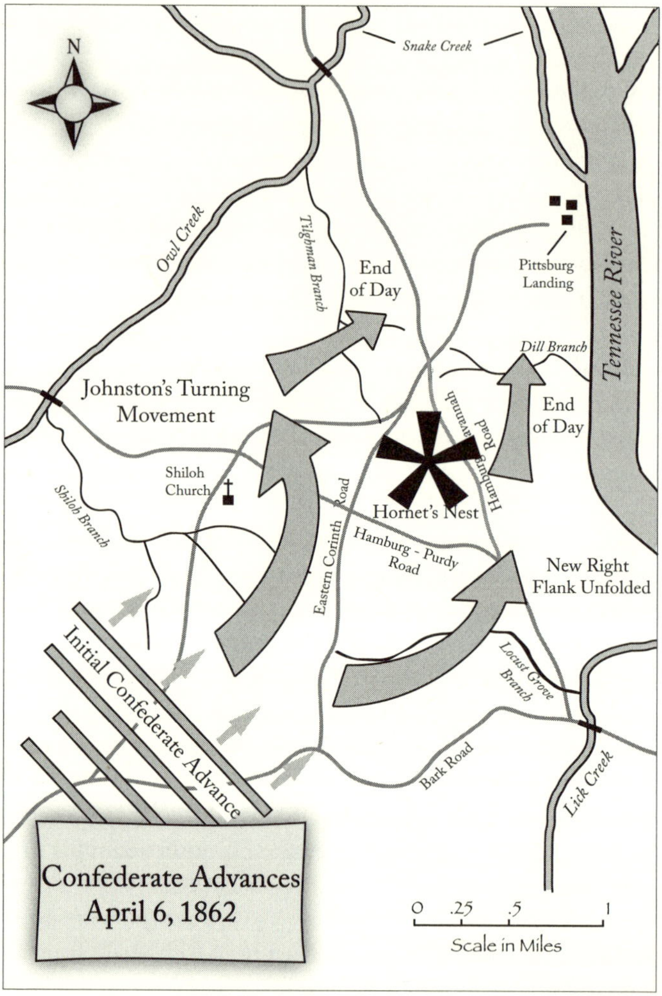


But Johnston soon learned, to his dismay, that he had acted too quickly. An engineer sent to scout the Federal left early that morning returned after Johnston had ordered the final push and reported that an entire Federal division was still lurking farther to the east. In actuality, it was only the understrength brigade commanded by David Stuart, not a full division, but Johnston did not know that at the time. Acting on this faulty intelligence, he immediately began to realign his army to take care of a major potential problem.[6]

Johnston basically unfolded another wing of his army out on the right flank. He recalled two brigades that were advancing on the right of the major attack at the Crossroads and sent them to the extreme new right of the army, while also sending two-thirds (two brigades) of the reserve corps to the area. The result was four brigades unfolded into line on the eastern third of the battlefield. These four units moved in an area far to the east of the Hornet's Nest. The two major wings of the Confederate army were thus moving away from each other along the lines of an obtuse angle. That left relatively few Confederate troops in the center third of the battlefield.[7]

The Hornet's Nest, therefore, formed inside a vacuum left by the Confederate movements. And it was a good thing early on, for the Union position was not as strong during the initial actions in the area as it would become later in the day. Two regiments of Colonel Thomas W. Sweeny's brigade had deployed on the right of the Corinth Road, but because there was little room left between them and McClernand's brigades, the other four regiments remained in the rear as a reserve. Colonel James M. Tuttle's Brigade of four Iowa regiments extended the line along an old road, with the 2nd Iowa (which connected with Sweeny's brigade on the road), 7th Iowa, and the right of the 12th Iowa fronting Duncan Field from behind a split-rail fence. The left of the 12th Iowa and the 14th Iowa faced a dense area of undergrowth along the Eastern Corinth Road, probably where a field had once been. But the 14th Iowa did not connect with anything. In fact, it was several yards between its left and the next units in line—Prentiss's division, and they were not terribly stable because of the trashing they had taken earlier that morning. Helping small portions of the 18th and 25th Missouri, 18th Wisconsin, and 12th Michigan hold the line was the 23rd Missouri, which arrived from Pittsburg Landing as the line was reforming and almost doubled Prentiss's command to about eleven hundred. It was Prentiss's command that ultimately connected with Hurlbut's units near the Peach Orchard. In addition, all or portions of six artillery batteries (Stone's, Welker's, Richardson's, Powell's, Munch's, and Hickenlooper's) studded the Federal line at various points. Still, a gap existed between Tuttle and Prentiss, and the Iowans on Tuttle's left went through several convoluted manual moves to try to shore up their flank.[8]

Within the context of the diverging wings of the Confederate army and the incomplete line of the Hornet's Nest early in the fight, gap and all, the first Confederate contact with the Hornet's Nest came around 10:30 a.m., when the extreme right of the major Crossroads attack stumbled into Duncan Field and quickly learned a strong enemy force was there. Colonel Robert Shaver's Arkansas brigade was moving on the extreme right flank of the eight-brigade

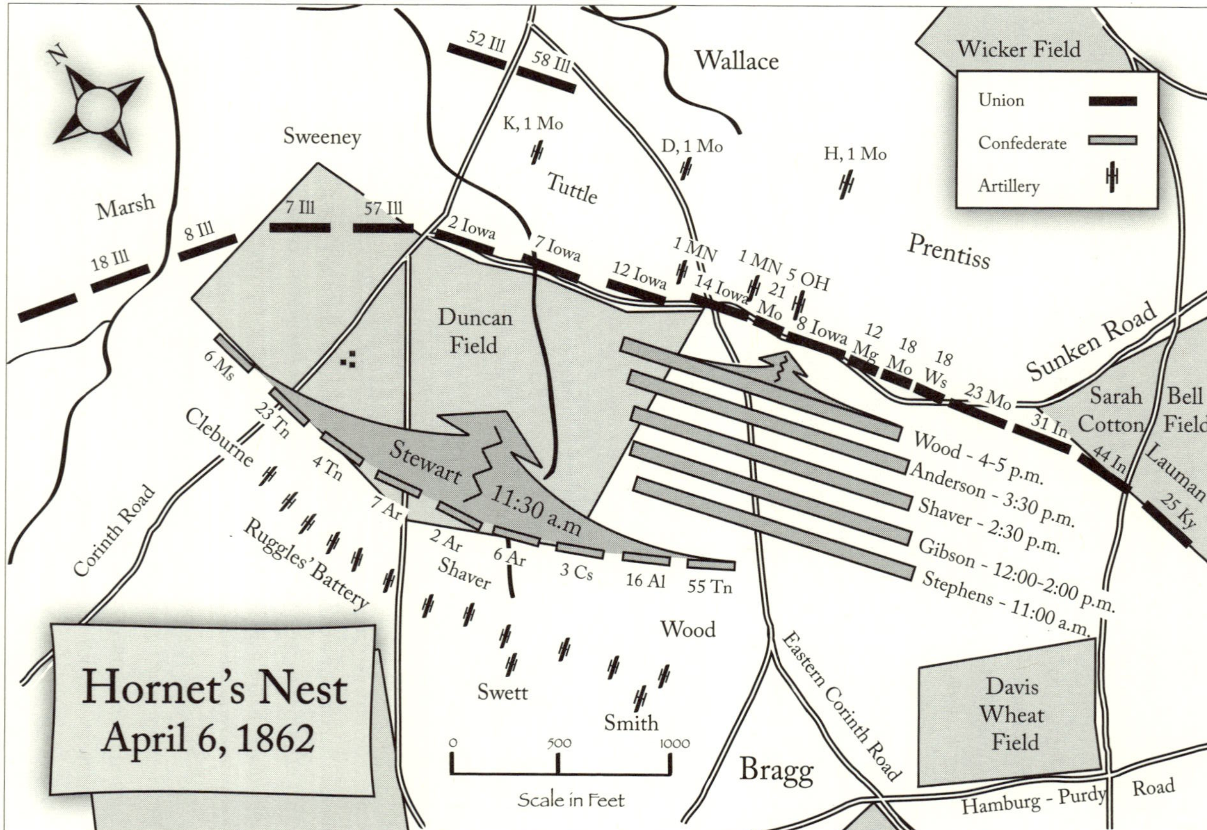

Hornet's Nest
April 6, 1862
Union
Confederate
Artillery
Wicker Field
Wallace
Sweeney
Marsh
Tuttle
Prentiss
K, 1 Mo
D, 1 Mo
H, 1 Mo
52 Ill
58 Ill
7 Ill
57 Ill
8 Ill
18 Ill
2 Iowa
7 Iowa
12 Iowa
1 MN
14 Iowa
1 MN
5 OH
21
Mo
8 Iowa
12
Mg
18
Mo
18
Ws
23 Mo
31 In
44 In
Lauman
25 Ky
Sunken Road
Sarah
Cotton
Bell
Field
Duncan
Field
6 Ms
23 Tn
4 Tn
7 Ar
2 Ar
6 Ar
3 Cs
16 Al
55 Tn
Stewart
11:30 a.m
Cleburne
Ruggles' Battery
Shaver
Wood
Swett
Smith
Wood - 4-5 p.m.
Anderson - 3:30 p.m.
Shaver - 2:30 p.m.
Gibson - 12:00-2:00 p.m.
Stephens - 11:00 a.m.
Corinth Road
Eastern Corinth Road
Bragg
Davis
Wheat
Field
Hamburg - Purdy Road
0
500
1000
Scale in Feet
N

mass attack (with an additional brigade in reserve) on McClernand and Sherman at the Crossroads. His attempt to flank McClernand's left brought him into Joseph Duncan's cotton field, on the other side of which lay W. H. L. Wallace's men along the old farm lane later termed the Sunken Road. As Shaver's boys, particularly the right-flank regiment—the 3rd Confederate Infantry—entered Duncan Field around 10:30 a.m., Tuttle's Iowa soldiers were waiting for them. Enfields made gruesome wounds to the Confederate infantrymen, who (all that could) quickly took cover in the woods to the rear. Shaver withdrew a short distance and reformed. The first shots in defense of the Hornet's Nest had been fired.[9]

While the Confederate units were forming, one Confederate brigade attacked of its own volition, marking the first actual assault on the Hornet's Nest itself. The Confederate second in command, General P. G. T. Beauregard, had sent Colonel William H. Stephens's small brigade to the right of the army; Beauregard told them to find the heaviest fighting and go in. Stephens's division commander, Major General Benjamin F. Cheatham, took the brigade to the right of the Confederate assault, which was Shaver's brigade, and no doubt learned from them the presence of the enemy to the front. Cheatham deployed Smith's Mississippi Battery and sent Stephens against the Hornet's Nest. About 11:00 a.m., Stephens led his troops into the teeth of the Federal line.[10]

Stephens's Brigade was not in the best of shape even before the attack. A portion of it, along with the brigade's normal commander, Colonel George Maney, was away guarding the bridge over Lick Creek. Stephens thus had a small brigade, fewer than a thousand muskets total. And Stephens himself was having a bad day. He had been sick and was extremely weak but had risen from his sick bed and accompanied his command into battle. Just before the assault, his horse took a shot and threw Stephens, causing further problems for the weak colonel. Under cover of the artillery, however, Stephens urged his men on, but there was no chance the small brigade would break the Federal line. The Tennesseans and Kentuckians met the massed volleys of the 12th and 14th Iowa as well as direct blasts from supporting artillery. One Federal officer remembered that "he made a bold attack on us, but [was] met with a warm reception." At least some of the assault was made through Duncan Field on the left, which caused even more problems for the units on the flank that had to charge through open territory. Cheatham described the results: "[T]he enemy opened upon us from his entire front a terrific fire of artillery and musketry . . . when another part of the enemy's force concealed and protected by the fence and thicket on our left, opened a murderous cross-fire upon our lines." The Federal fire was way too much, and the battered brigade withdrew to safety shortly after launching its assault. Some veterans later claimed that they launched a second assault, but no documentary evidence has surfaced to support that assertion.[11]

Both figuratively and literally blown away by the ferocity of the Federal defense, Stephens soon withdrew his now even smaller brigade and moved it to the right to connect with Breckinridge's new right wing, which he could see in the distance. He did not want a gap between his right and Breckinridge's left, but he also did not want to encounter the Federal line in the Hornet's Nest again. His troops moved to the right and connected with Breckinridge's brigades in front of a large cotton field. On the other side was a peach orchard in full bloom.[12]

At some point around 11:00 a.m. and Stephens's attack, the staunch defenders of the Hornet's Nest received a visit from their commander, Ulysses S. Grant. After arriving on the field, Grant made his way to the front lines and spoke to each division commander. Prentiss remembered Grant giving him the last orders he would receive—to hold his position "at all hazards." Prentiss would take the order literally, setting the stage for the future dramatic events that would occur that day.[13]

About the same time as Grant's visit, another group of Confederate officers were also growing concerned about the obviously strong position on the east side of Duncan Field. Shaver had just received its full force, and the racket made by Stephens's assault likely confirmed the suspicion in Confederate officers' minds. This led the ranking Confederate commander in the area just west of Duncan Field to pause from his advance to the northwest, in concert with Johnston's push to destroy the Federal army in the swamps, and focus his attention for a limited time on the Hornet's Nest line.[14]

With the wounding of the ranking Confederate in the area, Major General Thomas C. Hindman, Brigadier General Alexander Stewart became the commanding officer in the sector. He had commanded only a brigade that morning, but his own division commander (Brigadier General Charles Clark) had recently been wounded, which placed him in command of that unit. Likewise, Hindman, Shaver's division commander, was down, and Stewart received orders to take command of both units and attack the enemy. Leading Shaver's brigade as well as one regiment of his own brigade and the small elements of Brigadier General Patrick Cleburne's and Brigadier General S. A. M. Wood's brigades that had broken off their parent units and wandered into the area, Stewart managed to compile the largest order of battle that would assault the Hornet's Nest that day. Numbering some thirty-seven hundred men combined and supported by Swett's Mississippi Battery alongside Smith's artillery, the conglomerate of portions of four Confederate brigades trudged into Duncan Field about 11:30 a.m. They soon realized the folly of such a move.[15]

Stewart's command stretched from the main Corinth Road all the way across Duncan Field to the Eastern Corinth Road. The 23rd Tennessee and 6th Mississippi, lost from Cleburne's Brigade, manned the left with Stewart's 4th Tennessee next in line to the right. Next came the bulk of Shaver's Brigade, with the two lost units of S. A. M. Wood's brigade, the 16th Alabama and 55th Tennessee, manning the right of the line. The term "assault" is a misnomer; Stewart himself reported that his command merely "engaged" the enemy until Shaver sent word that his brigade was out of ammunition and was withdrawing. That, of course, effectively took any steam out of the attack, as Shaver's was the only full brigade participating. The other units soon also withdrew, some falling back for ammunition and others moving back over to the west, where the main effort was supposed to be occurring anyway. Shaver's brigade would take literally hours to rest and resupply its ammunition, taking it out of the effective ranks for that time period.[16]

Although Stephens and Stewart failed in their isolated assaults, the general Confederate advance against McClernand's Crossroads line to the west was very successful, but to different degrees depending on where it was along the line. Generally, the Confederate assault was more successful the farther west one traveled; this was because of many factors, including terrain, shattered defending commands, and the weight of Confederate mass on the extreme left flank. The result was that the Federals were driven toward Pittsburg Landing rather than away from it. The farther east along this line one traveled, the Confederate success became much less defined, with Shaver's right making no headway at all against Tuttle's Iowans and Stephens and Stewart being stopped in their tracks in Duncan Field and along the Eastern Corinth Road. The stiff resistance around Duncan Field thus alerted Confederate commanders of a new force that needed to be dealt with. Enter Braxton Bragg.[17]

The hard-luck commander of the Confederate second corps was the unfortunate recipient of a bungled operation at Shiloh. The original Confederate plan had called for an unwieldy attack order that soon broke down into chaos, with command and control rapidly deteriorating. The Confederate corps commanders thus acted on their own and divided up the line into sectors, with William J. Hardee taking the left, Leonidas Polk the center, and Bragg the right. (The fourth corps commander, John C. Breckinridge, was even then unfolding the new right, making Bragg's command the right center.) Bragg happened to get the area with the fewest Confederate troops in it. The bulk of the army had passed far to the west around the Crossroads, while Breckinridge was unfolding a new flank far to the east around the Peach Orchard.[18]

Bragg's center third of the battlefield had only three brigades on it, and one of those (Gladden's) was so badly mauled that it was essentially out of action for some six hours while another (Shaver's) was resupplying its ammunition and resting from what had already been hours of intense combat. Neither brigade would be a factor again until later in the afternoon. That left Bragg with one effective brigade in the area: Colonel Randall Gibson's. By this time, of sixteen Confederate brigades, seven (and one more in reserve) were off to the west while five (including Stephen's) were to the east. With few numbers and long odds, around noon Bragg finally arrived in the area and began his part in the famous operations against the Union Hornet's Nest.[19]

It was a good thing the initial Confederate assaults were either short on numbers in Shaver's and Stephens's cases or were logistically uncoordinated as in Stewart's case, because the yawning gap between Tuttle and Prentiss could potentially have caused problems for the position early in the day. Seeing the need to fill the gap, Prentiss asked for help and Sweeny sent one of his reserve regiments up to the main line. The 8th Iowa thus took position and soon was heavily engaged. Colonel James Geddes of the 8th Iowa reported he "immediately engaged a battalion of the enemy."[20]

The battalion described by Geddes was actually Gibson's Louisiana brigade. The result was a lot of dead and wounded Louisianans. Gibson himself described the attack: "The brigade moved forward in fine style, marching through an open [Davis wheat] field under a heavy fire and half way up an elevation covered with an almost impenetrable thicket, upon which the enemy was posted." Colonel William T. Shaw of the 14th Iowa reported that he ordered his men to lie down and wait until the enemy was within thirty paces before firing. "The enemy's first line was completely destroyed," Shaw remembered. The Louisianans and Arkansans could attest to his memory, one Confederate reporting that they were repulsed easily by "a battery . . . that raked our flank, while a steady fire of musketry extended along the entire front." Although regimental reports mentioned only three charges, Gibson reported the brigade fell back, reformed, and charged a total of four times. No matter how many times they assaulted the position, it was, in the words of one soldier, "impregnable to infantry alone." The jubilant Federals agreed. Colonel Joseph Woods of the 12th Iowa reported, "Again and again repeatedly did he attack us, trying vainly to drive us from our position. He failed to move us one inch." Part of the reason for the Confederate failure was that the artillery battery attached to Gibson's Brigade had been left in Corinth to help garrison the town while the army was fighting at Pittsburg Landing. With only long-range support from Swett and Smith, with an occasional fire from Robertson's Alabama Battery down the Eastern Corinth Road, Gibson's Brigade made those futile assaults into the teeth of the Hornet's Nest, losing more and more men as it charged time after time. For some two hours they fought, but Gibson finally admitted, "We were repulsed." To make the defeats even worse, the Federals counterattacked on a couple of occasions, driving the fleeing Confederates before returning to their original lines.[21]

Just as Gibson's fought-out brigade was falling back, from which position they ultimately moved to the right, Shaver's resupplied and replenished brigade came forward ready for action. Bragg, with Gibson's men incapable of making another attack, sent Shaver to the front once again. The Arkansas units strode into the teeth of the Hornet's Nest about 2:30 p.m., but the result was another failure.[22]

Shaver reported that Bragg ordered him to take the Federal line "posted in considerable force in a dense undergrowth in a heavy woods." Shaver's line moved forward until within fifty or sixty yards of the enemy line, when "a terrific and murderous fire was poured in upon me from their lines and battery. It was impossible to charge through the dense undergrowth." An amazed Tuttle, by now counting attack after attack, remembered that the enemy was "each time baffled and completely routed." Shaver wisely concluded that his fire was doing no harm to the enemy and he "had nothing left me but to retire or have my men all shot down." Shaver withdrew, and a disgusted Bragg ordered him to reform and resupply in the rear.[23]

Not only were the Iowa Federals in front pouring heavy fire into the oncoming Confederates, but so too were units on the flanks. With all the commotion along the Eastern Corinth Road, the portion of Sweeny's brigade that was on line in the northern part of Duncan Field shifted in order to take the Confederates moving along that route in flank. The 7th and 58th Illinois turned their lines to the left and occupied a position around Duncan's log cabin and a few cotton bales he had piled nearby. As the Confederates moved across their front, the Illinois soldiers poured a heavy fire into their exposed left flank. "The enemy's ranks were visibly thinned by the steady and rapid firing which the men with the utmost coolness poured into them," remembered one Illinois officer in Duncan Field.[24]

The next Confederate brigade to go in was Patton Anderson's, which had seen severe fighting on the Confederate left all day. He had heard the severe contest to his right and, acting on orders from one of Bragg's staff officers to go to the sound of the firing, had led his men to the right. He met Colonel Marshall Smith of the Crescent Regiment, and they decided to attack.

Smith was to go in on the left while Anderson led his men farther around to the right. He ultimately went in along the Eastern Corinth Road—precisely where Gibson and Shaver had assaulted before. As his brigade was moving forward through what Anderson described as "thick underbrush," they met survivors of the 13th Louisiana of Gibson's Brigade, who told them they "could not get through the brush." Anderson nevertheless tried, crossing the small hollow and beginning his "ascent of the opposite slope, when a galling fire from infantry and canister from howitzers swept through my ranks with deadly affect." Anderson remembered, "The thicket was so dense that it was impossible for a company officer to be seen at platoon distance." His brigade fell back under the brow of a hill, where several commanders reported "their men unable to make another charge by reason of the complete state of exhaustion they were in." The only success had been on the far left, where the Crescent Regiment, apparently aided by portions of A. P. Stewart's divided brigade, dislodged the Illinois boys of Sweeny's brigade from their flanking position along the main Corinth Road.[25]

By this time, about 4:30 p.m., the battle was beginning to simmer down to the Hornet's Nest alone. Indeed, the defenders were beginning to think something momentous was going on. "We held our position about six hours," one Federal remembered in amazement. But the Union line was not so secure on other parts of the battlefield, prompting Sweeny to send all three of his other reserve regiments to those threatened areas throughout the day. Sherman and McClernand had fallen back behind Tilghman Branch on the western side of the battlefield. Rather than follow and attack those units, most of the eight Confederate brigades on the western third of the battlefield wheeled to the right (according to the custom of moving to the sound of the guns) and moved on the flank and rear of the right of the Hornet's Nest. Similarly, Hurlbut's division had fallen back from the Peach Orchard, and those five Confederate brigades on the eastern third of the battlefield began to flank the left of the Hornet's Nest. More units arrived in front of the position as well, such as S. A. M. Wood's brigade, which massed alongside Shaver's men. Attending much of the Confederate infantry's move to the center was the accompanying artillery, which was put to good effect in a massed position later called Ruggles's Battery. By 5:15, the converging Confederate units had almost encircled the Federal center and were pouring the enemy lines with massed artillery along the western side of Duncan Field. In fact, the supporting Union batteries had fallen back and gone into Grant's next line of defense, leaving the infantry to hold the line alone. By then the Hornet's Nest was becoming untenable even for them as several rounds per second from Ruggles's massed guns fell in close proximity.[26]

But Grant was not giving up; he was busy forming another line to the rear. While McClernand, Sherman, Hurlbut, Prentiss, and Wallace held out, Grant had his chief of staff Colonel Joseph D. Webster forming all available units back near the landing. Beginning about 2:30 p.m., Webster located a battery of siege guns intended for use in a siege at Corinth and used them and their psychological advantage to stud a new Federal line. Webster also had no fewer than three other previously unengaged batteries to put into the line by midafternoon. And these overlooked huge, gaping ravines to their front—making their defensive line that much stronger. Two gunboats in the river on the left flank added to the initial strength of this new line. So the famous last line of defense was already very strong by 3:00 p.m. and became that much stronger as unit after unit fell back from the forward lines. For example, the Federal artillery that pulled out of the Hornet's Nest around 4:00 p.m. went into the line. By 4:30 p.m., the time Hurlbut, McClernand, and Sherman began their withdrawals into the last line, that line was already very strong. Prentiss and Wallace could have pulled out then and gone into the final line and held it all night long.[27]

But Prentiss and Wallace did not fall back. They interpreted Grant's orders to "hold at all hazards" differently than Hurlbut, McClernand, and Sherman had. The Hornet's Nest defenders literally held until they were surrounded and captured. After Hurlbut fell back on the left, Prentiss bent his flank back to the north to cover the area. Meanwhile, on the far right, several of Sweeny's and even Tuttle's regiments were almost magnetically drawn to the rear by McClernand's departure. That left Prentiss in his flank position and Tuttle's 12th and 14th Iowa, plus the 8th Iowa smudged in between, holding the line.[28]

Soon, even Prentiss and Wallace saw the need to withdraw, but it was too late. Wallace was mortally wounded trying to run the gauntlet of Confederate wings as they clamped shut on the Federal position. Prentiss could do nothing else but surrender himself and the twenty-two hundred men who had held out. They were now prisoners of war, but their step was somewhat lightened by the idea that they had hopefully given Grant enough time to build his next line of defense. So was born the thesis that Prentiss had saved the day at Shiloh, and it would get more and more attention as the years passed and the label "Hornet's Nest" became a household name.[29]

## Modern Analysis

But was all this action really that important? Did the stand made there that day save the Federal army? Were Prentiss and Wallace sacrificial lambs, offered to the Confederates so that the rest of the Federal army could survive? There is quite a bit of evidence that argues against the idea that the Hornet's Nest was the most vicious, focal, and important sector at Shiloh. Troop positions, unit casualties, contemporary veteran testimony, placement of burials on the battlefield, and battle context all paint a different picture than that of the icon established through the years after the war. It hints that the Hornet's Nest was not the line that saved the day for Grant.

Union troop positions show that the Hornet's Nest was not the most critical area on the field for much of the day. When they went into action, Colonel Thomas W. Sweeny's Union brigade of six regiments, positioned in Duncan Field north of the Corinth Road, did not have ample room to deploy. As a result, only two regiments went on line; Sweeny held the other four in reserve. Once the Union line began to fall apart on either side of the Hornet's Nest, Sweeny began to send his reserve regiments as reinforcements for the other more critical areas. He sent two Illinois regiments to the Peach Orchard sector and one to the north to aid McClernand. Only one regiment went to

The Sunken Road and Hornet's Nest have come to exemplify Shiloh, much as Pickett's Charge has Gettysburg and the Bloody Lane Antietam. But the term "Sunken Road" is somewhat of a misnomer, as this photo from the 1890s illustrates. The road was not terribly sunken, although any bit of protection was welcomed by the defending Union troops. (Courtesy of Shiloh National Military Park.)

aid the Hornet's Nest. Had the Hornet's Nest been the critical point with the most desperate and severe fighting, Sweeny certainly would not have sent his regiments away from the area.[30]

Casualty figures for the units engaged in the Hornet's Nest likewise do not point toward the most vicious fighting taking place there. Union colonel James M. Tuttle's brigade of four Iowa regiments, which held the Hornet's Nest and the Sunken Road in front of Duncan Field, sustained a total of 207 killed and wounded in the battle, far fewer than some individual regiments, such as the 9th Illinois (366) and the 6th Mississippi (300), sustained on other parts of the battlefield. On the Confederate side, casualties for brigades that attacked the Hornet's Nest were actually smaller than those of other brigades that came nowhere near the position during the day. The four Confederate brigades with the highest casualties were Pat Cleburne's (1,043), Adley Gladden's (829), Winfield Statham's (809), and Robert Trabue's (800), none of which attacked the Hornet's Nest en masse. For those brigades that did attack the area, their casualties stood somewhere in the middle of the Confederate army's casualties: Gibson's Brigade, with so many charges into the Hornet's Nest, ranked as eighth (of sixteen) among Confederate brigade losses, with William Stephens's and Patton Anderson's brigades ranking fourteenth and sixteenth respectively. S. A. M. Wood's and Robert Shaver's brigades ranked as fifth and seventh, but as part of the first wave of attack (Hardee's Corps), they had seen heavy fighting earlier in the day as well. Perhaps Colonel Henry W. Allen of the 4th Louisiana of Randall Gibson's brigade stated the case most clearly in his report made on April 10, 1862. After he had led his Louisiana boys into the teeth of the Hornet's Nest at least three and maybe four times, he wrote of another encounter as being the worst of the day for his men. "While drawn up in line of battle and awaiting orders[,] a Tennessee regiment immediately in our rear fired into us by mistake, killing and wounding a large number of my men," the future governor of Louisiana wrote. He went on to say, "This was a terrible blow to the regiment; far more terrible than any inflicted by the enemy."[31]

The number of dead in the area also demonstrates that the Hornet's Nest did not see the heaviest fighting at Shiloh. The Federal soldiers burying the dead on April 8 almost always buried the bodies of both sides at or near where they fell. With some thirty-five hundred bodies as well as hundreds of dead horses scattered throughout their campsite, they had neither the time nor the desire to haul the bodies any distance. An 1866 document produced by Captain E. B. Whitman, who was in charge of the laborers locating bodies on the battlefield for the new national cemetery, stated that the dead "marks most distinctly the progress of the fight, and the points where each party suffered most severely." Whitman reported the heaviest concentrations of dead were on the eastern and western sectors of the battlefield and that the dead were fairly light in the center, where the Hornet's Nest was located. "In the center there seems to have been less fighting as fewer graves are found," he testified.[32]

Moreover, placing the Hornet's Nest into the overall context of the battle shows that the center of the battlefield was the least fought over area for most of the day. Eight out of sixteen Confederate brigades can be documented as being located on the western third of the battlefield for the majority of the time between 10:00 a.m. and 5:00 p.m. Likewise, five out of sixteen Confederate brigades can be documented on the eastern third of the battlefield for the majority of those times. With Gladden's and Shaver's brigades out of action for several hours, this leaves only one lone brigade for the center third, Randall Gibson's, supported at various times by brigades that came and went quickly, such as Stephens's Tennessee brigade and Shaver's Arkansas brigade. For the majority of the time, Braxton Bragg had no mass of Confederate forces in the center to hurl at the Union line.[33]

Even more telling, what was happening to the rear of the Hornet's Nest supports the idea that Grant did not need Wallace and Prentiss to hold out and sacrifice themselves in order to save his army. The commanding general began establishing his final line of defense around 2:30 in the afternoon. Already formidable with two gunboats, three field batteries, five siege guns, and highly defensible terrain, the position became even stronger as units fled from the battlefield and were fed into line. Thus by the time McClernand, Sherman, and Hurlbut fell back from the flanks of the Hornet's Nest about 4:30 p.m., Grant had already had two hours to establish a very solid line, on very defensible ground, and it was augmented by the withdrawing divisions. While Wallace's and Prentiss's eventual stand in the Hornet's Nest did cause the Confederates to focus nearly their undivided attention on that position late in the day, had the center fallen back with the rest of the army they most likely would have gone into that last line and made it even stronger. We know that at least twenty-two hundred soldiers were eventually surrendered, and most of these would have been available to man that last line, which due to the terrain and strength would have no doubt held as easily at 5:00 p.m. as it did an hour later. Grant himself seemed to take this point of view, writing somewhat beratingly in his memoirs, "In one of the backward moves, on the 6th, the division commanded by General Prentiss did not fall back with the others. This left his flanks exposed and enabled the enemy to capture him with about 2,200 of his officers and men."[34]

The evidence points to the fact that the Hornet's Nest was not the most vicious, important, or decisive engagement at Shiloh. The soldiers themselves stated as much, the position of troops does not support the idea, and the casualties and burials firmly argue against such a notion. Most important, the Hornet's Nest, when viewed within the context of the battle as a whole, does not stand out as the dominant engagement at Shiloh.

## Hornet's Nest Historiography

Such evidence, then, begs the question of why the Hornet's Nest became so famous and important in Shiloh historiography. It was not always so. No one fighting in the "Hornet's Nest" knew it by that name. But then, no one participating in "Pickett's Charge" knew that it would be so named years later, and no one fighting at Antietam knew the road sunken into the earth would one day be called the "Bloody Lane." The Confederates apparently called the Union position as such that day because of the enemy bullets zipping past their ears, sounding like swarms of angry hornets. Such an expression was a common phrase at the time, however, but few if anyone used the term in reference to the position at Shiloh immediately after the battle. In fact, a diligent search has not yet turned up any mention of the name in contemporary literature; most likely, a search of all obscure Civil War newspapers, letters, and diaries might turn up a mention or two of the name, but as of now nothing has surfaced.[35]

The Hornet's Nest is not the only later-named position. No soldiers knew they were drinking from the "Bloody Pond"; no defenders knew they were holding "Grant's Last Line." In fact, the only two proper place names that consistently appear on contemporary maps are Pittsburg Landing and Shiloh Church. The rest are postwar names, and it is difficult to date the origin of these famous labels.[36]

The name "Hornet Nest" appears on a tantalizingly undatable map in the Library of Congress, but we cannot prove the map is of 1862 vintage. The map maker, Leon J. Fremaux, created several versions of his map (this is known because of several modifications), but it is not known when he drew the version that bears the famous name. The only known time and space connection that brings Shiloh and the term "Hornet's Nest" together during the war is an 1864 letter from a sailor aboard the USS *Tawah,* a wooden gunboat plying the Tennessee River. He remarked that his gunboat shelled the "historic Pittsburg Landing" but "failed in our object—that of stirring up a Rebel hornet's nest." And it would seem that another battle has as much claim to the historic name as Shiloh: a Confederate colonel in 1863 labeled a section of the line at Vicksburg as "a hornet's nest of lines and works, bristling with cannon and bayonets and crammed with soldiers."[37]

The term "Hornet's Nest" apparently did not surface in print, and as such in the major public's knowledge, until the late 1870s. William Preston Johnston, writing about his father's role at the Battle of Shiloh in *The Life of General Albert Sidney Johnston* (1879), remarked that the Union position "was nicknamed by the Confederates, by a very mild metaphor, 'The Hornet's Nest.'" Of course, Johnston would have been in a position after the war to hear tales of the story. Johnston's name for the Federal defense caught on somewhat. Other authors of the era also mentioned the Hornet's Nest, such as Manning Force in *From Fort Henry to Corinth* (1881). In addition, he first broached the idea that the country road on which the Federal regiments aligned was "sunk." P. G. T. Beauregard did not mention the name in his 1883 authorized biography by Alfred Roman, *The Military Campaigns of General Beauregard.* Neither did Ulysses S. Grant in his *Personal Memoirs of U.S. Grant,* published in 1885. Although the literature of the early 1880s began to mention the name, it clearly had not stuck.[38]

Then in 1885 came the first of a series of media productions that would forever make the name lodge in the minds of Americans and definitely sway the way we today look at the Battle of Shiloh. Under the direction of A. T. Andreas of the Western Art Association, Theophile Poilpot and twelve assistants produced in Chicago what must have been a remarkable panorama painting along the lines of the cycloramas for Gettysburg and Atlanta. While Poilpot had the entire battle as inspiration for scenes, including the legendary names of Shiloh Church and Pittsburg Landing, he chose to paint the action in the Hornet's Nest. "The name of 'Hornet's Nest' was given to our position by the rebels themselves," Hornet's Nest brigade commander James Tuttle remembered, "and the identification was made complete by some rebel officers in the fall of 1884, while making a survey for the picture at Chicago." He went on to say, "These soldiers had been in some of the charges made against our lines, and their decision in the matter is not disputed." Thus this panorama, with lectures at times by none other than Benjamin Prentiss himself, solidly fixed the term Hornet's Nest in the American mind. An accompanying publication, *Manual of the Panorama of the Battle of Shiloh,* increased the attention given to that part of the battlefield, testifying that the "Thermopylae of modern times, was the 'Hornet's Nest' at Shiloh" and "for some hours it was the turning point in the battle, and beyond doubt saved what was finally saved of the first day's wreck at Shiloh." The inclusion of several panels in the widely distributed *Century* magazine articles (now known collectively as the four-volume *Battles and Leaders of the Civil War*) took the name to more and more Americans, while L. Prang and Company's lithograph of Thure de Thulstrup's 1888 watercolor centering on the Hornet's Nest brought even more attention to Prentiss and his stand.[39]

The growing body of literature mentioning and illustrating the Hornet's Nest and the massive boost given the term by the panorama convinced the Union veterans of the worth of the name. Veterans of the Iowa regiments that had defended that section of line (the 2nd, 7th, 8th, 12th, and 14th Iowa) began talking of a veterans' organization of the defenders of the Hornet's Nest as early as 1884, during a visit to the battlefield. In 1887, the dream became a reality with the first meeting of the "Iowa Hornet's Nest Brigade." The veterans themselves, this time Union soldiers, carried on the by-now-common name, and they also continued the argument that the "Hornet's Nest Brigade saved the day at Shiloh."[40]

Several Iowa Hornet's Nest Brigade reunions took place over the following years. But the critical development in this veterans' association was not so much what they called themselves, although that in itself illustrated the growing usage of the term, but whom they produced. The 12th Iowa veterans, back at their first meeting in 1880, had elected themselves a historian. His name was David W. Reed. Historian Reed would also become a factor in the Hornet's Nest Brigade reunions and would ultimately take the growing fame of the Hornet's Nest and make it a household name.[41]

By the mid-1890s, Reed was ready to take the idea of the Hornet's Nest one step further, and he was possibly the only man in the United States who was in a position to do so. Congress has passed legislation to create a national military park out of the battlefield of Shiloh in 1894. The congressman who sponsored the legislation was another 12th Iowa veteran, David B. Henderson —soon to be Speaker of the House of Representatives. Once the bill was passed and the War Department began to make appointments to the governing commission, Henderson prevailed on Secretary of War Daniel S. Lamont to appoint his close friend David W. Reed to be historian. (He got other friends hired as well.) Reed thus began the historical work at Shiloh with a golden opportunity to shape how the battle was interpreted both in the creation of the physical battlefield and in the written version of the battle, neither of which had been fully done before.[42]

Reed not only produced a battlefield thoroughly marked with monuments and tablets that told the story of the Hornet's Nest as well as other positions on the field, but he also produced major media publications that took the story of the name one step further. Prior to Reed and his comrades' reunions, none of the major publications mentioning the battle had dwelt on the Hornet's Nest as the key to Union victory. In the *Century* articles, for example, the writers did not focus on that aspect of the battle or make grand arguments that the Federal stand there saved the day. It was Reed and his comrades who did.[43]

In *The Battle of Shiloh and the Organizations Engaged,* Reed subtly described the Hornet's Nest's role in the battle as one of extreme importance. He described in vivid detail how the units there defeated numerous charges upon the Union line, even counterattacking on a couple of occasions. He also made it clear that the entire Confederate army was involved in the capture of the Hornet's Nest defenders; at one point he made the correct assertion that adjoining Federal regiments surrendered to the two different extreme flanks of the Confederate army, which had overlapped in rear of the Union line. He also argued that the Confederate army had to "reorganize . . . for an attack upon the Union line in position near the Landing." In Reed's government published book, he never came out and blatantly said he and his comrades had won the battle, but he hinted that their stand had allowed the Federals to build another line in rear—one that held and ultimately secured the victory.[44]

The Iowa historian was not so subtle in his regimental history, *Campaigns and Battles of the Twelfth Regiment Iowa Veteran Volunteer Infantry,* produced a decade earlier but only published one year later in 1903. In it, he was able to tell what he and his comrades believed to be the real story of Shiloh—that the Hornet's Nest had been the pivotal action of the day, allowing the beaten fragments of Grant's army time to build another line of defense. Reed tantalizingly told his readers, "It has been claimed that the delay caused by the stubborn resistance of parts of five regiments at the 'Hornet's Nest,' even after the other troops had fallen back, saved Grant's army; and there is at least good reason for the claim." Reed then went on to give detail after detail from report after report on how the Hornet's Nest was the key event at Shiloh. At the end, Reed drove home the point: "To those comrades who survived that desperate struggle, and to the friends who still mourn those who fell on that glorious field, there is the consolation of knowing that, after years of waiting, the final summing up of the evidence will convince any unprejudiced searcher after the truth that the valor of the troops at the 'Hornet's Nest' *saved the day at Shiloh.*"[45]

For years, Reed's work on Shiloh was just about all that was produced on the battle, and his words convinced visitors and readers. With the Hornet's Nest growing into almost legendary status, however, one final media presentation made it the icon we know today. The National Park Service took over Shiloh National Military Park in 1933. Its historians began working on interpretive publications and services that would provide insight on the battle to a growing nonveteran clientele. By far the best known and most important

The Hornet's Nest became an American icon mainly due to the work of the Shiloh veterans who defended the area, chief of whom was David W. Reed. He became Shiloh National Military Park's first and foremost historian in 1895, fathering the school of thought that argues for the importance of the Hornet's Nest. He fought there in the 12th Iowa and is seen here later in life beside his regiment's monument. (Courtesy of Shiloh National Military Park.)

of these publications and presentations was the park's introductory movie, *Shiloh: Portrait of a Battle.* Written by park historian Charles E. Shedd Jr. and narrated by park superintendent Ira B. Lykes, the film was an overview of the battle with the Hornet's Nest as the central theme. Shedd had little more than Reed's books and the interpretation handed down from him through the years on which to base his narrative. No wonder he placed such high importance on the Hornet's Nest.[46]

The film was shot between 1954 and 1956 and was the first narrative-style motion picture shown at a national park site. That in itself, and even the fact that the movie firmly placed the Hornet's Nest as the key event at Shiloh, was not what made the movie so critical in the growth of the Hornet's Nest legend, however. Rather, that the movie was still being shown over fifty years later makes it remarkable for its longevity; it was by far the longest running National Park Service film in existence when it was retired in 2012. In that longevity comes the importance to the Hornet's Nest story; literally millions of people watched the film over the course of its fifty-six-year career, and they soaked up the story of the Hornet's Nest's importance at Shiloh.[47]

Thus the Hornet's Nest was the result of the veterans' later interpretation of the facts, not the facts themselves. And that interpretation, added to and strengthened through the years, has dominated Shiloh historiography to the point that the Hornet's Nest has become a legitimate icon. But a thorough examination of the historiography as well as battle accounts leads to a different conclusion, one that is very revisionist in nature and sure to cause some argument. But in seeking to find the objective truth, the historian must wade through decades of interpretations and test them for validity. Such an activity points to the importance of the future study of Civil War memory.

## Conclusion

The traditional view of the Battle of Shiloh is that the Hornet's Nest was the rock against which the Confederate tide crashed time after time, ultimately splitting itself and going around the flanks. The reality is that the center had so few Confederate troops in it that the strength of the Hornet's Nest was less because of the inherent power of the Federal line and more a result of the lack of numbers sent against it. The Confederates did not split their army on the immovable rock; the determined stand in the Hornet's Nest was the result of the split already occurring in the Confederate army. With major portions of Johnston's troops already going around the Hornet's Nest, that Federal position was bound to hold against the relatively minor forces thrown against it. The defenders of the Hornet's Nest actually saw less fighting than their comrades in arms; they just did a better job of getting their story out, thus creating the icon that today is the Hornet's Nest at Shiloh.

4

# A Case Study in Civil War Memory: Benjamin M. Prentiss as the Hero of Shiloh

Chaos and confusion were everywhere. The neatly aligned ranks of the Federal army at Shiloh had given way to a mass of straggling, running soldiers intent on escaping. To the defenders of the Union position known as the Hornet's Nest, the only hope for survival lay in running the gauntlet of crossfire in a place that would soon become known to history as "Hell's Hollow." Although these soldiers had defended their position in the Hornet's Nest nearly all day, they now learned the awful truth that the units on their flanks had not stayed in line. Their flanks were turned, and the enemy was in their rear, trying to shut off all hope for retreat. Making the situation worse, one of the two Federal generals in the Hornet's Nest was down. Brigadier General W. H. L. Wallace had been shot through the head about 5:00 p.m. and was presumed dead. That left only one other general officer to try to make some sense of the chaos. Brigadier General Benjamin M. Prentiss soon realized that the trap had shut. Just minutes after Wallace's wounding, he raised a white flag and surrendered the twenty-two hundred men with him. A shout went up from the conquering Confederates, prompting Prentiss to bellow, "Yell, boys, you have a right to shout for you have captured the bravest brigade in the U.S. Army." With those words, Prentiss became a prisoner, but more important, he began his trek toward becoming the "Hero of Shiloh."[1]

Historians ask questions. On the surface, the needed question in this case is whether Prentiss was actually the hero of Shiloh and, if not, why he is so often labeled as such. On a larger level, however, the story of Prentiss at Shiloh is a perfect topic for a case study in which to examine historical memory in general. There often is a vast difference between what actually happened and what the public has come to believe happened. In terms of Prentiss at Shiloh, what actually happened and what historians have generally said happened is very different, causing some confusion among the general public, which commonly accepts the story of Prentiss being a hero is spite of the actual events.

Historians of course are extremely important in the process, and the general public most often gets the story from them. As various schools of thought are reexamined and revised, the historiographical façade that develops becomes very important in understanding both the actual event and how it has been perceived. Civil War history offers many occasions to revise the deeply held beliefs of scholars and the public alike, and no better example can be used than Prentiss at Shiloh. This essay will thus examine Prentiss's role at Shiloh, looking not just at his actions and his perceived heroics but also at the episode as a historical memory exercise. Examining Prentiss at Shiloh in terms of what actually happened, what historians have said happened, and what the general public has come to believe happened will hopefully shed new light not only on Prentiss at Shiloh but also on the rewards of using memory in studying the Civil War as a whole.[2]

Benjamin Prentiss's direct ancestors came to America on the *Mayflower*. He was born in Virginia in 1819, but as a teenager he moved with his parents to Missouri, from which he moved to Quincy, Illinois. There, he first became involved with the militia, serving in the Mormon episode that expelled Brigham Young and his followers out of Illinois. He also fought in the Mexican War as a captain of an Illinois infantry company. When the Civil War broke out, Prentiss was appointed colonel of the 10th Illinois Infantry and then, along with Ulysses S. Grant and others, was appointed a brigadier general. He and Grant bickered over rank, but the two nevertheless worked together when they again found themselves together in the Army of the Tennessee. This time, there was no question of rank, however. Grant was commander of the Army of the Tennessee while Prentiss led its Sixth Division.[3]

Prentiss was still in the process of organizing his division when the Confederates surprised Grant's army at Shiloh on April 6, 1862. He fought hard but still lost the vast majority of his entirely green division. He reassembled his remaining men and took position between two stronger divisions. Later, the area came to be called the Hornet's Nest, and it was here that Prentiss won his fame.[4]

Prentiss's motley force held the center of the Union line for several hours, until the Confederates surrounded and captured them. The Illinois general became a prisoner of war for six months before being exchanged. Later in the war he held other posts, most notably at the Battle of Helena, Arkansas, on July 4, 1863. In later life he was a lawyer, postmaster, and pension agent, ironically appointed to that position by his former competitor, President Ulysses S. Grant. But nothing in his later life ever matched the fame he garnered from his role on one single day in the woods near Pittsburg Landing. There, Prentiss became what many today consider the hero of Shiloh.[5]

Benjamin M. Prentiss has been labeled one of the Union heroes of Shiloh, mainly because of his defense of the Hornet's Nest on the first day. While he was certainly a factor, most of the troops who defended the area were from W. H. L. Wallace's division, but he was killed in the action, leaving Prentiss to reap all the glory. Indeed, few modern general histories even mention Wallace, heaping all the praise on Prentiss. (Library of Congress.)

The story of Prentiss at Shiloh has unfortunately fallen victim to historians who have wrongly influenced the general public as to what happened at the battle. Modern scholars as well as Civil War buffs have all but made Prentiss the hero of Shiloh, and visitors to the Shiloh National Military Park have followed their lead, frequently mentioning him as the one officer who won the battle for the Federals. The visitors' thoughts were undoubtedly affected by the park's long-running film, *Shiloh: Portrait of a Battle,* which seemed to make Prentiss the hero. Millions of people saw the film over its fifty-six-year career. At one point, the narrator talked of veterans who would never be ashamed to say, "I fought with Prentiss in the Sunken Road at Shiloh." Even the park's brochure has on its cover Thure de Thulstrup's famous 1888 watercolor of the Hornet's Nest, with Prentiss centrally located on the canvas, bravely giving orders to his men. With all the media coverage surrounding his role in the battle, the public has justifiably come to think of Prentiss as the hero of Shiloh.[6]

Perhaps more illustrative of Prentiss's place in the mind of the public is the treatment he has received from academic historians. While the major authors of the battle of Shiloh, Edward Cunningham, James Lee McDonough, Wiley

Sword, and Larry Daniel, offer a balanced view of Prentiss's role at the battle in their in-depth studies, non-Shiloh-expert academics have built on the popular conception and in turn have fueled it even more. No fewer than fifteen major Civil War authors (James M. McPherson, Bruce Catton, Allan Nevins, Shelby Foote, T. Harry Williams, John F. Marszalek, Thomas L. Connelly, William S. McFeely, William C. Davis, Grady McWhiney, Charles R. Roland, Brooks Simpson, Nathaniel C. Hughes, Archer Jones, and Herman Hattaway) describe only Prentiss as the defender of the Hornet's Nest (a few mention W. H. L. Wallace in passing, but the emphasis is clearly on Prentiss). Most, by their coverage, seem to more than subtly view Prentiss as the hero who won the battle for the Federals. For instance, in *Battle Cry of Freedom,* James McPherson never mentions W. H. L. Wallace in the Hornet's Nest but wrote, "Although 18,000 Confederates closed in on Prentiss's 4,500 men . . . Prentiss surrendered his 2,200 survivors at 5:30, an hour before sunset. Their gritty stand had bought time for Grant." After mentioning that W. H. L. Wallace had pulled out, Bruce Catton stated in *Grant Moves South,* "Prentiss had done precisely what he had been told to do—hold on at all hazards—and so had his men." Most tellingly, in *P. G. T. Beauregard: Napoleon in Gray,* T. Harry Williams wrote, "Prentiss, under orders from Grant to hold to the last, fought on with 2,200 men. . . . If any one man saved the Federal army at Shiloh, Prentiss was the man." Although the word "hero" is not used in most of these accounts, the unbalanced concentration on Prentiss rather than Wallace, who commanded the vast majority of the troops in the Hornet's Nest, supports the idea that these historians viewed Prentiss as the one general responsible for the Union defense at the Hornet's Nest. Such wide-ranging praise for Prentiss alone does not reflect adversely on these authors or their scholarship, for they utilized the accepted story of Shiloh in admittedly general works that did not delve deeply into the battle, but this continued emphasis on Prentiss does tend to show the extent to which the Prentiss story is accepted.[7]

Most adulation of the general comes from his actions in three significant areas: the early morning patrol that uncovered the Confederate army, the defense of the Hornet's Nest, and Prentiss's role as the ranking officer who surrendered his men. In all these actions, however, he was not what he has been made out to be. The chasm between what actually happened and what many historians say happened is vast. Prentiss was hardly heroic.

For decades after the Battle of Shiloh, Prentiss was credited with sending out Major James Powell's patrol, which located the Confederate army in the early morning hours of April 6, 1862. The tablets in the national park mention a "reconnoitering party sent out by General Prentiss." Likewise, the park's film, *Shiloh: Portrait of a Battle,* does not say conclusively that Prentiss sent out

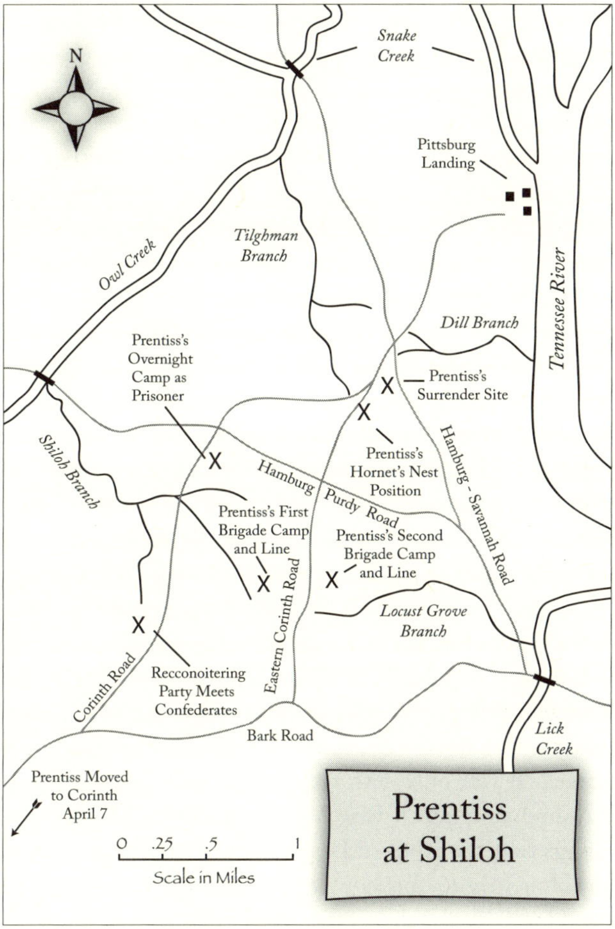


the patrol but gives that impression by merely stating that "a patrol moved out from Prentiss's camps at about three o'clock on Sunday morning to scout the countryside toward Corinth."[8]

Actually, Colonel Everett Peabody was the officer who sent out the patrol. In fact, he did so without orders from Prentiss and received a severe reprimand from the division commander because Prentiss believed this little patrol had started the battle. Hearing sounds of fighting, Prentiss rode to Peabody and, inquiring about the fighting, told him, "Colonel Peabody, I will hold you personally responsible for bringing on this engagement."[9]

The animosity between Prentiss and Peabody was evident in Prentiss's report, which conveniently failed to mention that Peabody had sent out the patrol. Prentiss took subtle credit, writing that the patrol "proceeded to the front" but never saying who sent it. Even worse, Prentiss failed to mention Peabody in the general narrative of his report, except merely to say that he had commanded one of his brigades. In a long list of adulation for other officers under his command, which included high praise for his other brigade commander Madison Miller (Prentiss says he "acted during the day with distinguished courage, coolness, and ability"), Prentiss never once mentioned that Peabody found the enemy first, made a desperate stand at his camps, and died from five bullets while trying to hold his line.[10]

In the years after the battle, it became commonly accepted that Peabody's patrol actually did important work. The Union army was going to be attacked anyway, so the patrol did not bring on a battle that would not have taken place otherwise. In an extremely convoluted and passionate argument over whether the Army of the Tennessee had been surprised at Shiloh, the topic of the patrol and its merits gained full credit for giving at least some warning to the camping Federals. Members of the Society of the Army of the Cumberland argued that the Confederates had surprised Grant and Sherman, while members of the Society of the Army of the Tennessee argued that there had not been any surprise. The patrol was an important issue when veterans debated the varying levels of surprise at Shiloh.[11]

But conversely, few people then or later debated who sent out the patrol. For decades, even into the 1950s, the idea that Prentiss had sent out the patrol was accepted. It was only with the emergence of the academic studies by Edward Cunningham, James Lee McDonough, and Wiley Sword in the 1960s and 1970s that the truth of Peabody's role finally came out. With that development, obviously learned by in-depth research in letters and diaries, Prentiss looked more like a self-servant than a hero, but by then the myth had caught on, especially with the major non-Shiloh-expert historians. It seems Prentiss had taken advantage of Peabody's gallant death and the silence it imposed and took the credit that was due the dead brigade commander, who was not able to defend himself.

This same situation is also evident in the defense of the Hornet's Nest. General studies of the Civil War and even some studies that focus exclusively on the Shiloh campaign describe the Hornet's Nest as being defended by Prentiss alone. In reality, the vast majority of troops in the Hornet's Nest were not Prentiss's, but under someone else's command, most notably W. H. L. Wallace, who commanded his division at the Hornet's Nest from 8:30 a.m. until his mortal wound at 5:00 p.m. Again, because Prentiss lived to tell his story and Wallace did not, Prentiss became the hero of the Hornet's Nest.[12]

Prentiss began the morning of April 6, 1862, with roughly fifty-four hundred men in his division. This number did not include several other regiments, such as the 15th and 16th Iowa and the 23rd Missouri, which were scheduled to join the division in the days ahead. When the Confederates attacked his original fifty-four-hundred-man line, the line broke between 8:30 and 9:00 a.m., the division scattering almost to the four winds. Some were dead or wounded on the field. Most, however, fled toward Pittsburg Landing and became the bulk of what many later described as a teeming mass of whipped Federals below the bluffs around the landing. As a testament to his courage, which is not in question here, Prentiss stopped and rallied a remnant of his division in the rear of what would become the Hornet's Nest line. But Prentiss could muster fewer than five hundred of his original fifty-four hundred soldiers, less than 10 percent. Some regiments, such as the 61st Illinois, reorganized and fought gallantly on other parts of the battlefield, but as an organized unit, Prentiss had lost 90 percent of his men. Nevertheless, he led them into line, where they fought the remainder of the day.[13]

The immediate question is not whether Prentiss was courageous, which by all accounts he was, or whether he made a stand, which he did. The immediate question is whether he was the hero of the Hornet's Nest, with the larger memory question revolving around the idea of what happened, what historians say happened, and what the public has come to believe happened that day in the center of the battlefield at Shiloh.

With fewer than 500 of his original division, augmented by around 575 fresh members of the 23rd Missouri who joined him in the Hornet's Nest, Prentiss's command was a vast minority in the Federal line holding the Hornet's Nest. The most detailed analysis has placed the number of Federal soldiers in the Hornet's Nest as 8,850. Thus Prentiss's 1,100 men made a total of 12 percent of the Federals in the Hornet's Nest. Clearly, the vast majority of the Federal soldiers in the Hornet's Nest were not Prentiss's. And Prentiss seems to make clear in his report that some of the original five hundred he rallied also fled to the river. He made the statement that after the initial assault on his new line about 10:00 a.m. (probably closer to 11:00 a.m.), he found his "command greatly reduced by reason of casualties and because of the falling back of many of the men to the river, they being panic stricken." Prentiss stated that his new line was so compromised that he had to call on Wallace to send reinforcements—the 8th Iowa Infantry of Thomas Sweeny's brigade. In actuality, the majority of the troops (nearly 90 percent) in the Hornet's Nest were from Sweeny's and James Tuttle's brigades under Wallace, who commanded them until his wound at 5:00 p.m. (a mere thirty minutes before the surrender), with the extreme right units of Jacob Lauman's brigade of Stephen Hurlbut's Division in the Peach Orchard also in the line.[14]

But Prentiss received all the glory. Few historians even mention W. H. L. Wallace when describing the defense of the Hornet's Nest. It was, again, because Prentiss, whether flagrantly or not, was able to tell his story in the years after the battle and Wallace, who was mortally wounded trying to force his way out of the trap just minutes before the surrender, was dead. If anyone should be given the credit for holding the line at the Hornet's Nest, it should be the martyr Wallace, not Prentiss.

By far, the greatest factor in why Prentiss gained more notoriety than Wallace was because of the third action that brings Prentiss credit—his surrender. By 5:00 p.m., Wallace lay mortally wounded on the battlefield and Prentiss was the ranking commander in the retreat. When the wings of the Confederate army closed in on him, Prentiss had no choice but to give up. He ultimately surrendered some twenty-two hundred soldiers to the Confederates, many of them wounded. But the majority of the troops Prentiss surrendered were Wallace's men, not his own. Roughly 75 percent of the men who surrendered were not from Prentiss's original fifty-four hundred men, but Prentiss, having taken command of those units just minutes before when Wallace was wounded, surrendered them and received the glory.[15]

The fact that Prentiss, in surrendering, became famous is in itself a curious case. He of course became a martyr, a reputation his six months in captivity added to and strengthened. Then, too, as the importance of the Hornet's Nest grew through the decades after the Civil War, so did Prentiss's defense. When historians concluded that the Hornet's Nest defense allowed Grant to form a new line and thus saved the Federal army from destruction, the fame heaped upon Prentiss only increased, despite the fact that he commanded only a slight minority of the men who fought in the Hornet's Nest. And in surrendering, giving up, he was made a national hero, which is only comparable to the surrender of Major Robert Anderson at Fort Sumter in the Civil War and has few comparable equals in military history. Most of the time, the dead, the killed in action such as Albert Sidney Johnston and Stonewall Jackson, become the martyrs, which in this case should have been Wallace. But Prentiss, not Wallace, became the hero as a result of a selective memory of the battle and the Civil War.[16]

In dealing with that selective memory, Shiloh's historiographical evolution has to be taken into account. Historians who painted the picture of Prentiss as the hero of Shiloh were not culpable of weak research or shoddy work because in almost every case they were working from primary sources that literally instituted the Prentiss myth a hundred years prior. The early historiography of Shiloh thus sheds critical light on how and why historians have wrongly shaped the general public's view of Shiloh.

Perhaps surprisingly to us today, in the immediate years after the Civil War, Prentiss, and for that matter the Hornet's Nest itself, was not the focus of Shiloh. Few if any writers from the 1860s to 1880s placed any great emphasis on either the Hornet's Nest or Prentiss's and Wallace's stand. But it is clear that when these authors dealt with the action in the center of the battlefield, it was both Prentiss and Wallace who deserved the credit, not just Prentiss, as later historians would argue.

For example, William T. Sherman was the first major Shiloh personality to write his memoirs, which appeared in 1875. In a chapter filled with after-action reports, Sherman basically detailed his division's action during the battle. In later commentary, however, he never mentioned the Hornet's Nest and never singled out Prentiss or Wallace for bravely holding the line and winning the battle. In all of Sherman's detail, he always mentioned each division on the field rather than singling out any one commander.[17]

In 1879, Albert Sidney Johnston's son published *The Life of General Albert Sidney Johnston,* which was a very detailed defense of his father in the Civil War. Although dealing mainly with Johnston and the Confederate side, the younger Johnston did make a successful attempt to deal with the battle as a whole. In analyzing the Hornet's Nest, which was the first time the name ever appeared in print, Johnston described both Wallace and Prentiss as being involved but offered some tinges of future arguments in later analysis that somewhat put the success of holding that position on Prentiss. Johnston remarked that Prentiss "determined on a bold course" and later stated that "in the writer's opinion, it saved both Grant and Sherman from capture." Significantly, however, Johnston gave Wallace's units just as much credit as Prentiss's. "With Hurlbut gone and Wallace gone," Johnston wrote, "Prentiss was left isolated. Struck in front, in rear, and on either flank, cut off in every attempt to escape, . . . what was left of Prentiss's division surrendered with the Eighth, Twelfth, and Fourteenth Iowa, and the Fifty-eighth Illinois Regiments, of Wallace's division." Very similarly, P. G. T Beauregard, in his 1884 authorized biography by Alfred Roman, stated, "But General Prentiss, unaware of the movement executed by Wallace's division, still clung to its position, together with the 8th, 12th, and 14th Iowa and the 58th Illinois, of Wallace's division, who were endeavoring to save their artillery." It seems that even the Confederates knew that Wallace and his units had been very much involved.[18]

As part of Scribner's Campaigns of the Civil War series, Manning F. Force wrote the only monograph to deal with Shiloh during this period, his

1881 *From Fort Henry to Corinth.* Where other writers were intent on saving reputations, Force wrote a detailed and objective account of the military action from Fort Henry all the way to the siege of Corinth. Shiloh was the central event, and Force continued the idea of giving both Wallace and Prentiss credit for holding the line until it was too late. Force chose to relate the battle in a series of division sketches. He first began with Sherman and then moved on to McClernand, and finished with Hurlbut. Importantly, Force chose to deal with Prentiss and Wallace together. He made clear that both Wallace and Prentiss "consulted and resolved to hold their positions at all hazards." Later, in dealing with the surrender, Force argued that the "Confederate left and right poured in and encircled Prentiss and Wallace." To Force, both were equally responsible for the stand.[19]

By the mid- to late 1880s, however, a change was beginning to take place in favor of Prentiss. While still not emphasizing the Hornet's Nest, later authors were beginning to view Prentiss and not Wallace as the defender of that section of the line. Don Carlos Buell did not emphasize the Hornet's Nest, although in a detailed article for *Century,* he gave Wallace some credit. Buell placed Wallace in the center of the action, but Prentiss was the main character for him. The general wrote specifically of Prentiss, saying, "On this line, between and under the shelter of Hurlbut and W. H. L. Wallace, Prentiss rallied a considerable force, perhaps a thousand men, of his routed division at 9 o'clock, and fought stubbornly until near the close of the day." In terms of the Hornet's Nest's importance, Buell did not argue that Prentiss's and Wallace's stand saved the army and allowed Grant time to build up his last line. Buell was only willing to go so far as to say that the stand "weakened the force of the attack which McClernand sustained in his seventh position."[20]

By far the most popular American of his time wrote what was evidently the most read description of Shiloh to that date. In his mid-1880s article for the *Century* magazine, which was basically the Shiloh chapter in his *Memoirs* (1885), Ulysses S. Grant had little to say about the Hornet's Nest. In fact, he actually laid partial blame on Prentiss for getting himself captured. Grant wrote, "In one of the backward moves, on the 6th, the division commanded by General Prentiss did not fall back with the others. This left his flanks exposed, and enabled the enemy to capture him, with about 2,200 of his officers and men." Grant and Prentiss had never been the best of friends and, as stated above, had actually had a small quarrel over rank early in the war. Perhaps some lingering animosity was still there. However, Grant later went on to say that Prentiss "was as cool as if expecting victory" when he last saw him around 4:30 p.m. on April 6. The main point is not postwar quarrels but what Grant thought was important enough to include in his story. That Grant did not dwell on the Hornet's Nest tells us he most likely did not consider it the key to the battle. He actually saw his last line as the key, as evidenced by his thorough discussion of it. Some veterans and historians alike later argued that Grant's last line was made possible by the stand in the Hornet's Nest, but Grant evidently did not hold this view either. He saw the defense by the entire army as the key to holding long enough for him to establish his last line. Grant used the phrase "in one of the backward moves," which insinuated that the steadfastness of the entire army rather than the stand of one division in the Hornet's Nest was crucial. Most important, however, Grant's treatment of the event shows the emerging popularity of Prentiss as opposed to Wallace. When dealing with the defense and surrender of the Hornet's Nest, although he never stated the name, Grant always cited Prentiss, never Wallace. By the 1880s, although he had not reached hero status yet because the Hornet's Nest had not yet been elevated to the key action on the battlefield, Prentiss had nevertheless begun to be seen as the chief defender of the Hornet's Nest. Grant's article, although somewhat negative toward Prentiss, also paid large dividends for the general in that it not only portrayed Prentiss (and not Wallace) as the chief defender of the Hornet's Nest, but it also forever put to rest the false rumor that Prentiss had been captured early in the morning.[21]

Thus the initial flurry of writing on Shiloh was often rambling and self-serving. Nowhere in the early literature, however, was the Hornet's Nest emphasized as the key to the Federals winning the battle, and likewise nowhere was Prentiss labeled the hero of Shiloh for holding the Hornet's Nest. Rather, the Hornet's Nest, when mentioned at all, was placed into the context of the entire battle as just another action among many during the fight. And in dealing with it in that context, both Wallace and Prentiss received the credit for holding that part of the line, although toward the end Prentiss began to slightly overcome Wallace in popular perception as the defender of the Hornet's Nest.

Paralleling the early battle historiography, and in a major way adding to it, Prentiss himself had a lot to do with the embryonic shift in public opinion in the mid- to late 1880s and played a major role in swaying later historians into wrongly telling the general public what had happened at Shiloh. Soon after being released from Confederate custody in October 1862, he wrote a report of his action, fully playing on the public's emotions. He began his report, "Upon my return from captivity in the hands of the public enemy . . ." As noted earlier, he then went on to subtly claim he had sent out the morning patrol that uncovered the Confederate army.[22]

In all fairness, the rest of the general's after-action report was a fairly accurate representation of what had happened at the Hornet's Nest, and Prentiss gave Wallace full credit for his actions. In a round of subsequent speaking engagements, however, Prentiss made more grandiose claims. On his way back home to Quincy from Confederate captivity, Prentiss spoke in Washington, D.C., Chicago, and many other cities, always to huge crowds who hung on every word he spoke. In each of the basically similar speeches, Prentiss recounted his capture and captivity, being extremely critical of his and his men's treatment in Confederate custody. He also began to make grand claims about his actions. Playing on the emotions of the crowd, Prentiss began his Chicago speech with the words "My friends, I feel free to-night; I am at home in Illinois." At the climax of the speech, Prentiss spoke of meeting with W. H. L. Wallace. "We had determined to hold our position," he thundered. "We determined to sustain our government; we determined there to save the army of Gen. Grant. I think we did it." Loud applause filled the building.[23]

But even as Prentiss was claiming he and Wallace had saved the army and the nation, he was already battling an unfounded rumor that cast doubt upon his heroism. Somehow, the rumor had begun that he and his division had been captured in the first few minutes of the battle and "had scarcely fired a shot." Prentiss even referenced this idea in his October 21 speech in Chicago. For twenty years, Prentiss battled this falsehood, even taking fellow division commander John A. McClernand to task for continuing this rumor in the 1880s. Perhaps the unfounded rumors explain Prentiss's determination to take the credit for the victory at Shiloh.[24]

By the mid-1880s, however, other generals were publishing their memoirs, most notably U. S. Grant, who firmly ended any thought that Prentiss was captured early in the day. Perhaps with that behind him, Prentiss again went on the offensive in the mid-1880s, often with such stirring lines in his speeches as, when ordered by Grant to hold his position, "I called upon God to help me obey that command. I held it.—I did." Of course, loud cheers erupted. Other veterans also began to come to Prentiss's side during this period. Andrew Hickenlooper, who had commanded a battery under Prentiss at Shiloh but later became a famous general, stated, "It has been asserted, over and over again, by Confederate writers that this delay at what they called the 'Hornets'-Nest' saved the Federal army. It certainly contributed more to this fortunate result than all the other causes combined."[25]

But Prentiss was in for even more notoriety in the mid- and late 1880s. As the story of the Hornet's Nest became more and more common, it began to take center stage in the battle. Much of this Hornet's Nest promotion was done in the mid-1880s with several famous paintings. In 1885, the artist Theophile Poilpot and twelve assistants produced in Chicago a Hornet's Nest panorama, which prominently featured Prentiss. None other than Benjamin Prentiss himself gave lectures at the panorama. An accompanying publication, *Manual of the Panorama of the Battle of Shiloh,* increased the attention given to that part of the battlefield, testifying that the "Thermopylae of modern times, was the 'Hornet's Nest' at Shiloh" and "for some hours it was the turning point in the battle, and beyond doubt saved what was finally saved of the first day's wreck at Shiloh." The inclusion of several panels in the widely distributed *Century* magazine articles took Prentiss's name to more and more Americans, and L. Prang and Company's lithograph of Thure de Thulstrup's 1888 watercolor, which centered on the Hornet's Nest and prominently displayed Prentiss, brought even more attention to the general. It is interesting to note that W. H. L. Wallace was not nearly as prominently displayed as Prentiss in the panorama, and he was not even pictured in the Thulstrup watercolor, although his regiments were prominent in both.[26]

Thus in large part because of his own actions, Prentiss was coming to be seen by the early 1890s as the key defender of the Hornet's Nest, which was

One of the reasons the Hornet's Nest became so popular, and helped propel Prentiss to hero status, was the famous *Panorama of the Battle of Shiloh,* which was displayed in Chicago in the 1880s. The painting was centered on the action in the Hornet's Nest, explaining that this was where Grant won the battle. At the center, of course, was Prentiss, and he actually gave lectures on the battle at the panorama site. (Johnson and Buel, *Battle and Leaders.*)

becoming known, although not yet entirely, as the key to winning the Battle of Shiloh. His telling of the story, whether accurate or not, would have a major effect on later historians and the memory of Shiloh.

In addition to Prentiss, there was yet another entity that seemed to make grand claims about the general's role at Shiloh. What began in the mid-1880s became by 1900 an accepted fact that Prentiss was the hero of Shiloh, and that change was solidified at the Shiloh National Military Park itself. By the end of Prentiss's life in 1901, his role in the Battle of Shiloh had been promoted literally in stone, and his fame as the hero of Shiloh would continue the climb that has only increased in the years since.[27]

It did not hurt Prentiss's reputation that the chief historian of the battle was David W. Reed, the "Father of Shiloh National Military Park." Reed had been a soldier at Shiloh and had himself served in the famous Hornet's Nest. So naturally he emphasized that portion of the field, especially after it had already started to become a household name in the mid- to late 1880s. But Reed's emphasis of Prentiss was somewhat odd in that Reed actually served in Wallace's division, not Prentiss's. One would think Reed would have immortalized his own division commander, but Prentiss became the focus at Shiloh instead. To be sure, Reed placed a division headquarters monument to mark Wallace's headquarters and a mortuary monument at the site of Wallace's wound, but each was one of five respective mortuary and division headquarters monuments placed on the battlefield. Where Prentiss actually surrendered, however, Reed placed an iron marker that read, "Brig. Gen. B. M. Prentiss surrendered here at 5:30 p.m., April 6, 1862." Although one of his brigade commanders and many other colonels and lesser officers surrendered too, only Prentiss received a personal marker.[28]

Reed's literary efforts, in addition to his marking of the battlefield, also helped propel Prentiss's hero status around the turn of the century. In *The Battle of Shiloh and the Organizations Engaged* (1902), Reed incorrectly gave Prentiss the credit for sending out the morning patrol that uncovered the Confederate attack. He also hinted that the Hornet's Nest stand had allowed the Federals to build another line in the rear—one that held and ultimately secured the victory. Reed was not so subtle in his non-government-printed version of Shiloh. In *Campaigns and Battles of the Twelfth Regiment Iowa Veteran Volunteer Infantry* (1903), Reed argued that the Hornet's Nest had been the pivotal action of the day, allowing the beaten fragments of Grant's army time to build another line of defense. Reed wrote, "To those comrades who survived that desperate struggle, and to the friends who still mourn those who fell on that glorious field, there is the consolation of knowing that, after years of waiting, the final summing up of the evidence will convince any unprejudiced searcher after the truth that the valor of the troops at the 'Hornet's Nest' *saved the day at Shiloh.*" In reference to Prentiss specifically, Reed (without explanation why) seemed to condone the bandwagon effect of solely giving Prentiss credit for holding the Hornet's Nest. In writing of his own regiment, he stated, "The 12th [Iowa] being so closely connected with Prentiss and he being the only General officer surrendered, the Confederate reports, and many of ours, for that matter, designate all the troops surrendered as Prentiss' division." Oddly, Reed stated no objection, but let it rest there.[29]

The extent to which the Prentiss myth was ingrained in the historiography as well as the park by the turn of the century is clearly seen in the cultural expressions on the event of his death. On February 9, 1901, the *Washington Post* ran Prentiss's obituary, which was titled "Hero of Shiloh Passes Away." Also in 1901, the Missouri legislature passed a resolution stating, "On the pages of history his name will appear as one on whose bravery and indomitable courage hung the fate of Shiloh battle field and perhaps the fate of a nation." Now, not only was Prentiss the hero of Shiloh, but some were also claiming that he had saved the nation by his actions.[30]

Many authors after Reed simply continued the Prentiss myth, further ingraining it into the public and academic mind. Shiloh National Military Park superintendent DeLong Rice wrote a little book named *The Story of Shiloh* (1924), which focused on the significance of the Hornet's Nest. Rice termed the Sunken Road the "grave of the Southern Confederacy." Elsewhere, Rice wrote of the Union center that "became as marble," deployed in the area "through which chance or God has carved that fateful 'Sunken Road.'" Most telling, Rice never mentioned Wallace in the Hornet's Nest, but he did talk about "the indomitable Prentiss." Otto Eisenschiml, in *The Story of Shiloh* (1946), wrote, "For hour on hour, Prentiss here held up the bulk of the Confederate army; when he finally did surrender, he had saved the day for Grant." Later, he wrote in more detail, stating that Grant "owed his own military survival and subsequent Presidential honors to Prentiss' stubborn and sacrificial resistance." In a caption for Prentiss's photograph, Eisenschiml labeled Prentiss the "real hero of Shiloh."[31]

After the National Park Service took control of the park in 1933, the agency's historians institutionalized Prentiss's heroics even more. The long-running text on the park's visitor brochure, handed to every visitor, mentioned Prentiss but not Wallace. In later years, the bland unicolor cover was replaced with the Thulstrup watercolor showing Prentiss in the Hornet's Nest. Likewise, as stated before, the park's 1956 film, *Shiloh: Portrait of a Battle,* heavily concentrated on Prentiss in the Hornet's Nest, leaving other actions relatively untouched. At one point, after mentioning Prentiss alone—not Wallace—the film narrator stated, "The troops in the Sunken Road held the key to the battlefield." Later, the film stated, "Prentiss's sacrifice had indeed not been in vain," and it then went on to describe how his stand had allowed Grant time to build a last line of defense. No wonder visitors to the park came away with a heavy emphasis on Prentiss.[32]

Today, Benjamin Prentiss widely holds the title of "Hero of Shiloh." But it is not a fitting label. Prentiss has been lauded for sending out the critical morning patrol, holding the Hornet's Nest, and then surrendering his men as a sacrifice so that his side could win the battle. In each case, Prentiss was not as heroic as legend says. He did not send out the patrol but took credit for it. The number of men he commanded in the Hornet's Nest was dwarfed by other commanders, namely Wallace, but he took credit for it. Finally, in surrendering, Prentiss did not save Grant's army, but in doing so he became a martyr—an honor that should have gone to W. H. L. Wallace, who was mortally wounded at the end of the defense. Prentiss's actions at Shiloh, while not cowardly by any means, were not heroic enough to warrant the attention given him. There is simply no factual basis for Prentiss's hero status.

The powerful action of Civil War memory and the major effect public opinion has had on how Americans then and now viewed the war has made Prentiss a hero. After decades of defending his actions, Prentiss began, in the mid- to late 1880s, to see a change emerge. Various paintings and written histories began to tell a different story—one with Prentiss as the hero. With the creation of Shiloh National Military Park in 1894, Prentiss's star rose even more as visitors could now see where the famous events took place. By the time of his death in 1901, Prentiss was publicly lauded as the hero of Shiloh, and later media presentations and literary efforts only added to the myth. But the hero Prentiss was a creation of Civil War memory, not of actions on the battlefield.

Modern historians have taken the early historiographical accounts as the truth and pushed this myth into even more general acceptance. Sometimes even though sources are considered primary, they still need to be looked at through the prism of historiography to calculate exactly where they fit in and how truthful they actually are. Modern historians have unfortunately, in the Prentiss case, taken the early primary sources from Prentiss himself and the early park officials and have dispersed the ideas encased within this myth. As an exercise in historical memory, the Prentiss myth can help warn modern historians of perpetuating inaccurate history just because it is widely accepted.

Finally, there is even some evidence that Prentiss was actually unheroic in his Shiloh exploits. It is known that he took advantage of Everett Peabody's death and took credit for sending out the famous morning patrol. It is known that he took advantage of W. H. L. Wallace's death and took credit for holding the Hornet's Nest. And it is known that the prisoner Prentiss willingly and freely gave out major bits of intelligence to his Confederate captors on the night of April 6, 1862. And after the war, he forcefully pushed several of these myths to raise his reputation. It seems Prentiss was not such a hero after all, and while his courage cannot be debated, perhaps his honor as an officer and a gentleman can. While it is up to a future biographer to examine Prentiss's entire life, it seems readily apparent that his Shiloh exploits were not the stuff of which heroes are made. But then Civil War memory is such a complex issue that the truth is often hard to discern, especially so when it is, intentionally or unintentionally, tainted by the participants.[33]

# 5

# Rewriting History: Locating Lew Wallace's Route of March to Shiloh

A variety of questions surround Lew Wallace's march to Shiloh on April 6, 1862. Why did it take all day to reach the battlefield? Was he really lost? What exactly did those elusive written orders tell Wallace to do? What was the exact route of his march? We may never know the answer to all of these questions, but fortunately, through new research, one of those mysteries has been solved. We now know the exact route Wallace took on his march and countermarch to Shiloh.

The last person known to purposefully traverse Wallace's route was Wallace himself, when he returned to the area in November 1901 and explored the roads in the company of various veterans and Shiloh National Military Park Commission members. Wallace had been in the area before, particularly in 1895. At that time, he had located what he thought was the correct route, but he had made several mistakes. In 1901, the group established what they all agreed on was the correct route and even marked some portions of it. Unfortunately, as the decades passed, all tangible evidence slipped away, and it has been more than one hundred years since anyone has explored and verified the original route.

But now, one hundred years of questions can be answered regarding the original route Wallace took to Shiloh. Using historic maps, overlays of modern topographical maps, aerial photographs, satellite imagery, and countless hours of research and ground truthing, it is once again possible to march Wallace's route, and one small group has done so. In the process, they have answered several nagging questions: What was the terrain like? In what condition were the soldiers once they arrived at Shiloh? What was the true distance of the route? And, most important, was Wallace slow on his march? The answers to these questions, gained by actually marching the route, force us to rewrite history.

* * *

Lew Wallace was one of the Union commanders who did not fare well at Shiloh. Castigated by a Grant public relations machine that labeled him as lost, Wallace never overcame the stigma, even with the publication of *Ben-Hur*. Wallace even came back to Shiloh in later years and tried to locate his route of march to prove he was not lost. (Library of Congress.)

*March 1862.* Lew Wallace's Third Division of the Army of the Tennessee, after an aborted raid on the Mobile and Ohio Railroad, had settled down in camp near Crump's Landing on the Tennessee River, halfway between Savannah and Pittsburg Landing. One of Wallace's three brigades was physically at Crump's Landing—his first under Colonel Morgan L. Smith. Wallace also kept his own headquarters there in order to keep communications open via the river. The second brigade, Colonel John M. Thayer commanding, camped at Stoney Lonesome, some two miles west on the Purdy Road. Colonel Charles Whittlesey and Wallace's third brigade camped another two and a half miles out the same road at the small hamlet of Adamsville. The division had reached its camps on March 13 and spent the most part of the next month there. It was not idle time, however. Several maneuvers and many precautionary measures kept the division busy.[1]

As soon as Wallace had made camp, he sent his cavalry to explore the surrounding area, particularly the roads to the south that would be his landward communications link with the rest of the army around Pittsburg Landing. Two roads ran to the Shiloh/Pittsburg Landing area. The eastern-most road, known as the River Road, paralleled the Tennessee River on high ground and was the direct route to Pittsburg Landing from Crump's Landing. It crossed the flooded Snake Creek bottom, which was not bridged at the time and was of unknown depth. The western road, known as the Shunpike, split off the Crump's Landing to Purdy Road at Stoney Lonesome (two miles west of Crump's) and crossed the same creek bottom as the River Road, but a few miles upstream and thus higher in the flooded watershed. In addition to crossing the Snake Creek bottom, the Shunpike also crossed two tributaries of Snake Creek: Graham and Clear creeks. The Shunpike joined the Hamburg-Purdy Road between Clear and Owl creeks, which then crossed Owl Creek and led to the main Corinth Road around Union general William T. Sherman's camps, about two miles southwest of Pittsburg Landing.[2]

After reconnaissance and consultation with other division commanders, Wallace developed a contingency plan by which his isolated division would be supported via the Shunpike if he was attacked from the west, which the Federal high command supposed would be the Confederate plan rather than an attack on the full army at Pittsburg Landing. Wallace and the other division commanders thus decided that the Shunpike would be the main connecting route with the rest of the army. After all, the Shunpike's head was at the center of Wallace's division near Stoney Lonesome, at which the brigades could concentrate fairly quickly in the event of trouble. Wallace also believed the Shunpike to be the shorter of the two routes to Sherman's camps at Shiloh Church. Wallace in fact later termed the Shunpike "the nearest and most practicable road to the scene of battle." Moreover, the River Road was completely flooded until April 3, that day being the first time cavalry made it across via that route. Even then, however, the road remained partially under water—not a good situation for moving artillery, wagons, and thousands of men. Because of this contingency plan, Wallace's men corduroyed the Shunpike, not the River Road, in the days before the battle, and as late as April 5, Wallace communicated with W. H. L. Wallace at Pittsburg Landing via the Shunpike, not the River Road.[3]

Already tense because of their isolated position and because of contact with the Confederates, the men of Wallace's division awoke Sunday morning, April 6, 1862, to the sounds of battle to the south. Hearing the cannon fire and presuming that the battle was on at Pittsburg Landing, Wallace ordered "the equipage of the several brigades" sent to the landing and made ready to march as soon as he received positive orders.[4]

Wallace ordered the first and third brigades to concentrate at Stoney Lonesome, the camp of the second brigade and also the turnoff onto the Shunpike. He then planned, once orders arrived, to march to the aid of

Grant's army. Using the contingency plan in reverse, there was no thought as to what road to take—the Shunpike was the most direct route to Sherman and the front of the army which, judging from the sound of battle, was evidently heavily engaged. While the brigades marched to Stoney Lonesome, Wallace himself remained at the river waiting for Grant, whom he knew would be on his way to Pittsburg Landing from his headquarters at Savannah. Grant's headquarters boat, the *Tigress,* soon steamed close in to Crump's Landing and stopped for a moment next to a boat Wallace had boarded. The two generals conferred. After a moment, Grant ordered Wallace to have his division ready to move "at a moment's notice" and also to make a reconnaissance out the Purdy Road, scouting for the enemy. Wallace replied that both had been done, whereupon Grant steamed on to Pittsburg Landing, telling Wallace to wait for orders.[5]

After his conference with Grant, Wallace rode to Stoney Lonesome, leaving a horse at Crump's Landing for the courier he knew would be coming with orders from Grant. Wallace later remembered the hours passing slowly: "Ten o'clock, and still the air laden with noises of the struggle going on . . . 10:30—Yet no order." At 11:30 a.m., Wallace finally received his orders from Grant, who had arrived at Pittsburg and decided the main attack was indeed taking place there. Captain A. S. Baxter, who had traveled by river to Crump's Landing, arrived at Stoney Lonesome on the horse Wallace had left at Crump's, now sweat-lathered from the two-mile gallop. Baxter carried the fateful order of the day. Almost immediately after Grant had arrived at Pittsburg Landing, he had ordered his assistant adjutant general, Captain John A. Rawlins, to send Baxter to order Wallace to march (as Grant remembered it) up the River Road and take a position on the Union right. Baxter was afraid he would "make some mistake" and requested written orders. These Rawlins produced on board the *Tigress,* and in a moment Baxter was off to Crump's Landing. Finding the horse left by Wallace, the quartermaster made his way to Stoney Lonesome and found Wallace. Their conversation "did not exceed three minutes," according to Baxter. After taking thirty minutes to eat, Wallace's brigades at Stoney Lonesome then moved toward the battle via the Shunpike, not the River Road.[6]

One of the questions that may never be solved concerns the written order. Wallace said it ordered him to move to the right of the army, which he had planned to do all along, moving via the Shunpike. Wallace also noted that the order was "*unsigned* by *anybody.*" Conversely, Grant later claimed that the order told Wallace to move along the River Road to Pittsburg Landing, but when pressed after the war he finally admitted that he had never seen the

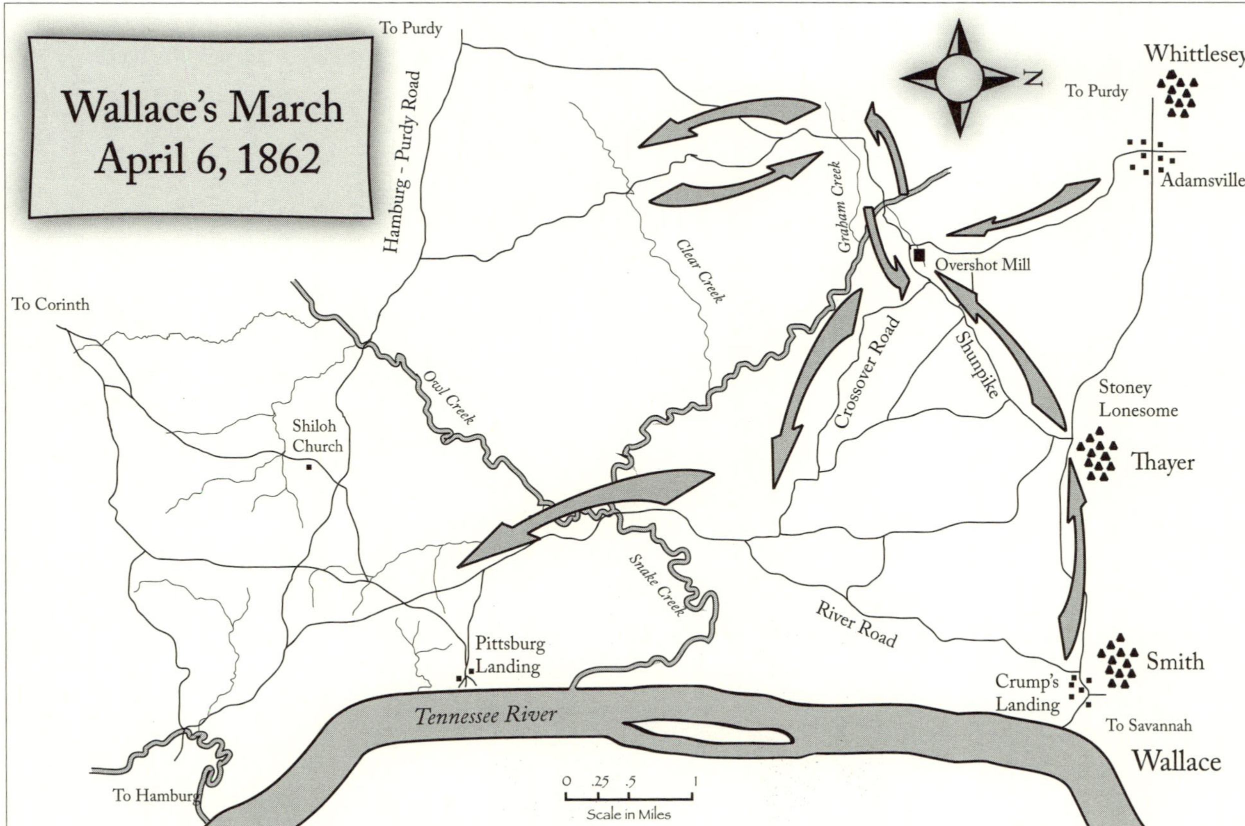

Wallace's March
April 6, 1862
To Purdy
Hamburg - Purdy Road
N
Whittlesey
To Purdy
Adamsville
Graham Creek
Clear Creek
Overshot Mill
To Corinth
Crossover Road
Shunpike
Owl Creek
Stoney
Lonesome
Shiloh
Church
Thayer
Snake Creek
River Road
Pittsburg
Landing
Smith
Crump's
Landing
Tennessee River
To Savannah
Wallace
To Hamburg
0 .25 .5 1
Scale in Miles

written order and thus was "not competent to say just what order the general actually received." A staff officer ultimately lost the original paper, but considering it had been from Grant to Rawlins to Baxter to Wallace, the order could have stated anything. Unfortunately, we will never know just what it said.[7]

Wallace nevertheless moved forward from Stoney Lonesome with two brigades. The third brigade was still at Adamsville and, through a mix-up, did not receive orders to move until 2:00 p.m. Two regiments and one gun were also left behind to defend the Crump's Landing area and the division's baggage.[8]

About the time he began the march, Wallace received a cavalry officer sent by Grant to hurry him up. This meeting was likewise quick, and the cavalry officer returned to Grant soon after noon. Apparently, the cavalryman misunderstood Wallace's reaction. He stated that the general had questioned receiving a verbal order and mentioned something about needing a written one. Wallace later vehemently denied this, and his actions verified his claim. He was on the move, after all. Moreover, Wallace later argued that the "cannonading, distinctly audible, quickened the steps of the men." By 2:00 p.m., the brigades had passed Overshot Mill and crossed Snake Creek.[9]

Wallace then received the shock of the day when an aide-de-camp to Grant, Captain W. R. Rowley, arrived just as the head of the division was nearing Clear Creek. In response to the cavalryman's report, Grant had sent Rowley back again to order Wallace forward once more. Rowley, traveling the River Road, soon came upon Wallace's deserted camps, which in itself indicated that the report about the verbal orders was untrue. Finding only a baggage wagon, itself leaving, Rowley inquired as to where the division was. The teamster pointed the way and Rowley hurried off. Seeing to it that he did "not spare horse flesh," as Grant had ordered, Rowley quickly came upon the rear of the division "at a rest, sitting on each side of the road, some with their arms stacked in the middle of the road." Rowley rode up to Wallace, who was at the head of the column on the high ground north of Clear Creek. Pulling Wallace to the side, the staff officer warned of the danger ahead: "Don't you know Sherman has been driven back. Why, the whole army is within half a mile of the river, and it's a question if we are not all going to be driven into it." Wallace admitted "myself more than shocked by this intelligence, heightened in effect, as it was, by Captain Rowley's energetic style of expression." He admitted being temporarily "struck . . . dumb—too dumb for question." Soon, however, he regained his composure. Wallace had sent his cavalry ahead to see if the enemy was in his front, and they soon returned with confirmation that the enemy was in fact between them and the rest of the army. Wallace wisely decided he had to turn around. "In this dilemma," Wallace remembered, "I resolved, as the most prudent course, to carry out *the spirit of General Grant's order and join the right of his army as it then rested.*" Rowley, at Wallace's request, stayed on as a guide, for Wallace knew little of the River Road that he would soon traverse.[10]

Instead of simply turning the division around, Wallace truly countermarched. Time was taken to march his first brigade the entire length of the division so it would be first again; then the second brigade did the same thing. Wallace wanted his best troops in the lead, because with such gloomy news from Rowley, he did not know what he could expect at Pittsburg Landing. He might have to fight his way in and thus wanted his best troops in the lead. Meanwhile, the third brigade, which had received its orders late and was complete with baggage and all, showed up behind the second brigade while the first was backtracking. Whittlesey had taken another road that connected Adamsville with the Shunpike, and his men stood in column for about an hour where the two roads joined at Overshot Mill.[11]

Wallace thus marched back past Overshot Mill, looking for a road that would take him across to the River Road. Wallace's cavalry found a young man named Dick Pickens near Overshot Mill and ordered him to guide the division to the River Road. Pickens led Wallace's division onto a small crossover road that began about half a mile north of the mill on the high ground north of Snake Creek.[12]

But more staff officers soon arrived at Wallace's mobile headquarters. By 2:30 p.m., Grant was growing extremely anxious. With no sign of Wallace, he sent Lieutenant Colonel James B. McPherson and Captain Rawlins to find out what was happening with the errant division. These two, with two orderlies, followed Rowley's route. Finding no one who could tell them where the division was, they proceeded to Crump's Landing. On the way, a surgeon told them the route taken by Wallace. The officers, along with the surgeon and a local citizen acting as guide, took the Shunpike and soon came upon the division at the opening of the small crossing road that led over to the River Road. The division was all the way back to within two miles of its camps at Stoney Lonesome and was turning onto the crossover road when McPherson and Rawlins found it. The first brigade, Smith's, had already turned onto the road, and the second, Thayer's, was at the junction. Thayer told the staff officers that Wallace was at the head of the column, so the party pushed on over the crossover road. They came upon Wallace about 3:30 p.m. McPherson and Rawlins filled him in on the situation at Pittsburg Landing and urged haste. Then the column, all three brigades now together, continued on the crossover road and finally reached the River Road. By all accounts, it was a harrowing march through very rough terrain.[13]

Grant's staff officers complained that Wallace moved too slowly on the march. They later reported Wallace ordered the division to stop occasionally and close up, to which Wallace later responded to Grant himself that "the *whole* division was what I supposed you wanted, and I was resolved to bring you the whole division." The staff officers also claimed Wallace demonstrated a lackadaisical body language that did not express a desire for speed. One staffer in fact wrote of Wallace at one point "dismounting from his horse, [he] seated himself on a log." Later, McPherson recommended that the artillery, in line behind the first brigade, be taken out of the column to make it move faster. Then, when the column came to the inundated Snake Creek bottoms, local citizens informed them that the enemy held the bridge across Snake Creek. So the column halted again. When this story proved untrue, the march restarted. Other delays occurred to close up the column and reconnoiter, but by this time it was of no use. The staff officers Grant had sent to hurry the column watched as "the sun sank to rest." Whatever had happened at Shiloh on April 6, Grant had done it by himself. Wallace, through no fault of his own but because he had become trapped in a no-win situation, had been of no help that day. [14]

* * *

After the war, debate raged over Wallace's march, mostly centering on what the mysterious order had said and who was at fault for the division's late arrival. But little interest was taken in the actual route. As time passed, however, more people began to get involved in tracing the exact course. There was some brief interest in the route in the 1880s when the *Century* magazine published an article on the march, with one officer even returning and trying to trace it. The debate over what route Wallace actually took became heated in the late 1890s, however, with several factors at work. Shiloh National Military Park had been established, and its historian, David W. Reed, was examining every piece of evidence to learn the truth about many Shiloh mysteries. In addition, Wallace was himself writing his autobiography and thus wanted the truth to be known. He of course believed the truth would exonerate him from any negligence.[15]

Although the mystery of the lost order was not solved at this time, several others were. One major controversy revolved around the location of the exact route of march on the crossover road. Wallace had been involved in trying to find it as early as 1895, when he employed the local Hardin County surveyor, George Harbert, to map his route. Wallace was present when the surveying was done, and so were several of his officers, including George McGinnis.

From the survey, Wallace and Harbert produced a map that was fairly accurate, but by then many memories had failed—Wallace's included. Wallace's two main errors in 1895 concerned the location where he had ordered the countermarch and where he had left the Shunpike to take the crossover road. Most important, Wallace incorrectly decided in 1895 that the crossover road he had taken in 1862 left the Shunpike at the Overshot Mill.[16]

The year 1895 was also the first year of the Shiloh National Military Park Commission. Chairman Cornelius Cadle examined the route that year, even finding Dick Pickens, who had guided Wallace over the crossover road in 1862. Later that year, Shiloh engineer Atwell Thompson also examined the route and mapped it. He also located Pickens, who led him over the route. The engineer described the 1895 condition of the route as an "old road, crossing fences and going through corn fields, pasture fields, and woods again." But Pickens had taken Thompson on the road that led directly away from Overshot Mill, and Pickens was evidently losing his grasp of the events. He also told Thompson that some of the division had marched on another road, and that the majority of Wallace's men had returned to Crump's Landing and moved to Shiloh by boat. To say the least, Thompson was not convinced he had found the correct road.[17]

In November 1901, Wallace returned to Shiloh to settle the issue (and others) once and for all. On November 20, Wallace and the foremost Shiloh authority, commission historian David W. Reed, accompanied by several other veterans and park engineer Atwell Thompson, rode to Crump's Landing. "General Wallace pointed out the spot where his headquarters tent stood," Thompson remembered, and located the campsites of Smith's brigade at the landing. After "devouring as many persimmons as the various conditions of their several anatomies would permit" and packing more seeds to plant in the North as memorial trees, the group left Crump's and traveled to Stoney Lonesome, where Wallace located the camps of Thayer's brigade. Moving on to Adamsville, the group ordered lunch at the new town hotel and went in the meantime to locate the camps of Whittlesey's brigade. After finding the spot, the party returned and had a feast. "General Wallace generously paid the bill for all," Thompson remembered.[18]

After lunch, the group began the process of finding the actual route of march. Following Whittlesey's route to Overshot Mill and the Shunpike, the group crossed Snake Creek and continued along the modern (1901) route across Graham Creek. Here a bit of uncertainty appeared. Thompson took the group along the route surveyed by the Hardin County surveyor in 1895, but the veterans were not convinced of its accuracy. "Here we halted for a little while until the gentlemen could renew their memories," Thompson explained.

Returning to the main route, the group decided it was the road traveled in 1862 and continued to Clear Creek, where all agreed that Wallace had turned around. By then, the day was "pretty well spent," so Wallace and Reed decided to continue on to Pittsburg Landing by way of the Owl Creek bridge and locate the rest of the route another day. As they moved on, Wallace became firmly convinced of his error in believing he had turned around at Owl Creek, not Clear Creek, in 1862.[19]

The next day was spent in examining Wallace's activities on the battlefield itself, but the group returned to the subject of his march on November 22. Thompson remembered Wallace as being "anxious to establish the place where he left the Shunpike Road and was guided by Pickens by the most direct route to the Wallace bridge." Having gone over the route with Pickens back in 1895, Thompson led the way. He first tried to find Pickens, but failed. Then he took the group to the road Pickens said he had used in 1862. It joined the Shunpike directly at Overshot Mill. Traversing this route, the group of veterans was not satisfied that it was the correct road. Examining the area more, Thompson led the group to another road half a mile north up the Shunpike, and all soon became convinced that this was indeed the road by which Wallace crossed over to the River Road. The group placed a sign at that point: "By this road General Wallace's army marched to Shiloh April 6th 1862."

One of the major locations along Wallace's route of march to the Shiloh battlefield was Overshot Mill. Here it is seen in the 1890s. The mill is long gone, but the remnants of Wallace's route of march are still remarkably intact. (Courtesy of Shiloh National Military Park.)

Rain began peppering the group as they finished the task, however, and they decided to return to the landing. For the next hundred years, few people traversed the route with Wallace in mind.[20]

Out of the agreement in November 1901 came an accurate map of the route. Wallace himself asked that park engineer Atwell Thompson make the map. Unfortunately, Shiloh's original commission map has apparently been lost, most likely with the abundance of papers and maps lost during the tornado of 1909 that literally blew away a priceless amount of original work on Shiloh. The only known copy today is in the Indiana Historical Society in Indianapolis. But there are published renditions of the map. Obviously using Thompson's map, Shiloh veteran Joseph W. Rich published his own map of the march in a 1909 *Iowa Journal of History and Politics* article. Later in 1920, Rich included it in another article in the same journal. But Rich left no doubt that he depended on Reed and the park staff for his map and information, even publishing a lengthy letter by Reed on the subject.[21]

* * *

The Thompson map (as well as the subsequent Rich maps), when overlaid with a modern topographic map, reveals many secrets. One is the amazing correctness of the road system on the map as compared with the modern system of roads. The main roads on the Thompson map line up exactly with the corresponding modern portions of the 1862 era roads. The validity and accuracy of the remainder of the route is thus verified.

But the accuracy does not end there. In places where the 1862 road system is not used by today's modern roads, extant evidence shows that the map is correct. Almost everywhere along the forgotten portions of the route, the roads are still discernable on the ground itself where the Thompson map says that portions of the route should be. Some portions are deeply cut, which most likely means that those parts of the route were used longer after the war; other, not-so-well-defined traces were evidently little used after the war. Even the places along the route with very little evidence remaining are still somewhat discernable, however, and match exactly where the Thompson map says they should be.

* * *

*October 2005.* Armed with historic maps and aerial photographs, and after many hours of study and ground truthing, I led a small group of eight people, including Shiloh National Military Park superintendent Woody Harrell and Lew Wallace biographer Gail Stephens, on Lew Wallace's famous route to Shiloh. It was hoped that several comparisons could be made with the original march, such as what condition the troops would have been in when they reached the battlefield (comparatively, of course; Civil War soldiers would have been in much better shape), how difficult the actual terrain on the march was, what the true distance of the march was, and, most important, a comparison of the time it took to march the route. Wallace has always been castigated for his slow march. If this small group could not beat Wallace's time (approximately seven hours) with all his problems of getting fifty-eight hundred men, artillery, wagons, and horses along a route covered with the fog of war and under battle conditions, no one could be justified in complaining that Wallace's march was slow.

Believing the route to be 14.2 miles (as measured by maps), the group set out from Stoney Lonesome at 9:00 a.m. on October 13. The route led (on private land) along the Shunpike past Overshot Mill and across Snake Creek. Reaching Clear Creek and beginning the countermarch, the group was approximately fifteen minutes behind Wallace's schedule. Countermarching at Clear Creek, the group recrossed Snake Creek and took the crossover road to the River Road, where it again crossed Snake Creek and a larger canal later dredged in the area. The exhausted group finally reached the high ground along Grant's last line of defense at 4:45 p.m.

It had taken a small group of eight people (at a brisk pace) longer than it had taken Wallace to march what turned out to be 16.75 miles (according to Superintendent Harrell's GPS unit). And this little band of hikers had a beautiful day, no high water, no battle conditions, and no wagons and artillery. The group did take approximately thirty minutes for lunch, which in all fairness requires that Wallace's starting time be pushed back to 11:30 a.m., when his men ate a thirty-minute lunch. Still, this group ran approximately fifteen minutes behind Wallace's original march: Wallace took seven and a half hours to eat lunch and make the march while the group took seven hours and forty-five minutes.

Lessons were learned on the march, including a new awareness of what the hike entailed for those soldiers of the Third Division and the meaning of Wallace's comment that the route was "out of one hole into another" (the route is continually up and down, in and out of creek valleys). More important, a true distance of the march was gained by the use of modern technology. Most important of all, the march showed that Wallace managed to get his division to Shiloh faster than a small, twenty-first-century group could over the same distance. All doubt about the speed of Wallace's march should thus be muffled forever.[22]

* * *

It is possible once again to traverse the route Lew Wallace took to reach the Shiloh battlefield. Trusting the accuracy of the Thompson map (which was made in concert with D. W. Reed, who traveled the route with Wallace in 1901 and verified to everyone's satisfaction the location of the route) and verifying it with aerial photographs and painstaking ground truthing, the route is once again found. We are now able to do what no one since that November day in 1901, and very few people since the actual events in April 1862, have been able to do: march the route Lew Wallace took to Shiloh on that fateful day of April 6, 1862. In doing so, we also need to rewrite the history of Wallace's original march.

# 6

# Secession at Shiloh: Mississippi's Convention Delegates and Their State's Defense

January 9, 1861, was a momentous day for the one hundred men gathered at the state house in Jackson, Mississippi. They were delegates to the Mississippi secession convention and were about to make a fateful decision, not just for their state but also for themselves. Some were wealthy planters who owned large plantations along the Mississippi River; they knew full well that secession would lead to war and war would lead to closed markets at best and total destruction at worst. While dedicated Mississippians, they were still unenthusiastic about secession. Termed "cooperationists," they tried to delay disunion. Others were more adamant about immediate secession, and they carried the day. The final vote was a dominating 84-percent majority for leaving the Union, and there was an immediate feeling of consequence when the deed was done. While casting his vote, James L. Alcorn explained that "the die is cast—the Rubicon is crossed—and I enlist myself with the army that goes to Rome. I vote for the ordinance."[1]

The delegates must have understood the significance of their action, but few realized the extent to which they would be personally involved. Most who were of military age, and a few who were not, opted to join the newly established military ranks during the excitement of secession and war, but the extent to which they would be called on to suffer and perhaps die was probably not foremost in their minds. It has often been noted that the signers of the Declaration of Independence in 1776 were potentially signing their death warrants; the same could be said of the Mississippi delegates in Jackson. For some, their action would literally consign them to death. Others would suffer terrifying wounds or imprisonment. Most would be economically and socially dispossessed. Their state would be devastated. It was a serious decision to make.[2]

Although a third of the delegates were too old to serve in the ranks (many still equipped companies from their locales or sent sons to the war effort), there were numerous delegates to the secession convention in the Confederate army by April 1862. During the initial year of the war, these delegates experienced only limited exposure to the war. There was some suffering, to be sure. The first delegate died in September 1861, but it was not on a battlefield or even in the army. And others were removed from Mississippi to defend other parts of the Confederacy. At least fifteen of the delegates, primarily those who first joined up and were sent to the Virginia front, served in the Eastern Theater eventually under Robert E. Lee. That was a long way from home.[3]

But the war began to come closer to Mississippi in February 1862, when a Union army under Ulysses S. Grant won impressive victories at Forts Henry and Donelson in northwestern Tennessee. That was uncomfortably close to Mississippi itself, and the fighting also caused the first delegate to die in action. Francis Marion Rogers of Monroe County, a wealthy lawyer, planter, and judge, was a captain in the 14th Mississippi Infantry, and he died defending Fort Donelson on February 15. At least four others, in addition to Rogers, had been at Fort Donelson and were either wounded or were now in Northern prison camps. But then, the news became much worse. Multiple Union armies began to trek southward toward Mississippi, intent on capturing the vital Confederate railroad crossing at Corinth in the northeastern corner of the state. The war was about to hit Mississippi itself.[4]

At least eleven delegates were a part of the army assembling at Corinth under General Albert Sidney Johnston, who soon advanced across the state line into Tennessee to attack Grant's army at Pittsburg Landing. He hoped to destroy that army before another Federal force under Don Carlos Buell arrived on the scene. In effect, Johnston was trying to defend Corinth, its railroads, the state of Mississippi, and the Mississippi Valley as a whole by going on the offensive. The result was the climactic Battle of Shiloh, fought on April 6 and 7, 1862.[5]

Of the eleven former delegates at Corinth, ten saw action at Shiloh. The eleventh, lawyer and future Confederate brigadier general Samuel Benton of Marshall County, was detached from his regiment, the 9th Mississippi, in order to form a new unit in the interior of the state. He left Corinth as early as March 24. The rest, however, went into the fight at Shiloh. On all, the battle would have a tremendous impact; for some, it would literally mean life and death.[6]

All ten delegates engaged in literally defending Mississippi at Shiloh were officers, as would be expected given their status as elected officials and the early Confederate practice of the men electing their own officers. Four were captains of companies, with another captain acting as a staff officer to Confederate general Braxton Bragg. There was also one major, two lieutenant colonels, one colonel, and a brigadier general.[7]

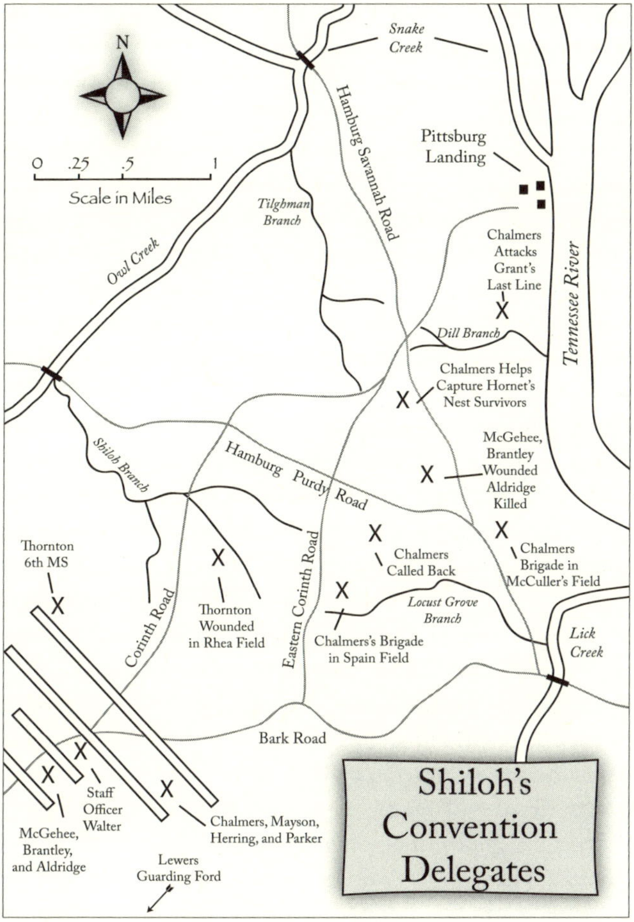


When the Battle of Shiloh began at dawn on April 6, these ten were arrayed throughout the Confederate army stacked in line four corps deep. The only delegate in the first line, William J. Hardee's corps, was Colonel John J. Thornton, commanding the 6th Mississippi Infantry in Patrick Cleburne's brigade on the extreme left flank. Thornton himself was somewhat of an anomaly. Representing Rankin County in the convention, the prewar doctor was so convinced that he should represent his cooperationist constituents that he voted against secession and then purposely stayed away from the convention the day the ordinance was officially signed on January 15. He became one of only two delegates who did not sign the ordinance, the other being a delegate who did not attend the January convention after the first three days;

he was not even there to cast a vote on the secession ordinance. Thus Thornton was the only active participant in the convention who refused to sign. Yet, having been a prewar militia officer, he was one of the first delegates to take up arms for the Confederacy.[8]

Thornton led his Mississippians forward on the bright morning of April 6, but Cleburne's Brigade soon ran into a swamp. The quagmire was so extensive around Shiloh Branch that it forced the brigade to split and go around on either side. Most of the regiments went to the west of the swamp, attacking at Shiloh Church, but Thornton's 6th Mississippi and the 23rd Tennessee went east and entered Rhea Field, where the 53rd Ohio was waiting.[9]

The result sounds like the stuff of legend, but it was true. Thornton and his Mississippians made three unsuccessful assaults across Rhea Field and through the enemy's encampments and were each time driven back by the Ohioans and an Illinois artillery battery on their flank. The regiment lost 300 of its 425 men engaged in that one field. Their colonel was one of the wounded. As Thornton led his men forward during one of the assaults, the regiment's flag bearer was instantly killed. Thornton grabbed the flag and continued on. Quickly, he also went down, severely wounded in the thigh. The Battle of Shiloh was over for him, ironically wounded in defense of the very act of secession he would not vote for.[10]

Thornton and his Mississippians' experiences were similar to those of the other units in Hardee's first line. Few of them made much progress for several hours, necessitating the Confederate high command to send forward the next wave of troops, Braxton Bragg's corps. In this line were numerous Mississippi convention delegates, including one of Bragg's staff officers, Assistant Adjutant General Harvey W. Walter, a prewar lawyer from Marshall County. Little is known of Walter's experience at Shiloh, but Bragg did commend him for his service when he wrote his official report later in April.[11]

The other Mississippians in this line were all in one brigade, James R. Chalmers's Mississippi brigade on the extreme right of this second line. The commander himself, a lawyer and large planter before the war, was a delegate to the convention, having represented DeSoto County. After the convention, Chalmers had quickly become colonel of the 9th Mississippi and then rose to brigadier general, now leading the brigade at Shiloh. Within the brigade, Lieutenant Colonel Hamilton Mayson, a lawyer from Marion County, commanded the 7th Mississippi in the absence of its colonel. There were also two captains, small farmers John B. Herring of Pontotoc County commanding a company in the 5th Mississippi and Daniel H. Parker of Franklin County, who like Thornton had voted against secession but quickly joined the Confederate army, commanding a company in Mayson's 7th Mississippi. The members of Company E, 7th Mississippi were thus inundated with secession convention delegates; their company captain had been there, as well as their regimental commander, brigade commander, and an officer on their corps commander's staff.[12]

Chalmers's Brigade moved forward in support of the Confederate right near Spain Field and aided the front line units, most notably Adley Gladden's brigade, in pushing Federal general Benjamin Prentiss's division back. Thereafter, when the Confederate high command realized there was a major threat farther to the right, Chalmers's Mississippians and an Alabama brigade were taken out of line and redirected to the east, where they soon fought David Stuart's Federal brigade in the ravines near the Tennessee River. Casualties were numerous as they fought their way up and down the slopes, but none of the convention delegates were hit.[13]

The Confederate advance stalled on this right flank, however, as it had begun to do all across the field, necessitating the Confederate high command to throw in additional units. Leonidas Polk's corps was next in line, but it contained no Mississippi convention delegates. The reserve corps, commanded by former U.S. vice president John C. Breckinridge, contained four more delegates, however. Lawyer, planter, and future Confederate general William F. Brantley of Choctaw County was the major of the 15th Mississippi and was in command of that regiment while its colonel, Winfield S. Statham, commanded the brigade. Prewar lawyer Francis Marion Aldridge of Yalobusha County was a captain in Brantley's regiment. Edward F. McGehee, who owned a large plantation and over seventy slaves in Panola County, was lieutenant colonel of what was once the 25th Mississippi but now was recognized as the 2nd Confederate Infantry. Brantley and Aldridge were in Winfield Statham's brigade while McGehee was assigned to John S. Bowen's brigade. In addition, planter Thomas D. Lewers of DeSoto County was a captain in Wirt Adams's cavalry regiment assigned to this reserve corps, but the troopers saw little action, their main job being to hold a ford on Lick Creek to the south.[14]

As Chalmers, Mayson, Parker, and Herring pushed forward to the east near the Tennessee River, Statham and Bowen led their brigades into the gap that was created when the Mississippians and Alabamians were earlier removed from the line. They took position on the south side of a large cotton field, with a peach orchard and a small pond on the northern fringes. There they were led by an impressive array of leadership, including army commander Albert Sidney Johnston, former vice president Breckinridge, and Tennessee governor Isham G. Harris.[15]

The famous assaults across Sarah Bell's cotton field and the Peach Orchard ultimately succeeded, but at a terrific loss of life, including Johnston himself. Death and injury also came to the Mississippi delegates. In these assaults, Lieutenant Colonel McGehee was terribly wounded in the left foot while urging his men forward. His regimental commander, John D. Martin, praised him as being wounded "while gallantly encouraging his regiment, without regard to his personal exposure." Brantley likewise was wounded while leading the 15th Mississippi onward. Both would survive, but Francis Marion Aldridge was not so fortunate. Hit while leading his company forward in the attacks, Aldridge was killed that day.[16]

The Mississippi delegates continued in the assaults throughout the remainder of the first day's action. With so many down, the only major unit containing delegates still in organized operation was Chalmers's Brigade. Chalmers, Mayson, Parker, and Herring thus led their men forward on the extreme right flank of the army, up and down the massive ravines near the Tennessee River. After aiding in the capture of the remnants of the Hornet's Nest defenders, their final action came near sundown when they attempted to assault Grant's final line of defense near Pittsburg Landing. With so much artillery, infantry, gunboats, and the leading elements of Buell's reinforcing army arrayed in this final Union line, the Mississippians' hope of breaking through was futile. They retired out of artillery range for the evening, although the Union navy's big guns peppered them throughout the night.[17]

It must have been a miserable night for all the delegates, especially Brantley, Thornton, and McGehee, all wounded severely during the fighting. Those who had not been wounded huddled helplessly as the naval guns and heavy rains bombarded them. Only the lifeless corpse of Francis Marion Aldridge rested peacefully that night.[18]

Had the Mississippians and the Confederate high command known what was coming the next day, they would have been even more uncomfortable. Grant and Buell counterattacked at daylight, driving the weakened Confederates backward throughout the second day's fight. With most of the delegates not in Chalmers's Brigade killed or wounded, only those in Chalmers's unit fought together as a group on the second day. They resisted the Union advance on the Confederate right near the famous Peach Orchard until Confederate commander P. G. T. Beauregard, having taken over for the deceased Johnston, realized the futility of further resistance. The delegates thus began the slow march back to Corinth. A company of Wirt Adams cavalry regiment was engaged the next day in combating the dismal Union pursuit, but Thomas Lewers's men were apparently not engaged.[19]

The Mississippi delegates at Corinth, as well as thousands of other Southerners, had attempted to defend Corinth, its railroads, and the state of Mississippi with a bold stroke. Now, with one of those delegates dead and three others wounded, the remainder prepared to resist the further Union advance toward Corinth. That came in May, and the healthy delegates, as well as an infusion of others who were part of regiments just then joining the army, unsuccessfully attempted to stop the Union progression. Although that attempt likewise failed, the war went on. Vicksburg would be the next major Union goal, and many of the delegates engaged in that campaign as well.[20]

But not all the ten delegates participated. Aldridge was eventually returned to his native Yalobusha County and buried. Thornton and McGehee, the two most dreadfully wounded at Shiloh, resigned and returned home. Thornton later dabbled in the militia but was not able to take the field again. McGehee noted that he was "now a cripple and will be more or less so for life." Only Brantley recovered and returned to the army; he went on to become a Confederate general.[21]

Most of the others not wounded at Shiloh rose in their respective ranks throughout the war. Chalmers became a major general, Braxton Bragg reporting that at Shiloh he had been "at the head of his gallant Mississippians, [and] filled—he could not have exceeded—the measure of my expectations. Never were troops and commander more worthy of each other and of their State." Herring and Lewers eventually rose to the rank of lieutenant colonel. On the other hand, Hamilton Mayson was driven from the army by Braxton Bragg in May, despite Chalmers's notation in his Shiloh report that he and the other commanders were "conspicuous in the thickest of the fight." Sadly, Daniel H. Parker returned home to Franklin County sick in May 1862. He died there on May 12 of typhoid fever.[22]

For those ten Mississippi delegates at Shiloh, they had given their all in defense of Mississippi, but their state was now the war zone. The feat of voting for secession—or not, in the cases of Thornton and Parker—had been the easy part. When it came to putting action to their words, however, they were just as resolute. They were perfectly willing to lay their lives on the line. And all suffered for it, some even being wounded terribly and unable to return to the war. And then there was Francis Marion Aldridge, who had literally signed his death warrant when he put his signature on the Mississippi ordinance of secession.[23]

# 7

# The Forgotten Inhabitants of Shiloh: A Case Study in a Civilian-Government Relationship

James Wood could tell something was amiss. He lived in a small house on the Corinth Road some three miles inland from Pittsburg Landing on the Tennessee River. There, he labored hard at his nearby cotton gin, working the fibers for the few cotton farmers who were his neighbors in the area. There was no ginning on this day, which was not surprising in early April, but there was no other type of work either. Nor had there been for weeks, because an entire United States army was camping on the surrounding land. Wood had seen column after column of blue-clad soldiers march past his house for several weeks as they went about maneuvers, training, and drill. There had even been some loud skirmishing in recent days as a few Confederates surveyed this Federal presence.[1]

But what was happening on this afternoon of April 5, 1862, was different. Now there were more than just a few roving bands of Confederate cavalry in the vicinity; thousands upon thousands of Confederates were gathering near Wood's house and were beginning to deploy in line of battle. Wood soon realized that something bad was about to happen, and fearing for his home and gin, but fearing more for the safety of his loved ones, he gathered his family and what possessions he could carry and set out south along the Corinth Road. What he saw confirmed his suspicions. Behind that initial line of Confederates were countless soldiers, in fact, the entire Army of the Mississippi. As the family slowly traveled southward against what must have seemed like an unending tide of Southern soldiers moving northward, they saw the Confederate army commander, Albert Sidney Johnston, who had set up headquarters under a post oak tree in a small glade. Surely Johnston would not be there if battle was not imminent.[2]

Johnston was indeed there to give battle to Ulysses S. Grant. It began at dawn the next morning, April 6, 1862, and has become known to history as the Battle of Shiloh. Yet as compelling as this scene is, few people stepping onto the battlefield of Shiloh or reading about the battle itself think of the civilians who lived on the field and endured the hardship of war. Few if any battle studies mention them, and when they do, it is normally in reference to some military aspect. But the study of the Shiloh civilians can offer a lot of knowledge about the terrain on which the battle was fought, the civilian surroundings of the area, and even about the battle itself. To be sure, the armies fought the Battle of Shiloh on common, everyday land where common people lived. Their houses, barns, and countless other trappings affected the battle to at least some degree, and the battle certainly affected them. Shiloh is a great case study in which to examine the impact of Civil War military operations on civilians.

But there is a larger story concerning the civilians of Shiloh than just the battle itself. Common people lived on the land that became the battlefield long before the conflict took place, and they have lived there ever since. Studying Shiloh's civilian population in a broader context can offer insights into governmental relations with the general public within the context of battlefield preservation and the larger issue of conservation. Shiloh's civilians were thoroughly affected by the battle as well as the commemorative results that came from those two days of conflict. Granted, they were probably more affected than the normal citizen in either 1862 or 2012, but their story, when examined as a case study of how the federal government has dealt with its citizens regarding the issue of conservation, can offer important clues into the historic civilian-government relationship in the United States.

The Shiloh civilians have endured more than just a normal amount of government intervention in their lives. The earliest settlers received government grants for land. As war loomed a couple of decades later, these people were forced to endure not only a horrific battle between huge contending armies but also weeks and weeks of Federal army occupation. After the war, the citizens of the area received a permanent government presence with the establishment of a national cemetery in their neighborhood, with a much larger national military park coming several decades later. Modern citizens of the general area are still very much affected by the existence of the park.

But while there are many locations that have seen much less government intervention than Shiloh, there are literally thousands of other areas in the United States that have seen as much and even more federal and state government involvement. The nearly five hundred national parks in the nation as well as the hundreds of preserves administered by other federal agencies, not to mention state, county, and city projects, have had a drastic effect on civilians in those areas. A study of Shiloh civilians can provide insight into the larger national, state, and city park systems around the country.

At Shiloh, civilians have been treated with the utmost kindness and offered ample reward or repayment for any land or possessions the government needed for the military park. The many stories about the government "stealing" land are simply not accurate. However, the simple fact that the land on which these civilians dwelled was historically important changed the normal citizen's relationship with government. Here is the story of that relationship.

* * *

Although there were certainly other civilizations present in the area before then, the first known inhabitants of the Shiloh area were prehistoric Indians in the 1050 A.D. time frame. These Mississippian period inhabitants left a vital record of their occupation in the form of seven large Indian mounds on a steep bluff on the west bank of the Tennessee River. Apparently the ancestors of the Chickasaw people, these natives left little record beyond the stately mounds. Archaeologists have sought, on numerous occasions, to excavate the mounds and unlock the hidden clues to the culture that once dominated that section of the Tennessee River valley.[3]

Although such digging has often occurred officially and unofficially over the years, the majority of the information on these natives has come from recent National Park Service–sanctioned archaeological investigations. The results have shown a political capital of a thriving civilization that ruled several locations within the Tennessee River valley. There were numerous inhabitants of this location, as shown by the many house mounds in the area (which are actually not mounds on which houses stood but rather the results of decaying and falling houses lumping on the ground after the decline of the civilization). The large mounds were used for ceremonial functions, with one being a burial mound for more than thirty people. The largest of the mounds, at the most prestigious location overlooking the river, apparently served as the chief's residence. There was also a temple nearby.[4]

The mound complex also served as a military fort. Recent excavation has shown that the mounds were constructed in layers, with each layer containing a red or white covering of clay, apparently signifying peace or war. The entire complex was surrounded either by steep ravines or a palisade wall with bastions. Such a configuration on high ground indicates that these mounds served as a refuge for the people in both times of flooding and times of war. The population of the site probably increased dramatically during both events as citizens in the outlying communities gathered there for safety.[5]

This early native population ultimately declined. By the 1500s, the area was home to the Chickasaw Nation. By this time, however, a civilization of white men of European descent had brought with them disease, modernity, and European ways, including settled governments. Westward expansion of the descendents of these white men eventually affected the Shiloh inhabitants. Tennessee became a state in 1796, although the Chickasaw tribal lands of West Tennessee were some of the last locations settled. By 1819, the area had become Hardin County, named for early surveyor Colonel Joseph Hardin. In 1820, the U.S. government brokered a treaty with the remaining natives for some ten thousand square miles of land. Thus, government affected early inhabitants even before white men flooded the area to take advantage of the numerous land grants along the Tennessee River.[6]

The offer of land brought settlement to the western side of the river, although most early settlers in Hardin County lived east of the river, where the town of Savannah emerged. The first grant on what would become the Shiloh battlefield took place in 1832, when the State of Tennessee granted John Chambers two hundred acres around what would later become Pittsburg Landing. Unfortunately, Chambers failed to develop it. In 1843, Thomas B. Stubbs received the same two-hundred-acre grant, by which time several other land grants to settlers had already been made in the area: Larkin Bell in October 1836, Robert Grissom in June 1840, and John J. Ellis in June 1841. Ellis, along with Jason Cloud and Jacob Wolfe, seemed to be the largest grant takers in the 1840s, and they eventually sold part of their holdings to other families moving into the area. Wolfe sold part of his land to John Rhea in October 1846 and another part to James M. Jones, who later sold it to John C. Fraley in January 1860. Both the Rhea and Fraley families lent their names to important fields where fighting took place during the Shiloh battle. Other families who would likewise become synonymous with the battle also took grants in the 1840s and early 1850s, people such as Peter Spain in February 1840, Lewis Wicker in May 1849, and Nancy Stacy in January 1851.[7]

As early as 1835, there was a Methodist Episcopal church known by the name "Union" near the park's modern-day Michigan monument, but like many other denominations, the Methodists split over the slavery issue in 1846. The southern branch went farther inland, where in 1851 John J. Ellis donated to the local school board land for a new school and to the church a parcel for a new house of worship. One story relates that when the local people could not agree on a name for the new church, they agreed to let the local schoolmaster, A. J. Poindexter, name it. He chose the biblical name Shiloh. The title seemed fitting at the time because of the quiet, rural setting. Meanwhile, a store and a few residences also sprouted on Stubbs's land near the river, where Pittser "Pitts" Miller Tucker operated a ferry to the east bank. He also opened a liquor store and tavern at the landing, which began to draw steamers on the river. The landing eventually became known as Pittsburg Landing.[8]

Despite the increase in river traffic, Hardin County developed slowly. By 1848, the population had reached only eight thousand people, with Savannah, on the east bank of the river, emerging as the county seat. Other hamlets grew, but almost all of them lay along the river, the central transportation artery in the county. Landings became particular havens for activity, including Crump's, Pittsburg, Brown's, and Hamburg landings in the Shiloh vicinity. Pittsburg Landing was the most important location. Several hundred yards long and sufficiently deep, the landing offered a gradual slope to the point that the river's notorious rapid rises and falls would not inhibit docking. The best roads of the time led north to Crump's Landing, west to Purdy, south to Hamburg Landing, and, most important, southwest to Corinth, Mississippi. Soon, Pittsburg Landing was the principal supplier of goods to Corinth and the surrounding area.[9]

The citizens of Shiloh faced an enormous tragedy as the battle at Shiloh raged. Most lost their homes and some lost loved ones. They returned to fields and farms covered with the debris of battle and the buried dead. But the experience of battle was but a small part of Shiloh civilians' larger context of civilian-government relations, which included many land grants to the original owners, the battle, a national cemetery, and eventually a national park, with which many of the local inhabitants found good government jobs. This photo shows local citizens after the war at one of the original cabins, the Sarah Bell home. (Courtesy of Shiloh National Military Park.)

By 1860, some of the first generation of land owners had died, men such as John Rhea, who had a heart attack in 1848 while getting water from the spring on his land, now known as Rhea Spring. The major landowners, such as Jacob Wolfe, John J. Ellis, and Jason Cloud, had either died or moved away since they no longer appeared on the 1860 census. The Tucker brothers, including Pitts, who lent his name to the landing, had likewise disappeared. Some of the earlier generation, such as Lewis Seay and John C. Fraley, still lived at Shiloh, but new families had moved in by that time, including Joseph Duncan, Daniel Davis, and William C. Barnes.[10]

More than three dozen families inhabited the Shiloh area by 1860. Most of them were small farmers, although there was an assortment of skilled artisans such as W. T Stratton, a shoe and boot maker, Patsy Fiffs, a weaver, George McCrary, a carpenter, and Charles Hopkins, a well digger. Zachariah Pickins listed his occupation as "squatter." Apparently there was some type of law enforcement or militia system, because John W. Sowell listed his occupation as "farmer and officer." Most had been born somewhere else in Tennessee, although several were settlers from states such as North Carolina, Virginia, South Carolina, Georgia, Alabama, and Mississippi. Not a single person living in the 15th Civil District of Hardin County listed his or her birthplace as being in a Northern state, although Thomas Walker in the neighboring 10th District listed his place of birth as England. It was Walker's testimony of the sights of the battlefield years later that spurred the romance of the Bloody Pond at Shiloh.[11]

The land itself was not well situated for agriculture, so most farmers eked out a bare subsistence with little left over to sell. One local historian concluded that "a more unprofitable spot of land, perhaps, could not have been selected . . . for a battleground, . . . with less loss to the county." John C. Rhea and Thomas W. Poindexter were early slaveholders, but there was nothing like a plantation anywhere. In 1860, only eight citizens of Hardin County's 15th Civil District owned twenty-three slaves. Joseph Duncan and John C. Fraley owned one each, while Lewis Wicker, Dudley Jones, and W. G. Wood owned two each. Margaret Shelby owned three, while the largest slave owners in the area were James J. Fraley with five and R. G. Wood with seven.[12]

The largest farmers seemed to be M. G. Wood, J. G. W. Hagy, J. A. Perry, and one woman, Mary Howell. Almost all the farmers listed on the 1860 agricultural census owned one horse, with more affluent farmers, such as Peter Wood, Mary Howell, and Lewis Seay, owning up to three or four. Each family likewise had at least two or three cows, from which they obtained milk and made butter. Only a couple of the wealthier farmers, such as J. G. W. Hagy and H. A. Pettigrew, had mules or oxen. All the farmers had swine,

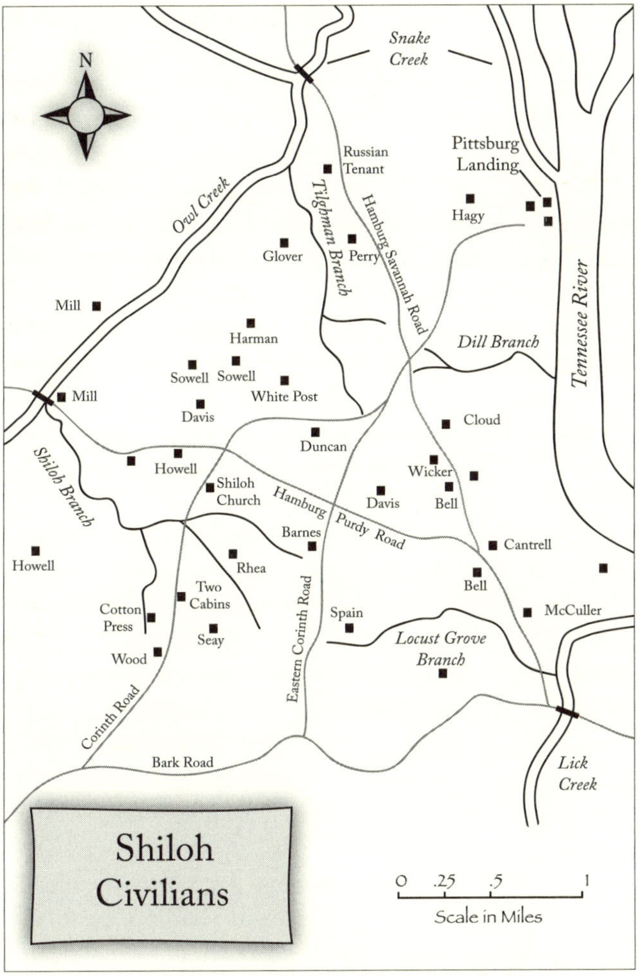


with most owning as many as ten or twenty and some such as John C. Fraley having as many as sixty. Many also had sheep.[13]

The dominant crop in the area was corn, which every farmer grew. Quite a few also planted wheat, peas, and sweet and Irish potatoes. Only a few farmers grew cotton, most notable among these being M. G. Wood, R. G. Wood, Lewis Seay, and H. A. Pettigrew. Only three raised tobacco. Lewis Seay and James Perry also produced beeswax, and a few more farmers had honey. Numerous farmers had orchards on their land, but not a single farmer in the area listed rye, oats, rice, barley, buckwheat, hay, or any type of cane as part of their crops.[14]

Most of the inhabitants lived in crude log cabins set in the small, cleared fields nestled amid the thick woods. Most of these buildings were small, one-room affairs with one window and a loft, which more often than not played host to father, mother, numerous children, and a few live-in hands. The Cantrell house south of Pittsburg Landing was apparently the best house on the field, with soldiers remarking on the apparent wealth of the Cantrells due to the house's clapboard siding rather than thick log walls. Most farmers had a barn, outhouse, and sundry other outbuildings to support their meager livelihood. They normally had wells or depended on fresh water springs for pure water. The farmers normally fenced their fields with rail fences in order to keep the roaming cattle and animals out of their crops. At the time, most farmers in the region used the open-range policy of letting their animals run wild through the woods, only gathering them when they needed them for work or slaughter. A spider web of roads and farm paths connected these dwellings.[15]

The locals worshiped at Shiloh Church or other nearby houses of worship, and many families buried their dead either in the church cemetery or in small family plots on their own land, some of which still exist today. They traded at the landing, where a small cabin offered available goods, or they traveled to local communities such as Adamsville or Corinth. What little cotton that was grown was ginned at James Wood's cotton gin on the Corinth Road. Many a young man of the neighborhood wooed and married nearby farmer's daughters, thus complicating and tangling many family trees. Such was the case of Manse George's wife Nancy, daughter of Sarah Bell, who lived on the next ridge.[16]

It was within this context of inhabitants that one of the bloodiest battles of the Civil War was fought. Most citizens of Hardin County did not want war. They had, in fact, voted against the secession of their state in 1861. War did come to the nation, but their area remained relatively quiet through 1861 and early 1862. When war came to the inhabitants of the Shiloh area, however, it came with a vengeance.[17]

Most of the fighting in early 1862 took place far to the north along the Kentucky and Tennessee border. The Federals made their first appearance in Hardin County in February 1862, when, after the fall of Fort Henry, Union gunboats plied the river as far south as Alabama. On March 1, 1862, two Union gunboats, the *Lexington* and *Tyler,* fought a small encounter at Pittsburg Landing with a portion of the 18th Louisiana and an artillery battery. The affair produced some dead and generally shot the place up, but the chief outcome of the fight was to alert the Union commanders of the landing's importance. By late March, much of the Federal Army of the Tennessee was utilizing that landing and camping at Shiloh.[18]

The arrival of five divisions of Federals, nearly forty thousand strong, in March 1862 was a shock to the inhabitants. Everywhere they looked, they saw a sea of white as the army camped in its large Sibley tents. Many of the civilians' cabins were taken by Union officers for headquarters, and the larger fields were used for drills and reviews. By April, the normal time for spring planting, the farmers in the area realized there would be no crop that year. Even if they could get seed in the ground, thousands of feet would trample it as the Union army prepared for future operations against Corinth, Mississippi, an important Confederate railroad junction just twenty two miles to the southwest.[19]

The Federals were not impressed with the inhabitants. One Federal officer described Shiloh Church as "the rude structure in which, within four months past, the voices of the 'poor white trash' of Tennessee mingled in praise to God." A member of the 18th Missouri, on April 4, 1862, described the origin of the name Pittsburg Landing by writing a friend that "[t]his Pittsburg took its name from a man that kept a one horse store at the place." But there was no report of Union stealing from the locals, despite the soldiers' disdain for what they encountered, although many residents hid the few valuable articles they possessed.[20]

What really caused problems for the inhabitants was the battle itself. By early April 1862, Confederate commanders at Corinth had realized that the Union army was about to double in size with the arrival of another large force from Nashville. The Confederates had no way to counter such a massive combined army, so they decided to strike before a Union merger. The Confederate Army of the Mississippi marched northward from the Corinth area and launched a surprise attack on the Federals at Shiloh on the morning of April 6, 1862. The two-day Battle of Shiloh was one of the bloodiest events of the war. As far as the inhabitants of the area were concerned, the battle was devastating.

Most families fortunately moved away from the scene before the battle. Lewis Seay had moved his family several days before the battle but returned to watch over his cabin during the fight. Miraculously, he survived. Wilse Wood lived at the famous two cabins, where Confederate commander Albert Sidney Johnston made his headquarters for a short time during the battle, but he likewise moved his family across Lick Creek before the fighting and did not come back until afterward. James Wood, the local cotton gin owner, evacuated south toward Corinth and right into the deploying Confederate army.

He did not get out in time and was pressed into service by the Confederates as a guide. J. J. Fraley moved his family away from the area on the morning of April 6 when a Confederate officer told him they were "in much danger, as the soldiers were drawing in line nearby for battle." Nancy George buried a set of silver goblets before hurriedly leaving her home. Sixteen-year-old Alex McDaniel was hiding from the army when the battle began. "Sitting on a log on the bank of Snake Creek fishing," he was frightened by the sound of the battle. The musketry "sounded more like a heavy shower of rain falling," while the cannon "roared like a heavy thunder." Soldiers found McDaniel and took his prized squirrel rifle.[21]

Although the vast majority of the inhabitants left Shiloh when the Federals arrived, and especially when the Confederates appeared in early April, a few families did not get out in time. Several family stories have survived, and they provide a clear picture of the horror and fright of being a civilian in the midst of a battle. Years later, members of the Wicker family could still remember the "sounds and smells" of the battle because they were right in the middle of it. For two days, the family hunkered in their tiny cabin, with bullets flying around and through their home. The only civilian casualty as reported by family history was George Washington Sowell, who lived on the western side of the battlefield near the modern picnic area. Like most people, he had moved his family away from danger before the battle but had returned to retrieve some valuables they had left behind. Unfortunately, he caught a stray bullet while on his front porch.[22]

The terrible battle destroyed almost everything at Shiloh, but the extent of the damage was not known to the families until they returned after the fighting was over. James Wood found his cotton gin burned to the ground and the cotton taken away. Wilse Wood found his two cabins destroyed. J. J. Fraley lost everything he had except one cow and a horse. Both were running wild in the woods on the morning of the battle, and he attributed the mare's survival to the fact that no one could "bridle her in the open." Artillery fire and flames produced by the battle destroyed countless other cabins. In fact, only a few structures remained. Orchards and any other structures or improvements were likewise heavily damaged.[23]

Perhaps the most famous icon of the battle, Shiloh Church itself survived the battle, although heavily damaged because it stood in the middle of some of the most intense fighting. It did not survive for many weeks, however. There is no conclusive story of what happened to the church, some accounts insisting that it was torn down by the Federals and used for firewood, bridges, and souvenirs. One Federal reported that, while eating a meal in the church, he saw a musket standing in one corner. Giving a good tug, he pulled the musket out of the corner and the entire church fell, injuring him and his companions. The adjacent cemetery was so devastated that it was hardly discernable to returning inhabitants.[24]

After the battle, the victorious but bloodied Federal army remained on the inhabitants' lands through April and into early May, when they departed for operations against Corinth, Mississippi. Still, however, Pittsburg Landing was an important supply station, and the 7th Missouri and the 14th Wisconsin remained there well into July. As foreboding, the local economy was shattered; one farmer bought a barrel of salt for thirty dollars in gold, only to have it taken from him by soldiers. Perhaps the most telling devastation to the inhabitants was the fact that their precious farmland, not good to begin with, was now covered with lead bullets, cannon balls, and any and all kinds of equipment left by the armies. Trees were shattered and filled with bullets, making lumber useless.[25]

Most gruesome of all, homes and farms were now part of a vast cemetery. Around three thousand men died during the battle, and almost all were buried on the field. Countless dead horses and mules also covered the field; most were eventually burned. Graves frequently washed open. Much of the drinking water was poisoned. The Shiloh battlefield was a place of horror, but it was home to the numerous families in the area. One by one, they returned to try to make a new life.[26]

Many residents immediately began to rebuild their cabins and lives. Manse George and his wife Nancy could locate only one of the silver goblets she had buried before evacuating the area. Of more concern, their cabin had been destroyed during the battle. George bought and moved one of the remaining cabins across the battlefield to his home place, where it still sits today, the only wartime structure remaining on the field. Shiloh Church was not rebuilt, at least not for several years. With no place to worship, locals built a brush arbor on the site of the church. They also held camp meetings "in the grove at Shiloh Spring." About 1875, the inhabitants were finally able to build a new church on the site of the original.[27]

Even as they struggled to start over, the inhabitants were never able to forget what had happened on their land. In 1866, a newspaper reporter visited the battlefield and saw horrifying sights. "I saw where hundreds of Confederate dead had been rooted out of their shallow coverings—I cannot call them graves—their flesh eaten by the hogs and the bones lying scattered and broken and trampled upon in every direction." Some of the locals who had returned to their homes told the correspondent that the hog meat was so offensive

The citizens of Shiloh continued their lives even amid the battle and the sometimes unpopular governmental involvement in their area. Here citizens and veterans attend a rebuilt Shiloh Church. (Courtesy of Shiloh National Military Park.)

"that it could not be eaten." They no longer ate the meat, being "afraid that they would be guilty of cannibalism to do so!" As late as 1878, visitors to the battlefield could still see bleached white bones all over the place.[28]

Farmers going about their daily routine even decades after the battle periodically uncovered human remains. Jesse Curtis found three Union soldiers near the Peach Orchard in 1880. As late as 1893, one veteran remembered that the farmers were "ploughing up their bones all over the field." In 1934, Mancil A. Milligan uncovered nine Union soldiers on his land just two hundred yards southwest of the national park boundary. Even as late as 1977, relic hunters found two Confederate soldiers buried on private property near the park.[29]

Most of the bones still on the battlefield decades after the war were Confederate, because most of the Federal dead had been buried in a brand new national cemetery at Pittsburg Landing. Established in 1866, the cemetery contained about thirty-six hundred Federal dead and four Confederates and was under the control of the Quartermaster Corps of the War Department. In 1867 and 1868, the area again saw Federal troops in the vicinity as Company F of the 25th United States Infantry established a post at Pittsburg Landing, presumably to help disinter the Federal dead and build the cemetery. The company remained at Pittsburg Landing from May 1867 to January 1868, at which time it returned to Memphis. After the initial construction, the cemetery came under the control of a local superintendent, who had several laborers on his workforce. Although not a major entity, the cemetery did mark the first organized, peaceful presence of the Federal government in the neighborhood of the Shiloh civilians, and it was one that would remain forever.[30]

What was most notable about the cemetery was how the Federal government gained title to the land. Because it was situated on some of the prime high ground at Pittsburg Landing, the owners were not pleased that their land had been chosen for the cemetery and burials had taken place even when it was still in their hands. The heirs of Thomas B. Stubbs, represented by Stubbs's daughter Mary A. Harmon, would not accept the government offer for the land. It was not until January 6, 1869, in *United States v. Mary A. Harmon,* that the U.S. District Court of the District of West Tennessee awarded the government title to the ten acres of cemetery lands for the sum of five hundred dollars. The governmental presence at Shiloh was growing.[31]

Clearly, some of the local population thought a ten-acre cemetery that was condemned by the federal government was an encroachment into their neighborhood. What occurred in 1894 was a much bigger issue, however. Congress established the multi-thousand-acre national park in that year, and in the months thereafter numerous veterans returned to the field to buy land, mark troop positions, and erect monuments and markers. The most important veterans were members of the three-man commission which had oversight of the Shiloh National Military Park. These three commissioners and those who succeeded them literally built the park itself as well as the history of the battle during the late 1890s and early 1900s.[32]

In the 1890s, there was still continuity among the families living on the Shiloh battlefield. While many of the patriarchs had died or moved away, many families tied to the area in the earliest days were still represented there. Numerous families present during the battle itself were still living on their homesteads when the park was established. Later generations of the Fraleys, Cantrells, Bells, Hagys, Duncans, Sowells, and Wickers were all still living on the battlefield when the park located land ownership tracts in 1895. Many of these, such as J. J. Fraley, who gave tours for twenty-five cents, were still involved in the history of the battle as well.[33]

The government activity that most affected the local residents of Shiloh was land purchase. The inhabitants watched as park engineer Atwell Thompson and his crews worked to determine boundaries, some remarking on the accuracy required and the amount of work performed. Some, however, complained of trespassing on their property. S. M. Rogers, for example, protested that Thompson's men had devastated his cornfield and requested payment for the damages. When told he would not receive any reimbursement, Rogers wrote Thompson tersely that "you will greatly oblige me by keeping off my land." In these days of Jim Crow racism, he continued, "I want to be treated like a white man, also an American Citizen." No doubt others similarly looked with disdain on the government's actions. T. J. Hurley took especial exception to the commission's work on his land along the Hamburg-Purdy Road just west of the park. One entry in the commission's "daily events" diary read, "Hurley is mad but can't help himself." Another stated, "Hurley wants to fight."[34]

Overall, however, despite the modern-day myth that the federal government stole the people's land and evicted them, the arrival of the park in the Shiloh area was a boon to the local inhabitants. Most thoroughly benefited from the park's establishment. The majority of the residents on the battlefield willingly sold their land for fair prices, about thirteen dollars an acre. Others cut free firewood from the trees felled by surveying parties. Local businesses saw an upsurge in activity, as when Armpy Johnson's sawmill, located near Owl Creek, received orders for thousands of wooden surveying stakes. Sam Chambers ran a small store and hotel just inland from the landing, and he continued the businesses after the park's establishment by obtaining a contract with the government. Later, others such as W. P. Littlefield ran the store and hotel, along with the ferry, under a similar contract. Many locals frequently gave tours to the visiting public and sold relics found near their residences. One local woman told the story of selling relics to visitors when she was a little girl. Her father told her to sell five bullets for twenty-five cents but to drop the price to fifteen cents if the visitors were not willing to pay the higher prices. When asked by visitors how much the relics cost, the small girl blurted out exactly what her father had told her. Of course, she only made fifteen cents for her efforts. Nevertheless, these businesses were of immense economic help to the inhabitants. Most important, the park eventually provided jobs for residents of the area, causing it to become one of the highest per capita income regions in the county. Workers stuck in hard farming jobs on terrible soil welcomed a set routine of government work for a dollar a day. The arrival of government checks every month created visible excitement. Displaying graphically how destitute the economy of the area was, local businesses could not cash the many federal checks that locals presented to them.[35]

There was one major land issue that caused problems, however, and this case probably fueled the surviving modern resentment among the twenty-first-century descendants of park inhabitants. W. C. Meeks, who owned 180.90 acres fronting on the Tennessee River, including Pittsburg Landing, was not willing to sell his land to the government at thirteen dollars an acre. Meeks asked twenty-five thousand dollars for his land. The commission would not pay such a sum and ordered the case to condemnation. The lawsuit went to trial and the court rendered a decision on April 27, 1897. In Cause No. 2274, *The United States v. W. C. and O. C. Meeks,* the Eastern Division of the Western District of Tennessee, District Court of the United States, awarded the United States title to the land for $6,000, thus bringing the price down from $138 per acre to $33, still a very good price and better than the average of $13 an acre.[36]

Although the government bought some thirty-six hundred acres of land at Shiloh within the first decade of the park's existence, the inhabitants were not evicted from their land or out of their houses. In the first thirty years of the park's history, only three tracts of land, including Meeks's, were condemned. Moreover, the bill creating the park allowed the secretary of war to enter into agreements with locals so they could remain in their dwellings and work their fields as tenants for subsistence and livelihood. The tenants, many of whom went to work for the park as laborers, were required to pay an extremely small sum of a dollar or two a month and were required only to preserve the historical features of the park, including maintaining wood and field lines and caring for the various monuments and markers that would eventually cover the battlefield. A good relationship developed between the federal park and the local residents, most of whom chose to remain in their homes with the option of life tenancy. The commission also made sure the tenants remained satisfied by providing many new services for the people living on the battlefield, including modern wells at each site and material to keep the grounds clean and sightly. Other byproducts of the park aided the locals as well, such as the standardized arrival of mail and steamboats at the landing. In sum, no one was cheated, no one was ejected out of a home, and most were better off economically than they had been before the park's establishment. One local summed up the experience when he wrote how his family "made money hand over fist [working for the park] so we kept on living right on the park."[37]

Still, the often reckless locals caused problems for the park administrators. One member of the commission wrote in 1913, "Very few tenants have remained in the same places. . . . They are constantly changing places, as some go out of Park employ and others come in to occupy houses made vacant. There are also frequent exchanges of places." One local gave the reason for so much movement: "If someone would leave that had a better house than ours, we'd move into it with the permission of the superintendent." The park's

Many of the local citizens went to work for the park as laborers, bringing home large government checks on a regular basis, something the hard-luck citizens of the area had never had before. Here a crew hauls rock for the park's roads around the turn of the nineteenth century. (Courtesy of Shiloh National Military Park.)

historian, David W. Reed, called the people of the area "lawless characters that invest the region" and had "4 bad women" evicted from a house near Brown's Landing in 1899. In addition to prostitution, other offenses ranged from throwing mud on park signs to outright murder. Park officials prohibited gambling in the park and enforced laws banning alcohol. On Memorial Day, May 30, 1901, for example, Mrs. Chambers found a box of beer and a jug of whiskey in a storeroom above her store. The commission confiscated the alcohol, and "destroyed [it] by pouring it upon the ground." Range Rider Francis A. Large frequently arrested drunks on the park grounds.[38]

Two episodes clearly illustrate the local mentality and the government view of it. On January 14, 1899, Perry Jones, a park employee, argued with "one of the Wicker boys." Wicker shot and killed Jones, whereupon Jones's son stabbed Wicker four times. Park engineer Atwell Thompson reported, "I presume that some of the Wicker relations will kill young Jones, and the two families [will be] 'wiped out' before they get through." He continued, "I wish our neighbors . . . were more civilized." Later in the year, in June 1899, vandals shot thirteen times into G. W. Moore's house in Cloud Field and set it on fire. Moore emerged from the house only to become a target again. He survived the affair and was even able to put out the fire. Somewhat callously, Thompson informed Reed of the matter, stating, "I regard this with some concern." He continued, "It concerns us as it was a deliberate attempt to destroy U. S. property."[39]

Over the years, the locals nevertheless continued to benefit from the park. By the 1930s, there were two stores on the grounds, one at Pittsburg Landing run by L. T. McDaniel, who also served as the postmaster, and the other in the old church formerly used by the northern branch of the Methodist Episcopal Church. As modernity set in, other conveniences arrived, such as telephone service and electricity. Of course, many locals continued to work for the park, particularly after it was transferred to the National Park Service in 1933. Even the top spot at Shiloh, the superintendent who took over after the veteran commissioners died away, was a local himself. Robert A. Livingston, who had been born on the battlefield in 1892, served as clerk for many years and became superintendent in 1929, holding that position well into the National Park Service years. Although not technically owning their land, the inhabitants were well taken care of in the early twentieth century.[40]

The federal government also aided the Shiloh inhabitants during the hard Depression years of the 1930s. Several New Deal agencies, most notably the Civil Works Administration (CWA), employed men from the local area. A temporary relief agency, the administration provided funds to put men to work all over the nation in order to get them through the hard 1933–34 winter. Such was the case at Shiloh, where the majority of the workers supported archaeologists at the Indian mounds within the park. At times, the number of CWA men working at the mounds site was over a hundred, and they severely taxed the two archaeologists who supervised them. The local workmen were neither trained in archaeology nor particularly careful about their work. A recent study of the CWA digs laments the fact that the work was done mostly with shovels rather than trowels, and that the trenches were not even straight. The locals were somewhat less than careful in their work, with records noting "skull smashed in finding" or "skull when found was in good condition but was damaged by visitors during our absence." In all fairness, however, the government had workers at Shiloh to get them through the long, cold winter, not necessarily to locate miniscule clues to a civilization that had disappeared eight hundred years before.[41]

By the 1940s and 1950s, the civilian presence at Shiloh began to come to an end. The National Park Service began implementing a plan to remove the inhabitants from the park and raze the nonhistoric structures. One by one the families left, and now, in the early twenty-first century, there are only five houses for employees left on the reservation. There are, however, numerous local families living nearby whose ancestors once owned the land within the park. Families with names such as Hagy, Tillman, Sowell, Wood, and Bell still inhabit the area surrounding Shiloh National Military Park, providing a remote but solid connection with Shiloh's beleaguered civilians of times past.

* * *

It is fitting that so many families with connections to Shiloh still inhabit the area, for the Shiloh National Military Park holds a special place in their hearts. The park, just like other parks, actually belongs to all the American people, but the citizens of today's Shiloh community feel a special bond with the land, and well they should. It was the land of their forefathers, where many of the old-timers still alive even today were born, and where many of their ancestors rest in peace. Shiloh is special to many people, but none more so than those whose families once owned the battlefield.

And therein lies the conflict. These families are just as connected to their land as other Americans, yet it no longer belongs to them except in the largest context as American citizens. The mere fact that something extremely important to their nation's history occurred on their land caused this disruption in their normal familial existence. Had the Battle of Shiloh not taken place there, the area certainly would not be a national park today.

Yet there is a park there, and it is the culmination of years of governmental involvement in the Shiloh civilians' lives. The government first gave their ancestors grants for the land, but the 1862 battle ruined almost life itself. From then on, the ground was stained and marked, never again to be the same. Some, such as the patriotic, saw it as glorious; others, trying to rebuild lives, saw it as a disaster. Still, the armies that fought at Shiloh opened a non-ending Federal presence there, first with the dead of the Shiloh National Cemetery and later with the Shiloh National Military Park itself. Ultimately, these families would sell their land and eventually move off the park. Life for these civilians was inextricably altered with the first shot at Shiloh.

But the story of government intervention at Shiloh is not one solely of losing land and homes. Weighed against the national need to commemorate and memorialize, the inhabitants gained many advantages. The locals were able to sell their hard-scrabble land, made even more so by the remnants of the battle still there today, for a good price and go to work for the park at a good wage. Moreover, they were allowed to remain in their homes for several generations. Even after the decision was made to remove all nonhistoric houses, the park still employed many locals and has ever since. Perhaps the biggest positive in both the historic and modern period was and is the tourism the park has brought to the area. Visitors to the park helped store and hotel owners make decent livings in the early days, far better than what could have been attained working the poor quality land. Today, the number of national and international visitors that flock to Shiloh is remarkable; cars from every state in the Union appear in the remote section of the Tennessee countryside. These visitors eat in local restaurants, stay in local hotels, and shop in local stores, all benefiting the local economy.

So the story of Shiloh's civilians is a paradigm of heartbreak, recovery, and perpetuity. The locals through the years have had their homes destroyed and their land made into a national park, but the federal government responsible for those negative actions has more than compensated their families in return. The inhabitants were given fair prices for their land, good jobs, and nearly free housing for decades. In a larger sense, few American families can boast of a national park preserving their homelands, but this is the case at Shiloh. The "forgotten inhabitants of Shiloh" will always be remembered in the preserved land they once owned.

# 8

# A Case Study in Change: The New Deal's Effect on Shiloh National Military Park

The last week in October 1929 was calm at Shiloh National Military Park, the government reservation in West Tennessee set aside as a memorial to the great April 1862 Civil War battle. Matters had calmed down considerably since late September of that year when the superintendent, DeLong Rice, had died in an accidental park explosion. The new superintendent, Robert A. Livingston, knew his duties, however, having been on the park staff since 1916. Still, there were many matters of Rice's estate to take care of, such as his belongings and the pay and death benefits due to his family. Superintendent Livingston corresponded with the Rice family that week, no doubt with a heavy heart over the shock that was just then beginning to wear off. Meanwhile, at the Shiloh National Cemetery immediately next to the park, the superintendent there, R. E. Gatewood, took care of similarly mundane matters. He reported that the cemetery was in fine shape, "except for some leaves that blew down in the last few days." It was business as usual in late October 1929 at Pittsburg Landing.[1]

It was not similarly calm elsewhere in the United States. The same week that Livingston settled Rice's estate and Gatewood worried about fallen leaves, the stock market crashed in New York. On October 29, 1929, Black Tuesday, stock market investors lost millions of dollars and a worldwide Depression ensued. While the isolated, poverty-stricken area of western Tennessee heard little of the news, those events would eventually have a profound effect on life and times at Shiloh and the surrounding area. In fact, within the next decade, the park would undergo a transformation unlike any seen since its foundation in 1894. The decade of the 1930s would see a literal makeover of Shiloh National Military Park.[2]

Although the Great Depression began in 1929, it was not until the 1932 election and the 1933 inauguration of President Franklin D. Roosevelt that the massive government action known as the New Deal took place. Roosevelt began a multi-agency process of relief and recovery that came to affect all of

America, even Shiloh. Within months, workers for such bureaucratic sounding names as the Civilian Conservation Corps, Civil Works Administration, and Public Works Administration swarmed over the park, reshaping it into a modern national park equipped with modern facilities.[3]

Shiloh National Military Park had been established in 1894 under the auspices of the War Department. In the early years, five congressionally established battlefields, Shiloh included, were the department's shining light. Famous and revered Civil War veterans managed them, and thousands upon thousands of other veterans flocked to them for reunions and as individual visitors. As the nation began to change in the 1910s and 1920s, however, the battlefield parks became less important to the War Department bureaucrats. World War I and the second industrial revolution produced dramatic effects such as modernization, mobilization, and urbanization. American life became increasingly hectic, and the quiet battlefield parks lost their predominant roles. By 1930, these parks were viewed more as a bother than a benefit. As a result, by 1933 the parks were run down in all areas of management, interpretation, and care.[4]

The New Deal years would change all that. By 1940, the Shiloh park and its surrounding area would see dramatic physical, social, economic, and political changes that would forever alter the region. Other military parks and countless other historic sites throughout the United States received the same attention. A thorough study of the New Deal's effects on Shiloh thus presents an opportunity to see how major anti-Depression local projects, funded federally, transformed individual localities. Taken together, such work transformed the nation. Historians study change over time, and Shiloh can offer a glimpse into one local change phenomenon that, taken with all the others, helped transform America.

* * *

The first and foremost federal activity which affected Shiloh National Military Park was Franklin D. Roosevelt's executive order of August 10, 1933, which transferred Shiloh as well as the other military parks from the War Department to the National Park Service of the Department of the Interior. National Park Service officials had desired such an action as far back as the mid-1920s, and even some in the War Department finally realized that an agency mandated to preserve and interpret America's natural and historical treasures would no doubt have more insight into managing the parks than the War Department. Thus Shiloh became a National Park Service entity, and the

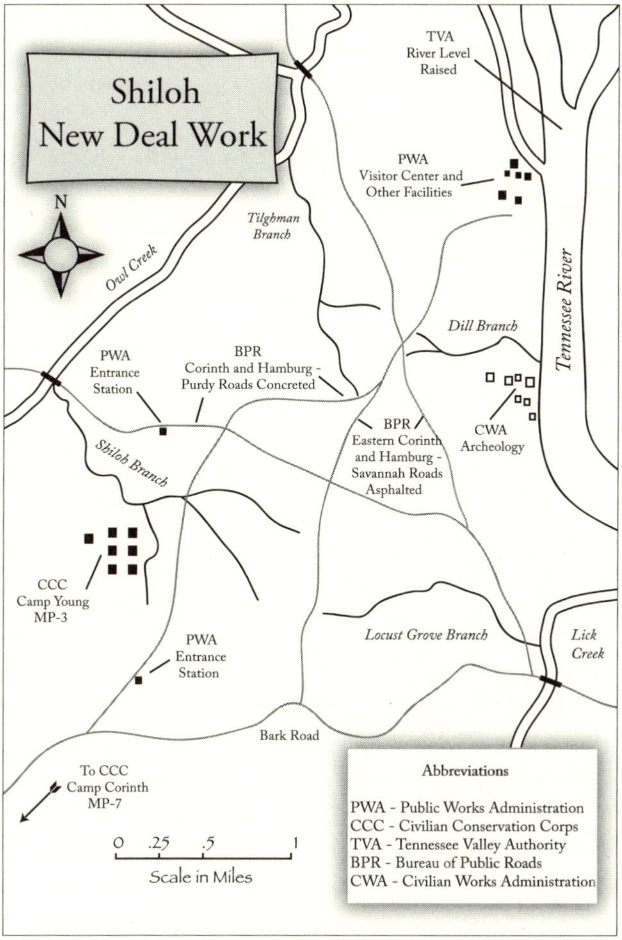


change was dramatic. The Shiloh superintendent had enjoyed wide discretion throughout the 1920s as the War Department had shifted parks from department to department within the army with no one quite sure what to do with them. In the National Park Service, however, bureaucrats in Washington and regional offices became heavily involved even in day-to-day matters.[5]

There was also a symbolic change that took place amid Roosevelt's reorganization of the parks. Since their establishment, the battlefields had maintained a firm connection to the veterans who had fought at the battles and then built the parks. Even after members of the original veteran commissions died, the parks remained under superintendents who, almost to a man, were veterans, sons of veterans, or had worked at the various parks for many years with the veterans. Thus the connection to the Civil War was present, even as late as the early 1930s. The martial air of being a part of the War Department only added to that idea.[6]

When the National Park Service took over in 1933, however, the veteran connection was both symbolically and literally severed. The military parks were no longer military; they were now civilian. The emphasis was no longer on battle, but on more visitor-oriented topics. And as time passed, more and more veterans died. Most important, the War Department superintendents who stayed on under National Park Service control did not last long. The service had its own way of doing things and wanted its own people doing them. Shiloh and all the military parks thus experienced rapid change in philosophy and administration.[7]

Creating further impetus for change was the introduction of the influence of a variety of New Deal government agencies at the Shiloh National Military Park.

## Tennessee Valley Authority

The Tennessee Valley Authority (TVA) was one of Franklin D. Roosevelt's 1933 "one hundred days" legislative achievements. The TVA took the isolated and poor Tennessee River valley region and transformed it. Flood control provided by nine large dams on the river and numerous smaller dams on its tributaries allowed for a tamer and more certain life along the river. The dams also produced hydroelectric power for the economically lagging region, bringing some modernity to even the backwoods. The heightened water level, with locks on the major dams, allowed for continuous river barge traffic in the channel, opening the interior of the South to commercialism. The lakes created by the dams offered southerners and tourists recreational opportunities.[8]

Although it did not work directly on the park, the TVA nevertheless affected Shiloh. Two dams affected the battlefield area. Just fifteen miles south of the park, Pickwick Landing Dam created a vast reservoir that produced electric power as well as recreational opportunities for local citizens. This dam was upstream from Shiloh, however, thus reducing the river's fluctuations but flooding many Civil War–era river landings. The dam with the most affect on Shiloh, however, was Kentucky Dam, more than a hundred miles north of the park. This dam, the largest on the river because of its relative nearness to the Tennessee's mouth, backed up what is actually Kentucky Lake all the way to Pittsburg Landing.[9]

The Kentucky Dam thus had a profound impact on the battlefield. Although Kentucky Lake at Shiloh National Military Park still resembled a river, the water level there was much higher than it had been in 1862. Thus the view shed of the river was dramatically changed. Likewise, the rise of the river's level caused 1862-era land to be submerged along the battlefield's eastern border. At Pittsburg Landing, the water submerged a large portion of the historic site.[10]

Erosion, always a problem along the river, was made worse when TVA altered the Tennessee River. Shiloh lay in a great bend of the waterway, and the normal historic current ate away at the bluff on which a set of Indian mounds sat. With the higher water level and the resultant increase in river barge and recreational traffic, the endless waves ate away at the park's land more rapidly. An unwise policy of cutting riverbank trees to widen the channel only compounded the problem. Erosion became such a problem that, in 1954, some twenty thousand cubic yards of Pittsburg Landing actually fell into the river. Another major slide occurred in the early 1970s, and more recently, Riverside Drive had to be closed due to erosion. (It has since been repaired and reopened.) While TVA has produced many positive changes around Shiloh over the years, its negative effects on the military park are also clear.[11]

## Civil Works Administration

The Civil Works Administration (CWA) was a temporary New Deal effort to provide jobs for millions of Americans in order to get them through the hard winter of 1933–34 while the other, more permanent agencies swung into full gear. An outgrowth of the state-run Federal Emergency Relief Administration, the CWA was different in that the workers were federal employees. Begun in December 1933 and lasting only through April 1934, the CWA employed more than four million Americans building roads, schools, playgrounds, and airports. The agency also hired teachers, writers, artists, and archaeologists. The CWA provided money for starving families and placed millions of dollars into the American economy.[12]

Working with Superintendent R. A. Livingston was the CWA superintendent Lewis M. Anderson. These two men oversaw a variety of projects, although the majority of the CWA work at Shiloh took place at the Indian mounds located on the Tennessee River on the eastern edge of the battlefield.[13]

The mounds had apparently once served as the capital of a Native American group and by 1933 contained six large ceremonial mounds, one large burial mound, many house mounds, and the remnants of a palisade wall used

The government became even more involved at Shiloh in the 1930s, when several agencies such as the Works Progress Administration, Civil Works Administration, and Civilian Conservation Corps sent men to work at Shiloh during the Great Depression. Here several African American World War I veterans who were members of the CCC camps fill in archeological digs at the Indian Mounds site. The excavations had been dug by locals hired through the CWA program and were overseen by Smithsonian archaeologists. (Courtesy of Shiloh National Military Park.)

for defense. The area had been preserved in the national military park in 1894, although the park commissioners, who were not trained in archaeology, dug into the burial mound in 1899.[14]

In the 1930s, an archaeologist from the Smithsonian Institution, Frank H. H. Roberts Jr., decided to study the mounds to learn their secrets. A Harvard PhD who was part of the Bureau of American Ethnology at the Smithsonian, Roberts had previously excavated many Native American sites in the Southwest. Assisting him at Shiloh was a young Mississippian, Moreau B. C. Chambers, who was fresh out of the University of Chicago and had previously worked with some of the best known archaeologists in the Southeast. These two men directed the digs at the mounds site, using CWA labor for the physical work. To their great chagrin, the CCC had just completed a system of trails and steps on and around the mounds, and now most of this earlier work would be dug up.[15]

Roberts arrived at Shiloh on December 19, 1933, and immediately ran into problems. His field notes contain a simple entry: "Cold and raining. Found only very poor quarters for living. Discouraging start." In the next few days, however, Roberts began to work through his troubles. He examined the mounds on December 20 and met with the CWA officials who would provide the manual labor for the digs. He also arranged for tools to be loaned from the park. Roberts began work on December 21.[16]

Roberts and Chambers oversaw the work through several crew bosses that were listed only by last names: Combs, Dillon, Atkins, Leith, Smith, and Hagy. These foremen led the crews, many of them park residents, in the dirt removal. The CWA workers and two archaeologists first began by cutting trenches inside the plaza area but then moved on to the larger mound structures. Several mounds where houses once stood were then trenched, as were a few areas of the remains of the palisade wall that once provided defense for the area. The crews found numerous pieces of pottery, stone and bone tools and warheads, and other artifacts. Numerous human burials were located as well, mostly in what they named Mound C. Some care was taken with this evidence, but modern archaeologists cringe when comparing the methodology then and now. One writer has even found fault when comparing the Shiloh dig to other contemporary efforts of the time. In all fairness, however, the main reason the government had crews there was to put them to work to get them through the long, cold winter, not necessarily to locate miniscule clues to a civilization that had disappeared eight hundred years earlier.[17]

At times, the number of CWA men working at the mounds site was over a hundred, and they severely taxed the two archaeologists who oversaw them. Moreover, the local workmen were neither trained in archaeology nor particularly careful about their work. A recent study of the CWA digs laments the fact that the work was done mostly with shovels rather than trowels, and that the trenches were not even straight. The workers were somewhat less than careful in their work, with records noting "skull smashed in finding" or "skull when found was in good condition but was damaged by visitors during our absence."[18]

The Shiloh mounds project lasted only from December 21, 1933, to March 30, 1934. During that period, however, much information was gleaned from the dig. In all, two major mounds, several small mounds, the plaza area, and the palisade wall were excavated, as well as several more recent log cabin structures. In his 1935 report, Roberts also mentioned more recent battle relics found, and he noted an interesting fact that tied the Battle of Shiloh to the Smithsonian Institution. The archaeologist wanted his readers to know that the organizer and first director of the Smithsonian's Bureau of American Ethnology was Major John Wesley Powell, who as a captain had commanded an Illinois battery at the battle and had lost an arm doing so.[19]

Roberts also described an episode that indicated that the park managers and CWA officials viewed his archaeological investigation more as a means to work unemployed men than as a major scientific effort. "Because of the large trees growing on these mounds, which the Park Service was particularly anxious to preserve," Roberts wrote, "it was not possible to investigate them thoroughly." In fact, National Park Service associate director Arthur Demaray ordered the park superintendent to send a "landscape foreman and forester" to the site to look into allegations of tree damage.[20]

Although the mounds were the CWA's primary work at Shiloh, several of the men also worked on erosion projects, road construction, cleanup at Shiloh Church, and similar tasks. One of the most interesting CWA projects was a program set up for local writers to examine the history of the area. Although the park staff as well as other agencies' historians produced 106 "historical reports" prior to 1936, thirteen different CWA-paid historians produced twenty-nine histories ranging in topics from the Battle of Shiloh and nearby Corinth to more generic items such as fortifications and armaments of the Civil War. Lera Durbin, who taught at the local Shiloh school, wrote on the battle, while C. A. Duke obviously had a fascination with Corinth, because he wrote four different reports on that town during the war. Archaeologist Moreau Chambers wrote a report on the work done at the mounds site. These reports varied in quality and information, with most of them ranging from ten to forty pages and many of them footnoted. Most of these reports, on file at Shiloh National Military Park, are still useful to park staff and researchers today.[21]

In all, the CWA work at Shiloh produced many changes, including physical alterations to the battlefield. The knowledge gained about the mounds was also worthwhile, but more important, the societal aid rendered by the program allowed many destitute locals to make it through the long, rough winter of 1933–34.

## Public Works Administration

The Public Works Administration (PWA), part of the National Industrial Recovery Act, emerged in 1933 as the federal version of the earlier state-aimed Federal Emergency Relief Administration. The PWA provided funds for constructing thousands of schools, courthouses, and hospitals. PWA workers also built railroads, tunnels, and bridges, and even built navy ships such as the aircraft carriers *Yorktown* and *Enterprise*. Millions of Americans employed by the PWA thus put a new face on America's public places and in the process earned money for their families.[22]

Shiloh superintendent Robert A. Livingston applied for as much PWA money as he could get. He put in requests for all sorts of projects, from new buildings to the purchase of the Cherry Mansion in nearby Savannah, Tennessee, which Major General Ulysses S. Grant had used as his headquarters before the battle. He also solicited funds to revamp electrical, water, sewage, and telephone systems at Shiloh and to finish the uncompleted shell of Shiloh Church on the battlefield. The church rebuilding had been started in the 1920s, but the Depression that spurred the PWA had slowed its progress. Livingston wanted it completed.[23]

The sewage, water, and electrical systems were revamped, but the major work funded by the PWA consisted of the erection of public buildings for use by the park. The first round of construction saw the building of two entrance stations, four houses for staff members, and a large administration building. One of the entrance stations sat on the south entrance of the park on the Corinth Road, by then known as Tennessee Highway 22. The other station went up on the Hamburg-Purdy Road on the western side of the park. These stations provided contact points whereby staff members could welcome visitors and give them directions. Construction of the entrance stations began in February 1935 and was completed by July of that year.[24]

The four homes the PWA provided sat immediately to the rear of the headquarters area. White with large porches and comfortable settings, these wood dwellings offered first-rate accommodations for park staff. Later, garages were also added. These houses, begun in November 1934, were completed by July 1935 and were still in use in 2013.[25]

The major construction was a new brick administration building. The park had had no such building for the first sixteen years of its existence. Because of a massive tornado in 1909 that swept away the hotel used as an office, the park had then received a building of its own. By the 1930s, however, that administrative building was too small, and Livingston jumped at the chance to secure funding for a new one. The long winter of 1934–35 caused some delay, with a massive rain in November 1934 resulting in the basement "being flooded to a depth of sixteen inches." Completion of the building was also delayed due to a slight change in position to allow the retaining of large oak trees. "Work was suspended a week pending decision on question of location of the bldg.," the weekly report stated. Nevertheless, the McDonald Construction Company of St. Louis waded through the delays, working anywhere between ten and twenty laborers, masons, plumbers, and carpenters on any given day. The massive visitor center, still in use today, was thus laid out in November 1934 and, despite disruptions in the work, was completed by July 1935.[26]

Livingston then razed the old administration building and replaced it, on the same spot, with a concessions building that would serve for years as a post office. In 2013, it serves as the park bookstore. The PWA money spent at Shiloh National Military Park has passed the test of time.[27]

## Civilian Conservation Corps

The most enduring of the New Deal activities at Shiloh National Military Park was the work of the Civilian Conservation Corps (CCC), another of Franklin D. Roosevelt's 1933 "one hundred days" legislation. Initially known as Emergency Conservation Work, the CCC employed young men from eighteen to twenty-five years of age on national and state parks and other areas to perform reforestation, erosion control, and fire maintenance. Also part of the CCC were World War I veterans who were employed in the CCC primarily because of their 1932 protest as the "Bonus Army." Some two hundred thousand World War I veterans ultimately joined the CCC, thirty thousand of them black veterans, with the total number of men enrolled in the military style camps reaching two and a half million by its demise in 1942.[28]

Two different African American CCC camps existed at Shiloh National Military Park in the 1930s and early 1940s. One, Tennessee Camp MP-3, was established on July 15, 1933, and was physically located on the park. Made up of men from Company No. 2425, MP-3 was situated at "Camp Young" in the southwestern corner of the Shiloh park. At first, the men lived in tents "deep in the shade of the large white oaks of the park," as one eyewitness described it, while they built their permanent buildings (which were completed in November 1933) just across Shiloh Branch. Ultimately, the camp boasted eighteen buildings, with the four barracks aligned in two rows with "a beautiful green carpet of grass . . . between the barracks, on the side, and the mess hall and recreation hall on the ends." Large oaks and numerous flower beds beautified the camp. Made up of enrollees from numerous southern states, MP-3 boasted an enrollment of about two hundred.[29]

The other company, Tennessee Camp MP-7, was established nearly a year later, on June 14, 1934, and was located two and one half miles northeast of Corinth, Mississippi, some twenty miles southwest of the park. Called "Camp Corinth," MP-7 did the majority of its work on the Shiloh-Corinth Road, which was owned by the government and operated as a part of Shiloh National Military Park. Original park engineer Atwell Thomson had surveyed the roadway in 1900, but appropriations for its construction had never emerged from Congress. A private turnpike company later built the road, for which they charged tolls. Because the tolls proved very unpopular, the government bought the road in 1924 and retained control over its maintenance and patrol operations during the CCC period. The enrollment of MP-7 fluctuated more than that of MP-3, with the number of enrollees usually ranging between 150 and 200, most also being from the South.[30]

Both camps had basically the same organization and work process, as well as similar campsites, extracurricular activities, and educational and religious functions. Each individual camp was under white officers; a captain in the army or lieutenant in the navy normally served as camp commanders. There was also a junior officer to serve as second in command, with a camp surgeon similarly detailed from the military. In addition to the white military officers and white civilian foremen, each camp had a set of white technical officers who advised on such matters as engineering and forestry. Within the ranks of the black enrollees, men with special skills were detailed as foremen, drivers, clerks, storekeepers, or cooks, based on their specific ability. All the common laborers in the field or in camp were black. The Shiloh National Military Park superintendent developed the work programs for the camps.[31]

The Corinth camp enrollees worked on the seventeen miles of government-owned "Shiloh-Corinth Military Highway" within the park. Their two major duties were road improvement and telephone-line construction along the route. The workers maintained the highway itself as well as the right of way and adjoining areas. They graded the sides of the road, seeding and sodding grass along the way. The enrollees also planted trees and shrubs, working with the local landowners by taking plants from their land and replanting them on the highway and the farmers' adjoining land. At places where drainage and erosion were problems, the laborers built check dams and riprap on sloped banks. The men also placed pipe lines and conduit along the road and removed unsightly stumps. These efforts were not lost on the local population, who had caused the problems in the first place by what one official described as "excess pasturing and cultivation." The locals were "encouraged . . . to begin work on their farms," which resulted in terracing and better methods of farming. The goal of all the work was the "general beautification of [the] highway."[32]

Enrollees at the Shiloh CCC camp worked on a wider variety of jobs in the park itself. They performed road work, erosion control, and landscaping work, as well as additional duties in forestry management and fire prevention. Erosion had become a major problem in the park by the 1930s, and the laborers streamlined drainage and streams on the park as well as in the national cemetery area. Small dams were constructed at various areas to keep the battlefield from eroding. For example, at the death site of Confederate general Albert Sidney Johnston, the men built ninety-six dams. They also filled in and beautified an eroded area called "Dead Man's Gravel Pit," which was so named because of an 1899 rock slide that had killed three workers. In order to test new methods of erosion control and new types of wood and stone dams, the company created a test area in Rhea Field on Shiloh Branch. There, they learned which methods worked and which did not.[33]

The major differences between white and black camps in the CCC were the segregation and other forms of racism that pervaded camp life and the local opposition that the black camps encountered. It appears that, at first, Tennessee state officials were uncertain how even to manage the public reaction to such camps. The state commissioner of agriculture, O. E. Van Cleve, mentioned to Tennessee governor Hill McAlister that "should you be called upon to designate a particular project for colored camps you might suggest the National Parks." Federal officials agreed, directing "complete segregation of white and colored enrollees" and establishing the black camps at Shiloh and other "military reservations."[34]

Despite the precautions, area residents complained about having black camps nearby. U.S. Senator Kenneth McKellar of Tennessee told Governor McAlister, who had chosen the camp locations, that the "colored camps are problems, and the only way they can be managed is to take them up with the local authorities before making a recommendation." Likewise, the governor felt that "it [is] far better for the colored race not to have these camps in our State if they must be established where race hostility will immediately develop." McNairy County was particularly vocal in its objection to black camps, with citizens issuing a statement in the *McNairy County Appeal* that "[voiced] the sentiment of our entire population." "We do not want them here," the statement read, "as ours is not a negro community, and we do not know how to handle them." The locals raised such a furor that the projected camp at nearby Adamsville was changed from a black to a white camp.[35]

Public opinion also ran against the camp at Corinth, Mississippi. In 1937, a resident of Corinth wrote to President Roosevelt himself:

> The Negro CCC camp is near here and the houses are rented to these Negros [sic] and family while the land is rented to the Government. A poor farmer is unable to pay big rent for a house and has to have land to work so they are left out here. While the Negros [*sic*] feed families and relatives from the camp. Aren't these barracks built for them. Please look into this.[36]

Segregation was the norm. Although the enrollees had built picnic areas at the Indian mounds and Rhea Springs, they were not allowed to use them because the areas were reserved for whites only (they had to build their own picnic area adjacent to their camp on Shiloh Branch). When family and friends visited, the enrollees had to remain in designated areas. Such face-to-face encounters with segregation and other forms of racism at Shiloh remained in the minds of the black veterans who had served their country twice on battlefields: first in combat and later in conservation.[37]

Conditions were such that some of the enrollees complained. An enrollee at Camp Corinth, writing under a pseudonym, complained to the Veterans Administration about "this commander that won't proper feed us" and accused the commander of diverting money allotted for food to buy paint for his own quarters. "We feel we should have a fair deal such as is due," he protested. "Please let someone come." In response, the Veterans Administration sent a special investigator who, upon discovering that the signature (I. E. Smart) was fictitious, concluded that the letter had been written in reaction to the camp's strict discipline. The investigator told the enrollees that "they should be appreciative of what the Government is doing for them." An enrollee at Camp Young similarly wrote to the National Association for the Advancement of Colored People (NAACP) in the fall of 1937 about the treatment of blacks at Shiloh. "We are advised," the NAACP leadership informed the CCC, "that a gang of outsiders working around the camp steal the clothing and shoes of the enrollees for which the enrollees have to pay; that no serious

Black CCC laborers performed many different duties at Shiloh, such as erosion control, masonry, fire prevention, and picnic area construction. Here workers beautify a road. (Courtesy of Shiloh National Military Park.)

effort is made by the officers to patrol the camp so that the property of the enrollees can be protected; that there is a further complaint about food." The letter prompted another investigation by CCC leaders.[38]

The racism at Shiloh was nothing out of the ordinary for the time, however. Rather, it was indicative of the racism that existed in the CCC and many other New Deal agencies. Housing segregation in the Tennessee Valley Authority and Federal Housing Authority occurred frequently. Blacks were often paid less than whites in many New Deal programs. Racial discrimination and segregation ran rampant particularly in the South, where federal officials deferred to local laws and practices.[39]

The contributions of the CCC and other New Deal programs to the development and management of the national parks are comparable to those of the National Park Service's Mission 66 program, however. The long list of projects at Shiloh alone illustrates the enormity of that legacy and the importance of understanding the diversity of the CCC experience in evaluating the resources where CCC activities took place. More difficult to quantify but of tremendous significance was the impact that the CCC camps had on their enrollees. The thirty thousand black World War I veterans were a small but important part of the New Deal effort. In many national and state parks, they performed good, solid work and made substantive and lasting contributions to the nation. However, their CCC experience was a double-edged sword: The vocational, financial, and educational opportunities the CCC provided lay under the mantle of segregation and other forms of racism that affected African Americans nationwide. While work and camp life were supposed to be regulated uniformly across all camps, black enrollees had to endure prejudicial treatment that white enrollees never faced, much of it codified by the federal government. Sadly, African American veterans were denied full equality in the CCC camps, even on a hallowed battlefield where their very freedom and citizenship had been partially gained.[40]

At the same time, the New Deal's relief and recovery programs also helped African Americans on a fundamental level by providing work, food, housing, and educational opportunities to those in need of assistance. Although segregation had permeated New Deal programs, the New Deal marked an important point in the steady march toward equality for African Americans that led to the desegregation of the U.S. military in 1947 and the civil rights movement of the 1950s and 1960s.[41]

Despite strict racial segregation, the men did well in monthly and annual inspections concerning their work, recreation, education, and basic camp status. The Shiloh camp won the title of best in its district for 1935, along with a tremendous compliment paid by the army inspector: "It is with great pleasure that I select Co. 2425, MP-3, as the outstanding company in my entire district. The appearance of the camp is excellent. The morale is high, and the conduct of the members is highly commendable. I do not believe that I have seen a better camp in my two years of contact with the CCC." The Corinth camp won the award in 1936.[42]

Camps Young and Corinth continued to function independently until October 31, 1941, when the two were joined into NP-9 and enrollees worked on both the park and the roadway. Some of the men were assigned to a short-term "side camp" at Lookout Mountain in Chattanooga, Tennessee; others worked at nearby Pickwick Dam. The outbreak of World War II marked the beginning of the end for the CCC camps, however, with the extra manpower and labor redirected toward the war effort. Shiloh's combined CCC camp, reduced in status to a side camp, was disbanded on April 15, 1942.[43]

## Bureau of Public Roads and U.S. Geological Survey

Although not officially New Deal organizations, other government agencies were also hard at work at Shiloh during the 1930s and used New Deal labor. The Bureau of Public Roads (BPR) was the federal government's agency for all road building and thus it had jurisdiction over the process on national parks. As part of the Department of Agriculture, the bureau worked closely with the National Park Service and other government agencies, such as the U.S. Geological Survey (USGS), to complete Shiloh's road program.[44]

The USGS created a modern topographic map of the battlefield, the first since original park engineer Atwell Thompson had surveyed the park around 1900. Complete with accurate topographical lines as well as designations of markers and monuments on the park, the new map was indispensable to road building and repair. The Geological Survey concluded its work by May 1934, just in time for major planning for the road work to begin.[45]

The BPR used the new map information in their surveys and plans for the new road system at Shiloh. Treatment of the roads was varied, the roads "fall[ing] generally into groups which are related as to nature of traffic and historic significance." Several old roads were obliterated, while two major groups of the heaviest traveled roads in the park saw much attention. One group of secondary roads was treated with a gravel base and covered with a "light bituminous surface," basically a form of asphalt. These included such roads as Peabody, Eastern Corinth, and Hamburg-Savannah roads, a total of almost four miles. These secondary roads saw a fair amount of traffic from park visitors but were not major thoroughfares requiring heavy construction to meet the growing demand of the highway traffic through the park.[46]

By far, the most important road construction came on the two major roads within the park—the main Corinth-Pittsburg Landing Road and the Hamburg-Purdy Road. Both of these were state highways until bypasses were routed mostly away from the heart of the park. The Corinth Road was Highway 22 and the Hamburg-Purdy Road served as Highway 57. In order to provide a solid foundation for these highways, the BPR laid reinforced concrete slabs along these two routes. Total distance for the two roads was nearly seven miles.[47]

Both projects were completed by 1936, although some experimental work, such as tests for material to fill the cracks between slabs, went on for several years. Several permanent changes were made in the process. The engineers were only somewhat concerned with the roads "following in a general way the existing roads," so their work made alterations to the historic landscape. Likewise, although old battle-scarred trees were saved when possible, some were destroyed. "The principal obstacles were trees," one report read, "especially those old enough to have existed at the time of the Battle of Shiloh." The writer reported, "It was of course impossible to avoid cutting some trees." During this time, the park managers also conceived of and received approval for a plan to alter the original road names. Arguing that the roads were, "for the sake of convenience," becoming known simply by numbers, park managers "recommended that they be given short historical names." After 1936, the Eastern Corinth Road became Hornet's Nest and Gladden Road, while the Corinth Road became Confederate Drive and the Hamburg-Purdy Road became Federal Road.[48]

## Superintendent, Shiloh National Military Park

All the New Deal agencies and federal government bureaus working at Shiloh National Military Park had one common denominator—the park superintendent. No matter what work took place, the park superintendent was in the middle of it, and most of the time he selected and approved the various tasks to be performed. That made sense because the incoming bureaucrats and workers had little knowledge of the park and what needed to be done. It was up to the superintendent to guide them and their efforts.

Robert A. Livingston had been born and raised on the battlefield and grew up with the veterans who had established the park. He became the park's clerk in 1916, and after serving time in the army during World War I, he returned to Shiloh and spent the next several years as clerk. Then, in 1929, when Superintendent DeLong Rice was killed in an accidental explosion, Livingston became the park superintendent. But little activity took place during his early tenure, prior to 1933.[49]

When Roosevelt transferred the park from the War Department to the National Park Service in 1933, Livingston became the first National Park Service superintendent at Shiloh. In that position, he dealt with the CWA officials and accounted for the money spent in that program while keeping a careful watch over park resources. Livingston also worked with the CCC officials and selected projects for the camps to undertake. The same occurred with the PWA leaders constructing buildings and the road workers improving the roads. Livingston was very much involved in each endeavor, often making decisions about how the work should be done. In all, Livingston had a massive, nearly impossible job to do: monitoring rapid changes to the park while maintaining its historic conditions.[50]

Livingston's supervision of the work at Shiloh was not carried out without complaint. Coming after the eloquent and extremely sociable DeLong Rice, Livingston was curt and short. For example, he stopped the annual revival meetings at Rhea Springs, which Rice had allowed for a number of years. Church officials and other local people tried to persuade Livingston to reconsider, but he refused to budge. The annual revival preacher, N. B. Hardeman, told Livingston (addressing him by a nickname), "Arby, do you know what I should have done? When I baptized you, I should have just held you under the water a while!"[51]

Livingston's demeanor eventually caused him trouble with elected officials as well. Primarily, Livingston crossed a U.S. senator from Tennessee, Kenneth D. McKellar. The superintendent was an avid and outspoken Republican, which did not sit well with the solid Democrat McKellar. And Livingston was apparently not the only government bureaucrat to earn McKellar's ire; the senator seemed to thrive on confrontation, even leading an investigation against the War Department during World War I and later taking on TVA head David E. Lilienthal. Now, another War Department bureaucrat had crossed him, and he pounced. The trouble began in 1930, when Senator McKellar and several of his colleagues visited Shiloh. Desiring a tour of the park, the senator phoned Livingston from a local hotel. Livingston said he responded that he would come and give them a tour but that the senators had left before he reached the hotel. McKellar insisted that "Livingston said he was too busy and that he didn't have time to go down there." McKellar was clearly unhappy and waited for an opportunity to teach Livingston a lesson.[52]

Livingston's personality and demeanor also caused some trouble with the local population, because numerous complaints against him were filed and investigated. In November 1935 Senator McKellar took advantage of the growing anti-Livingston faction. He persuaded the Senate to pass a resolution to appoint a special committee to look into Livingston's dealings with CWA officials. The Senate subsequently charged two counts to Livingston: "That as supervising officer for the Civil Works Administration, the said superintendent did on or about January 11, 1934, make a false certification of certain pay rolls" and "That in November 1933 it is alleged that he offered a bribe of a position to be paid out of Government funds." McKellar came all the way to Tennessee to hold a hearing on the matter at the Shiloh Hotel on November 18–19, 1935. Senator McKellar, Senator Lynn J. Frazier (R) of North Dakota, and Livingston's attorney, R. D. DeFord, examined various witnesses in two days of hearings, but the charges were never proven. Technically, Livingston had signed payrolls for men who had not worked their time in the CWA, but he did so unknowingly because the CWA men had used the "stagger system." "Big-hearted" men alternated work weeks with others not on the rolls and then signed over their checks to the men who had actually worked in their place. The bribe charge similarly never amounted to anything.[53]

Disappointed, McKellar tried to find anything he could to get rid of Livingston. He alleged during the hearing that the superintendent undermined his employees, changed work orders to harm local businesses, used government gas for personal benefit, and obtained government services for his own advantage. Once again, the senator could not make any of these charges stick. For everyone that would testify against Livingston, the superintendent's lawyer found someone who would explain the situation adequately.[54]

The hatred between Livingston and McKellar was evident in the testimony. One witness hoped "the wound that the Senator feels so much, can be healed and once more the good feeling of so many years can be restored." But McKellar would not budge. After Livingston's testimony, McKellar responded, "I want to say now, in reply to that statement, that there is not one single word of truth in it. It is a deliberate falsehood from beginning to end. Now, Senator Frazier, I want to turn the witness over to you. I won't examine a witness who will make a statement that hasn't even a scintilla of truth."[55]

Ultimately, McKellar won. Livingston accepted an offer of a transfer from the director of the National Park Service. He resigned as superintendent in April 1936, remaining on duty until May 14. National Park Service bureaucrats Charles S. Dunn, William W. Luckett, and Blair Ross all served as Shiloh superintendents during the New Deal years, but none of them had Livingston's knowledge of or longtime service with Shiloh National Military Park. Livingston eventually retired to his farm adjacent to the park and became involved in later park matters, such as securing funding for the 1950s-era film *Shiloh: Portrait of a Battle.*[56]

* * *

The changes at Shiloh caused by the New Deal were more than the typical natural evolutionary changes present in most national parks. The New Deal produced at Shiloh a massive shift, a radically different park in 1940 from what had existed in the 1920s.

One of the greatest changes occurred in the topographical makeup of the battlefield. With TVA damming the Tennessee River, the water level rose and forever changed the 1862-era landscape. Not only did the river become much wider and as a result the adjacent land areas smaller, but the erosion caused by the cutting of trees along the river bank, a wider channel, and increased river traffic all caused major changes in the historic lay of the land. Such a dramatic change was probably unforeseen in the mid-1930s, when TVA planned the work, but the resulting alterations have been of major consequence.

Similar to the change in terrain was the massive infrastructural change produced by the New Deal work on the battlefield. What some called progress and others called destruction of a historic site nevertheless caused the battlefield to take on an entirely new look and feel. The effects of concrete roads, new administrative and concessions buildings, and numerous erosion and landscape projects significantly altered the aesthetic look of the historic battlefield.

The changes produced by the New Deal went further than battlefield preservation or even infrastructural upgrades, however. The social and economic effects the programs had on the park were as significant as the physical changes. The influx of money into the park set up a situation rarely seen in Shiloh's history. The 1930s were fat years in the midst of an almost total lean fiscal history of the park.

The New Deal programs also had a major effect on the people living within the park and in the surrounding area. The jobs produced during the 1930s provided work for many park residents, which in turn provided money for their families to survive. Without government paychecks, many families might have succumbed to the despair-ridden Depression era. Likewise, the services the New Deal work provided allowed for modernity to change an otherwise rural and poor region of the United States. The electrical power provided by TVA, the better roads provided by numerous agencies, and the increased self-esteem given to unemployed men boosted social, cultural, and family pride.

The housing of some four hundred African American veterans of World War I in two CCC camps significantly altered the racial makeup of the area. But while some racism and segregation prevailed, no major problems developed between the races. Even more telling, the fact that the black veterans were even allowed into the New Deal service at all, particularly in a southern state like Tennessee, was a testament to the increased participation of African Americans in society as a whole.

The political change produced by the New Deal years had special significance for Shiloh and the National Park Service as a whole. The Livingston episode demonstrated just how much of a political entity the park service was and demonstrated the growing surveillance and watchfulness by politicians during the government-increasing New Deal era. That a U.S. senator could be offended by a park superintendent and ultimately cause him to vacate the position demonstrated the increasingly political nature of the National Park Service.

Perhaps most important, the commemorative change produced by the New Deal caused the park to have a very different historical nature in 1940 than it did as the 1930s began. Shiloh National Military Park was a rather obscure battlefield in 1930, overseen by the military and run with that type of martial mentality. The park superintendent was only the fourth in its history, and although Livingston was not a Civil War veteran, he had definite connections to them. Livingston had grown up on the battlefield and thus knew the original veterans who had built the park. Later, he had served under Superintendent DeLong Rice, who had been tutored at the feet of the "Father of Shiloh National Military Park," battle veteran David W. Reed.

By 1940, however, the park had been transferred from the military to a civilian department more inclined to education and interpretation than military ways. The staff for the first time was made up of men who were neither from the local area nor had connections with the veterans. Now the staff was made up of professional bureaucrats brought in from other sections of the country. Moreover, with the resignation of Livingston, all direct connection with the original establishing commission was lost. No one in the 1940s had known the veterans that established the park. From the New Deal on, the park was a political entity, not the passionate obsession to which many of the veterans and their protégés had given their lives.

* * *

The New Deal was thus an amazingly productive time of change for America. The economic, political, and social changes produced nationwide were evident at Shiloh, as were many of the physical and aesthetic alterations. Arguably a backward step in terms of pristine battlefield preservation, the New Deal nevertheless changed Shiloh, turning it into a modern park with modern facilities. But the New Deal projects at Shiloh, although highly significant in the history of the park, were but miniscule parts of what was happening elsewhere. All over the nation, the same agencies that transformed Shiloh were at work on countless other parks, forests, and cities, producing local results which collectively demonstrated that the New Deal had literally transformed the United States. When taken as a snapshot of the work performed by Depression-era workers and multiplied infinitely, the work at Shiloh National Military Park illustrates well the broad and massive scope of the New Deal, at a time when a nation literally pulled itself up out of chaos and turmoil. Perhaps in that sense, Shiloh is a fitting example, for the New Deal–transformed park itself memorialized a former age when the nation had done the same thing.

# 9

# History in the Making: *Shiloh: Portrait of a Battle* Fifty Years Later

The elderly, white-haired woman walked out of the auditorium at the Shiloh National Military Park visitor center with a quizzical look on her face. She had just seen the park's introductory film, *Shiloh: Portrait of a Battle.* Walking up to the front desk, the woman asked a park ranger matter-of-factly, "Was that movie made from actual footage?" Anyone who has seen Shiloh's long-running film will know what the woman was talking about. First shown in 1956, the film eventually became a historic artifact in its own right. When it was shown to park visitors on April 7, 2006, the film celebrated its fiftieth anniversary. It was only retired after fifty-six years of service on the battle's anniversary in 2012.[1]

Reactions to the movie varied with the visitor but typically fell into two distinct camps: people either loved it or hated it. Everyday visitors to Shiloh who knew little about either movie making or Civil War history tended to think the movie was a work of art. They were captivated by the old look and original feel. Those with a little more technical background in movie making or with a deep interest in the Civil War typically had a less positive view. This group noticed problems with the acting, props, and plot. Reenactors tore it apart because of the lack of total accuracy in terms of uniforms and equipment. As one group of Confederate reenactors walked out of the film, one of them was overheard to say, "That was worse than that movie we made that time."[2]

Whether an individual visitor loved or hated the movie is somewhat unimportant, although park managers desire that all who come to the battlefield make a strong emotional and intellectual connection to the site and what happened there. What is more important is the massive effect the movie has had on how visitors think about the Battle of Shiloh and how it has affected interpretation issues at the battlefield. *Shiloh: Portrait of a Battle* was the longest running interpretive film in the history of the National Park Service when it was retired, and literally millions of visitors through the years saw its rendition of the battle. Whether or not critics thought the fake beards were good, whether or not reenactors thought the uniforms were correct, and whether or not visitors thought it was made from original footage, few people actually questioned its historical content. The result is that *Shiloh: Portrait of a Battle* has had more of an impact on how Americans view Shiloh than all the books, magazine articles, and interpretive tours through the years put together.[3]

For those who either loved or hated the film, *Shiloh: Portrait of a Battle* must be viewed in its original context. First filmed in the 1950s, the movie was made before the advent of popular historical event reenacting. There was no large pool of reenactors answering the call to film a great epic like *Glory, Gettysburg,* and *Gods and Generals,* all recent Hollywood productions. Consequently, viewers cannot expect to have the quality of accuracy on arms and equipment that is so common in today's films. Second and more important, the park orientation film was made in the mid-1950s and therefore predated all the modern academic studies of the battle. Its factual content was the history published by the original park commission that developed the park in the 1890s. Later research uncovered many new sources and theories that shed much more light on the battle, but this research was unavailable to park managers in the 1950s. Third, the movie must be viewed in the context of its being the first film production in a national park, coming at a time when National Park Service films were nonexistent. *Shiloh: Portrait of a Battle* was thus a pioneer and literally blazed a trail that millions of Shiloh visitors have journeyed. Its influence has been immense.

* * *

The idea for a motion picture at Shiloh National Military Park dated to 1937, when park officials realized the need for a film to orient visitors to the battle and battlefield. Shiloh superintendent Charles S. Dunn noted that considerable talk had occurred about "animated devises to explain troop movements." The first idea was an electric map, but Dunn and others soon concluded that an electric map's "results . . . could not compare with those of motion pictures." Dunn asked the director of the National Park Service for a 16-millimeter projector. Nothing ever came of the notion.[4]

Fifteen years later, the Shiloh superintendent was Ira B. Lykes, a former U.S. Marine Corps major who brought to Shiloh not only a military background but also quite an imagination. He first envisioned a slide presentation about the battle, complete with music and narration. Lykes and park historian Charles E. Shedd Jr. soon produced a new slide show totally with park resources. Shedd wrote the script and Lykes narrated the presentation as well as painted several images for the slides. The national park now had a slide presentation to orient visitors. Lykes named his project "Shiloh: Portrait of a Battle."[5]

Lykes and Shedd's original presentation had seventy-eight slides, complete with narration, music, and sound effects. They soon decided, however, that the program was too long; they cut it to forty-two slides, thus creating a twenty-four-minute show. The slide show reviewed the beginning of the war through the battle and carried the story of Shiloh through the eventual military results, culminating in the Vicksburg campaign. Thus the program placed the battle in its correct military context.[6]

The presentation also sought to provide insight into the battle itself, including slides on the fighting at Shiloh Church, the Hornet's Nest, and Bloody Pond. Even today, few visitors realize that places such as Jones Field and Shiloh Branch were key points on the battlefield, but Lykes and Shedd included them in their presentation. In the end, however, their program emphasized the Hornet's Nest, Sunken Road, and associated events, such as the deadly fire from Ruggles's Battery, as the most important parts of the battlefield.[7]

First shown at Shiloh on November 9, 1953, and shown daily thereafter, the film gained public as well as National Park Service approval. The Shiloh park staff then carried the presentation all over the Southeast, showing it to conventions, schoolchildren, and interested groups. At one point, they showed it at the Peabody Hotel in Memphis, although its show time had to be altered due to a conflict with the Ole Miss–Memphis State football game occurring in the city the same day. In all, thousands of children and adults saw the presentation in the early 1950s, with one newspaper reporting that over fifty thousand people had viewed the presentation in its first two years. It was a grand beginning, indeed, a first that other superintendents in the National Park Service soon emulated.[8]

But Superintendent Lykes was not satisfied. "The slides were static," he reasoned, and "could not convey the great motion of the battle." A bigger problem was that the program required the presence of park staff to run the fairly complicated machinery and make sure the slides and the sound effects were synchronized.[9]

Lykes wanted a better, livelier presentation that also was not so demanding on park staff and resources, so he decided to develop a thirty-five-minute full-color motion picture. He did not intend to produce a Hollywood-caliber film, yet he knew that even a self-produced movie would be far beyond his normal park budget. But that did not stop him. He was determined to have his Shiloh movie.[10]

Lykes, with a large group of local park supporters aiding him, began to find the money. The Shiloh Park Citizens Association, a precursor to today's national park friends groups, offered him support in his effort. They liked Lykes's new and innovative ideas and approved the concept of a film, which would replace the "time-honored and now really worn out slide presentation which met with such wide acceptance." With the association providing the avenue for funding, the film was actually made and copyrighted in the association's name. Its treasurer was R. A. Livingston, who had at one time been superintendent of the park in the 1930s until he crossed U.S. Senator Kenneth McKellar.[11]

In October 1954, the association began soliciting donations from every conceivable area group. Most gifts were of small amounts, ranging from schoolchildren's donations to families' gifts of one dollar. In addition to the many small gifts, the group received larger donations. Several local banks, clubs, and heritage organizations donated as much as one hundred dollars for the film, but three groups gave even more. The Corinth Centennial, a group celebrating the one hundredth anniversary of the city, gave five hundred dollars, while the Eastern National Park and Monument Association, a cooperating association now known simply as Eastern National, donated one thousand dollars. By far the largest sum came from the Tennessee Historical Commission in Nashville, which donated twenty-five hundred dollars for the project. They also helped in other ways. When the National Park Service decided to transfer Ira Lykes in the middle of the venture, the commission helped to get the transfer stopped so that Lykes could finish his job.[12]

The association soon realized how large an endeavor they were undertaking. The officers incorporated to protect themselves legally and ultimately copyrighted the new film. In doing so, the association gained much attention. The *Jackson Sun* reported that the "production of this picture is attracting national interest as a 'first' in publicizing national military parks." It went on to say that the film would replace the slide presentation of the same name, which "also was a 'first' in the park service."[13]

With money for the film's production coming in, Lykes began to create his dream. In late 1954, he had the park historian, Charles Shedd, alter the old slide show script for use in the movie, and Lykes himself prepared to direct and produce the movie. As more money accumulated, Lykes became more and more consumed with producing his film.[14]

Superintendent Lykes first produced animated maps, creating most of them himself. He painted a large number of canvases, working through the Bureau of Public Roads' Motion Picture Division to record them on film. In

Shiloh National Military Park superintendent Ira B. Lykes was a World War II U.S. Marine veteran, a visionary, and a thinker. He came up with the idea of a motion picture to introduce visitors to Shiloh, and the result was *Shiloh: Portrait of a Battle.* First shown in 1956, it was the first of its kind and became the longest running film in Park Service history, only being replaced in 2012. Here are Lykes (*left*) and historian Charles E. Shedd, who wrote the film's script. (Courtesy of Shiloh National Military Park.)

1954, some government agencies were further along in audio-visual technology than the National Park Service, so the "promise of help and technical advice" from the Bureau of Public Roads proved extremely important.[15]

The imaginative and talented Lykes also constructed a scale model of Fort Sumter, which was used in the beginning of the film to vividly portray the opening shots of the Civil War. He also produced two scale models of Union gunboats, the *Tyler* and *Lexington*. The models briefly appeared in the film with their heavy cannon firing during the night of April 6. Lykes used special effect shots to show cannon being fired at night. In all, the realism of Lykes's models was amazing.[16]

Lykes was able to get the job accomplished with a minimum of cost. He narrated the film himself with a bounding yet soothing voice. The musical score was more of a concern as it required more talent than the park staff could provide. The Music Department at Memphis State University came to the rescue in October 1955 with professors Raymond Haggh and Paul Eaheart writing the score and directing the university band to produce the musical soundtrack for the film. The university chorus also sang several patriotic songs for the opening and closing. In thanking the musicians for their aid, Superintendent Lykes reported, "Our one concern now is that the picture be good enough for the wonderful music which has been written for it."[17]

By far, the most significant production activity was filming the live scenes, for which Lykes used borrowed cameras from the National Park Service's Washington office. Actual filming, which needed to be done in the spring of the year to make the battle scenes more accurate, began in mid-March 1955.[18]

Lykes rounded up an assortment of participants to film the scenes. Members of the Brice's Crossroads Memorial Association traveled up from Baldwyn, Mississippi, to film scenes in the Peach Orchard. Under the leadership of local historian Claude Gentry, the Mississippians were an assorted bunch ranging from high school students to middle-aged men. The local school superintendent let several of the high school boys out for a couple of days to support the film. Of course, he did not have to beg the boys to go. "We were gung ho at that time," Clyde Tapp remembered later. Lykes soon got the boys' attention, however. "He was full military," John Cunningham remembered of the former Marine. "No question about it—you thought you were in the Marines. . . . When he hollered you had to obey—no backing up on him." With such eager reenactors, some of the Peach Orchard scenes were filmed that mid-March, although Lykes had difficulty finding peach blooms that early in the year.[19]

Later in March, students from the Memphis State University drama department filmed scenes that involved generals and civilians. Donald C. Streeter, who played Tennessee governor Isham G. Harris, remembered that the day was extremely cold. Several scenes at the Cherry Mansion in Savannah, Tennessee, had to be deleted because the cold weather (reported as nineteen degrees) would not allow "some nice scenes of the two Cherry sisters, in their crinolines and bare shoulders, watching from the verandah as Grant and his officers climb[ed] the long flight of stone steps leading from the river to the mansion." Admittedly not a horseman, Streeter's problems became much worse when the Albert Sidney Johnston death scene was filmed later. The horse to which he was assigned was in heat and "other horses kept bumping against her and I could do little to control her movements," Streeter remembered. Another horse was brought in and the show went on.[20]

The majority of the filming took place April 4–5, 1955, when the Baldwyn contingent was joined by local students and Mississippi and Tennessee National Guard troops, in all about 150 participants. For this shoot, Lykes and his staff amassed a conglomeration of equipment and people through newspaper ads and other forms of invitation. Park staff met with the prospec-

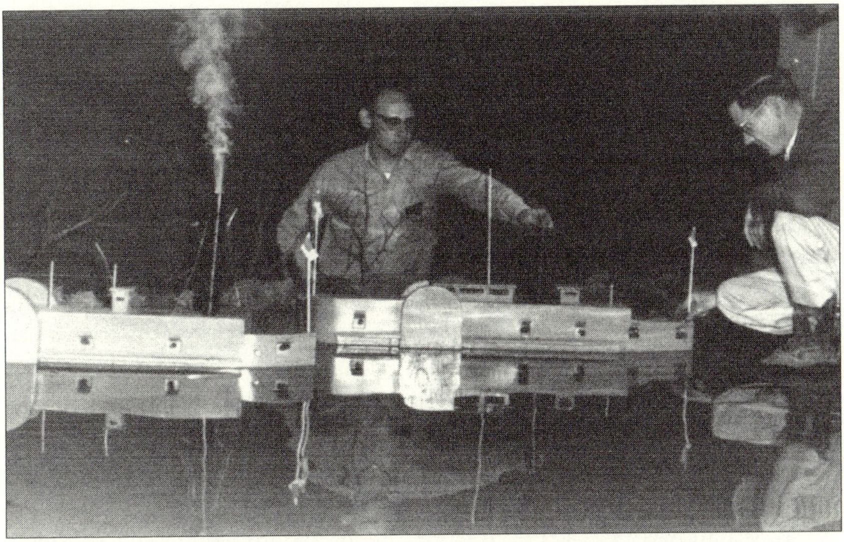

Lykes built models for his film *Shiloh: Portrait of a Battle,* including these two of the Union gunboats *Tyler* and *Lexington*. Here Lykes (*left*) is shown with one of the park's staff, J. B. Jordan, filming the scenes involving the gunboats' action. (Courtesy of Shiloh National Military Park.)

tive actors before the filming and gave them the details of what they would be doing, when it would occur, and how to prepare (for example, not to shave). In the meantime, staff had to borrow rifles, horses, saddles, wagons, and uniforms, and many of their owners subsequently appeared in the film. Many other participants wore civilian clothes. James Lewis remembered that "a lot of them just wore regular clothes and they told us fix up an old pack like [that which] came across our shoulders."[21]

Although some parts were filmed in Corinth and Baldwyn, Mississippi, most of the battle scenes were filmed in the park. Lykes of course took precaution to keep angles just right so that monuments and tablets would not appear in the film. When it was impossible to cut out the tablets and monuments, the park staff cut bushes to cover them. Lykes also tried to film parts of the movie where the events actually happened. The filming soon took on the feeling of a grand adventure for many of the young participants. One Tennessee National Guard member, just barely out of high school, remembered they "rehearsed a little bit and kind of got it under way." He recalled that "every time we would change scenes, . . . they would get us all together and tell us what we were going to do." Apparently, Lykes let the reenactors run through their motions with little direction. "I think they just kind of filmed what they wanted and then we got stopped," he remembered. By all accounts, it was enjoyable. James Lewis remembered, "We had a lot of fun over there . . . [but] we got serious when we needed to."[22]

Former Marine drill sergeant Lykes put on quite a show for the young boys involved in the film. He was "rather an impressive guy," Henry Outlaw remembered, describing him as very serious with tall leather boots and a megaphone. "To him it was just like a real battle," Outlaw remembered fifty years later; "we were going to war." Yet Lykes sometimes confused the boys, as with his use of the word "sequence" to describe what would happen in the next sequence of filming. One young participant remembered that he had never heard that word before and did not know what it meant. The boys thus began to call Lykes by the nickname "Sequence," behind his back of course. Another youngster was not so sly. After some of the boys discovered they could shoot peas from their rifles during the filming, one reenactor shot the superintendent and was quickly sent home.[23]

Lykes allowed the actors to camp on the park, setting up a few tents in Duncan Field. He fed them breakfast at Ed Shaw's restaurant at Shiloh one morning and threw a big barbeque one evening for supper. But this was no normal meal. Lykes barbequed half of a buffalo for the youngsters. John Cunningham fondly remembered the buffalo fifty years later and recalled that "after that a crap game broke loose." By all accounts, everyone had a big time.[24]

Although he had an able historian in Charles Shedd, Lykes consulted other historians and technicians. To make the movie more realistic, he gathered the support of the Third U.S. Army and the U.S. Army Signal Corps to stage explosions on the battlefield. The ordnance men also facilitated the supposed discharge of the cannon, at which one participant marveled that "black smoke would just roll!" They also produced smoke for the battle scenes. Lykes also asked for help from a Philadelphia historic uniform dealer and borrowed nine Civil War rifles from the Fredericksburg National Military Park. University of Mississippi history professor James W. Silver was on hand to help with accuracy. Physician Reuben B. Caldwell of Baldwyn, Mississippi, participated in the tent hospital scenes.[25]

By June 1955, Lykes had all the recorded scenes "rough edited" in Washington, D.C. He returned to Shiloh with a Moviola film-editing machine and began the process of choosing which scenes to include and which to cut. On site at the park, Lykes and his historian pored over reels of footage looking for the right combination of scenes. By early 1956, they had made those decisions.[26]

The process of actually putting everything together then began. For example, the original musical score recorded in Memphis in October 1955 had to be transferred onto the narration recording, to which was added battle sounds and sound effects. All this then had to be synchronized with the film itself and all placed onto one master recording. Jack Robertson at the University of Mississippi did most of this work.[27]

Due to the donation of time and resources, Lykes was able to produce the film at a reasonable cost, what he described as "somewhere in the neighborhood of $10,000." Some of the work was too technical for volunteers or park staff, however, or even for the imaginative Lykes himself. For this technical work, Lykes contracted work out to various laboratories and firms. "Network engineers will have charge of the actual mechanics of recording for I do not feel that anyone less qualified than professional engineers should be entrusted with this important work," Lykes reported. The superintendent used Byron, Inc. in Washington, D.C., and local educational facilities for editorial work on the film. For example, the association paid the University of Mississippi over thirteen hundred dollars for film production in the final stages. (Ole Miss experts put in more than 166 hours in developing magnetic film, editing, and recording the narration.) Still, Lykes was very concerned about money and counseled his staff that they "may be able to squeek [*sic*] through. So we better nurse what we have or go out and get more."[28]

In April 1956, Superintendent Lykes described the project as "in the can," the movie term for completed. He premiered the film at Shaw's Restaurant in Shiloh on Saturday night, April 7, 1956. That showing was closed to the public and only seen by invited guests and donors. The next week, Lykes began showing the film at Shiloh.[29]

The National Park Service and the Department of the Interior approved the results. In March 1957, Secretary of the Interior Fred A. Seaton issued a Unit Citation for Meritorious Service to the Shiloh National Military Park staff "for outstanding performance in producing the motion picture 'Shiloh-Portrait of a Battle' during the period November 1954 to April 1956." The director of the National Park Service, Conrad L. Wirth, sent a copy of the movie to each of his regional directors with a memorandum that stated, "This film was recently previewed in this Office and met with such favorable acceptance that I have ordered enough prints to permit distribution of a copy to each of the Regional Offices." Wirth reminded his regional directors that the "film was made entirely at the field level and with funds donated from private sources." Obviously converted by the audio-visual, Wirth still told his underlings, "This office does not advocate the making of motion pictures of this nature at the field level," but he went on to say that Shiloh did so well because of "almost unanimous community backing and financial support." Realizing most parks would not be so blessed, Wirth advised tackling such projects on a regional level in the upcoming Mission 66 program, a ten-year, service-wide upgrade program implemented between 1956 and 1966.[30]

The result has been more than anyone at the time could have envisioned. Those who made the film are justifiably proud. One participant described it as "a defining moment" for him and many others. It was also a defining moment for the National Park Service. Not only was it the agency's first movie, but it also turned out to be the longest continually running film in service history at the time it was retired. Surely Lykes could not have envisioned that level of success. In 1956, he admitted, "No, I'd not want to live through these last couple of years again, since I had to learn so much about movie making on my own, from financing to making animated drawings. What I'd like to think is that this will be the first of many for our national park shrines. But that, of course, is up to the budget bosses." Lykes's hopes were realized. He would no doubt be proud to know that almost every site in the service had an audio-visual program at its park fifty years later, and especially proud to know, fifty years later, that his film was still being shown every day at Shiloh National Military Park.[31]

* * *

The making of the film is an interesting, important story. So too is the story of fifty years of reactions to the movie. Some more recent viewers have pointed out that the film was not accurate. Most keyed in on problems with equipment, guns, and other fabricated props. For instance, the uniforms in the film were not totally authentic. Nor were some of the guns. At one point in the film, soldiers were seen wearing tennis shoes. At another point, bolt-action rifles were used. Some even complained about the fake beards used to dress the actors.[32]

These shortfalls were not really shortfalls at all. People judged the film by twenty-first-century standards and held it up against *Gettysburg* and other modern movies. Today, we have thousands of eager reenactors who travel long distances to volunteer their time to participate in movies. But this pool of reenactors was nonexistent in the 1950s, before the Civil War centennial and the birth of the reenacting hobby. As a result, the knowledge of Civil War weapons and equipment was much less prevalent then than it is today. The movie was made between the time the veterans themselves died away and when major reenacting efforts began. The knowledge of topics related to Civil War soldiers was thus limited, and the reenactors in the film had a much different standard than reenactors of today. As historian Ed Bearss has stated,

"Didn't bother me at that time whether the reenactors were all farbs—which they are . . . didn't really bother you that some of them have on tennis shoes and some of them have bolt-action weapons."[33]

The fake beards were another well-worn complaint concerning the movie, and in reality they did not look real. One has only to compare Grant's beard in *Shiloh: Portrait of a Battle* to James Longstreet's beard in *Gettysburg*, however, and Grant's does not look all that bad. Noted historian William C. Davis has labeled the *Gettysburg* facial hair as a "restless beaver apparently cast to be Longstreet's beard."[34]

More important than the lack of accuracy with weapons and equipment was the liberty the film took with the story of Shiloh. Two major problems emerged, one being the extremely narrow view of the battle. The film did not make inaccurate statements so much as it left out a great deal of information. The film completely concentrated on the Hornet's Nest. In fact, one could leave a viewing of the film with the idea that the battle took place only in the Hornet's Nest and surrounding areas. Very little was said about the Peach Orchard and Shiloh Church, both of which saw as heavy or even heavier fighting than along the Sunken Road. Absolutely nothing was said of the Crossroads, Dill Branch Ravine, or Rhea Field, where very heavy and important fighting also took place and where some historians argue that the battle was won and lost. The movie tended to draw the viewer into the Hornet's Nest and Sunken Road, thus propelling those locations into icon status.

Lykes and Shedd's script, however, followed the accepted consensus of the 1950s. Almost everyone agreed that the fighting at the Hornet's Nest decided the battle. For years after the Civil War, veterans of the Hornet's Nest emphasized their role in the battle, claiming that their sacrifice had provided Grant with enough time to establish a last line of defense. Division commander Brigadier General Benjamin M. Prentiss wrote a widely circulated report after the battle that emphasized his role as well as that of his troops. After the war, veterans who had fought in the position claimed the defense of the Hornet's Nest was the central event of Shiloh. A veterans' organization, the Hornet's Nest Brigade, held annual reunions. Congress established Shiloh National Military Park in 1894 to preserve the battlefield, and the secretary of war appointed a commission to oversee its building and development. Although made up of veterans, the commission relied heavily on its appointed historian, who wielded much power in locating troop positions, making sense of the confusing reports, and interpreting the battle to the public. The appointed historian was David W. Reed, a member of the 12th Iowa, which had fought squarely in the Hornet's Nest. With images of battle in his mind and a growing consensus that the Hornet's Nest was the central event of Shiloh, Reed developed the Hornet's Nest interpretation of the battle in his government-published history, *The Battle of Shiloh and the Organizations Engaged.*[35]

Reed's book became the standard treatment of the battle for decades. Other historians, such as DeLong Rice and Otto Eisenschiml, wrote popular versions of the battle, and each built on Reed's idea of the Hornet's Nest's importance. It was not until the appearance of *Shiloh: Portrait of a Battle,* however, that the story really became well known. Readers of Reed, Rice, and Eisenschiml could in no way match the number of visitors who saw the movie.[36]

In all fairness, then, park personnel and movie producers had only Reed and his followers' versions on which to base their film. No wonder the movie stressed the Hornet's Nest and Sunken Road. The film appeared some twelve years before the first academic study of the battle, a 1966 dissertation, and some twenty years before the first published scholarly study in 1974.[37]

The lack of any academic treatment of Shiloh and the resulting lack of research on which to construct the movie allowed several factual inaccuracies to creep in. For instance, the film made the assertion that the dawn Union patrol that encountered the Confederates on the first day was the result of Benjamin Prentiss's efforts, not Colonel Everett Peabody's, a fact which later research developed. The film showed incorrect tents for the Federals, who utilized Sibley tents instead of the pup tents shown in the film. The standard Confederate battle flag in the film was the Confederate battle flag rather than the individual corps flags actually carried in the battle. Some uniforms were better than others, but some infantrymen in the film were shown with red piping and stripes, which was used by the artillery; the infantry had blue trim. At one point, a cannon fired while the artilleryman was still holding the lanyard. Most important, tactical formations in the film were lacking. Due to the lack of a large pool of reenactors, the Union line in the Sunken Road looked more like a skirmish line than a standard two-rank, shoulder-to-shoulder line of battle.

By far the greatest inaccuracy of the film was the depiction of the action at the Hornet's Nest. The movie described some eleven Confederate charges against the Union position, while in actuality only seven or eight can be documented (depending on the sources). The narration also spoke of "wave after wave" of assaults moving against the Union position. Likewise, the vast majority of the attacks that did take place did not move wholly across the open Duncan Field, as depicted in the film, but mostly through the woods along the Eastern Corinth Road.

Despite several problems as viewed from toady's standpoint (its tunnel vision of the Hornet's Nest, its misrepresentation of the action at that place, and its lack of technical skill in terms of tactics and equipment), *Shiloh: Portrait of a Battle* was still a fairly accurate depiction of the Battle of Shiloh. For decades, it offered park visitors a good introduction to what happened in April 1862 and to what they were about to see when they toured the park. Moreover, taken in context of time and resources available, it was a revolutionary piece of narrative film work. And that is exactly how we should view it today.

* * *

Originally the film was shown on a reel-to-reel projector in what are now offices in the visitor center. The construction of an auditorium in the early 1960s provided a much larger and more comfortable area for viewing the film. In 1976, Shiloh park managers determined the need to condense the film into a manageable length whereby it could be shown every thirty minutes on the hour and half hour, with time for visitors to enter and exit the auditorium in between showings. About twelve minutes of the film contained background information on the war itself, beginning with Fort Sumter and including other details deemed unnecessary. Ironically, the full version was returned to service later, but like a well-worked farm animal that is long overdue for pasture, the movie was replaced in 2012. *Shiloh: Portrait of a Battle* had its place and time, and it performed pioneering duty. As historian Ed Bearss said of the film in terms of its functionality, however, "The Donner Party was pioneer[ing] too."[38]

Even with all its problems and its recent replacement, *Shiloh: Portrait of a Battle* must be taken in its original context. Doing so takes the edge off the inaccuracies and misrepresentations. Judging the film by today's standards is like judging a Civil War commander's actions in terms of today's military process. Problems aside, the film was an extremely popular movie that served its purpose well. It furnished millions of visitors to Shiloh National Military Park with an introductory audio-visual program and it did so with cutting edge-technology for the time. Beyond its special commendation from the secretary of the interior, the film won accolades from thousands of devoted fans and the literally millions of visitors who saw it through the years. Within that longevity lies the real importance of *Shiloh: Portrait of a Battle.*

# Notes

## Preface

The essays cited in notes 3–11 have been reprinted in this volume in slightly different form by permission of the original publishers.

1. Ulysses S. Grant, "The Battle of Shiloh," in *Battles and Leaders of the Civil War,* 4 vols., ed. Robert U. Johnson and Clarence C. Buel (New York: Century, 1884–87), 1:465.
2. Timothy B. Smith, *The Untold Story of Shiloh: The Battle and the Battlefield* (Knoxville: Univ. of Tennessee Press, 2006).
3. Timothy B. Smith, "'Difficult and Broken Ground': The Terrain Factor at Shiloh," *Tennessee Historical Quarterly* 70, no. 3 (Fall 2011): 170–95. © The Tennessee Historical Society.
4. Timothy B. Smith, "To Conquer or Perish: The Last Hours of Albert Sidney Johnston," in *Confederate Generals in the Western Theater: Essays on America's Civil War,* vol. 3, ed. Lawrence Lee Hewitt and Arthur W. Bergeron Jr. (Knoxville: Univ. of Tennessee Press, 2011), 21–37.
5. Timothy B. Smith, "Anatomy of an Icon: Shiloh's Hornet's Nest in Civil War Memory," in *The Shiloh Campaign,* ed. Steven E. Woodworth (Carbondale: Southern Illinois Univ. Press, 2009), 55–76.
6. Timothy B. Smith, "Shiloh's False Hero," *Civil War Times* 47, no. 6 (Dec. 2008): 28–35.
7. Timothy B. Smith, "Why Lew Was Late," *Civil War Times* 46, no. 10 (Jan. 2008): 30–37.
8. Timothy B. Smith, "Secession at Shiloh: Mississippi's Convention Delegates and Their State's Defense," *Hallowed Ground* 13, no. 1 (Spring 2012): 16–22.
9. Timothy B. Smith, "The Forgotten Inhabitants of Shiloh: A Case Study in a Civilian-Government Relationship," *Tennessee Historical Quarterly* 67, no. 1 (Spring 2008): 36–55. © The Tennessee Historical Society.

10. Timothy B. Smith, "A Case Study in Change: The New Deal's Effect on Shiloh National Military Park," *Tennessee Historical Quarterly* 66, no. 2 (Summer 2007): 126–43. © The Tennessee Historical Society.
11. Timothy B. Smith, "History in the Making: *Shiloh: Portrait of a Battle* Fifty Years Later," *Tennessee Historical Quarterly* 65, no. 2 (Summer 2006): 147–61. © The Tennessee Historical Society.

## 1. "Difficult and Broken Ground"

1. *War of the Rebellion: A Compilation of the Official Records of the Union and Confederate Armies,* 128 vols. (Washington DC: Government Printing Office, 1880–91), ser. 1, vol. 10, pt. 1:464–67 (hereafter cited as *OR;* all references are to series 1).
2. Warren E. Grabau, *Ninety-Eight Days: A Geographer's View of the Vicksburg Campaign* (Knoxville: Univ. of Tennessee Press, 2000), xv–xvii; James F. Gentsch, "A Geographic Analysis of the Battle of Shiloh" (master's thesis, Memphis State Univ., 1994), 29–31. For Champion Hill, see Timothy B. Smith, *Champion Hill: Decisive Battle for Vicksburg* (New York: Savas Beatie, 2004). For a broader look at environmental history, see Ted Steinberg, *Down to Earth: Nature's Role in American History* (New York: Oxford Univ. Press, 2002) and Louis S. Warren, ed. *American Environmental History* (New York: Wiley-Blackwell, 2003).
3. John Keegan, *The Military Geography of the American Civil War* (Gettysburg, PA: Gettysburg College, 1997); Grabau, *Ninety-Eight Days;* Robert K. Krick, *Civil War Weather in Virginia* (Tuscaloosa: Univ. of Alabama Press, 2007). See Harold A. Winters, with Gerald Galloway, William Reynolds, and David Rhyne, *Battling the Elements: Weather and Terrain in the Conduct of War* (Baltimore: Johns Hopkins Univ. Press, 1998) for a standard text on military terrain.
4. James Lee McDonough, *Shiloh: In Hell Before Night* (Knoxville: Univ. of Tennessee Press, 1977), 50; O. Edward Cunningham, *Shiloh and the Western Campaign of 1862,* ed. Gary D. Joiner and Timothy B. Smith (New York: Savas Beatie, 2007), 85–87; Wiley Sword, *Shiloh: Bloody April,* rev. ed. (Dayton, Ohio: Morningside Bookshop, 2001), 26–27; Larry J. Daniel, *Shiloh: The Battle That Changed the Civil War* (New York: Simon and Shuster, 1997), 102; David W. Reed, *The Battle of Shiloh and the Organizations Engaged,* 2nd ed. (Washington DC: Government Printing Office, 1909), 9; Gentsch, "Geographic Analysis of the Battle of Shiloh."
5. Smith, "Forgotten Inhabitants of Shiloh," 42.
6. For the width of the Civil War–era river, see Reed Map, First Day, 1900, Series 6, Box 1, Archives, Shiloh National Military Park, Shiloh, Tenn. (hereafter cited as SNMP).
7. Ibid.
8. Ibid.

9. Ibid.
10. Ibid. There is some debate as to whether there was a bridge or just a ford over Lick Creek during the battle.
11. Reed Map, First Day.
12. Grant, "Battle of Shiloh," 472; William P. Johnston, *The Life of Gen. Albert Sidney Johnston, Embracing His Services in the Armies of the United States, the Republic of Texas, and the Confederate States* (New York: D. Appleton, 1878), 569.
13. Don Carlos Buell, "Shiloh Reviewed," in *Battles and Leaders of the Civil War,* ed. Johnson and Buel, 1:495; Sword, *Shiloh,* 27; Cunningham, *Shiloh and the Western Campaign,* 85; Gentsch, "Geographic Analysis of the Battle of Shiloh," 100. One Confederate writer described the battlefield as a "quadrilateral of great strength." William Preston Johnston, "Albert Sidney Johnston at Shiloh," in *Battles and Leaders of the Civil War,* ed. Johnson and Buel, 1:551–52.
14. Reed Map, First Day.
15. Gentsch, "Geographic Analysis of the Battle of Shiloh," 26.
16. Buell, "Shiloh Reviewed," 495.
17. Reed Map, First Day.
18. Grant, "Battle of Shiloh," 469; Buell, "Shiloh Reviewed," 495–96; Gentsch, "Geographic Analysis of the Battle of Shiloh," 26.
19. Grant, "Battle of Shiloh," 472; Buell, "Shiloh Reviewed," 495; P. G. T. Beauregard, "The Campaign of Shiloh," in *Battles and Leaders of the Civil War,* ed. Johnson and Buel, 1:585.
20. Grant, "Battle of Shiloh," 472; Reed, *Battle of Shiloh,* 9; Gentsch, "Geographic Analysis of the Battle of Shiloh," 29–31.
21. Gentsch, "Geographic Analysis of the Battle of Shiloh," 84, 105.
22. Reed Map, First Day.
23. Ibid.
24. Buell, "Shiloh Reviewed," 495.
25. Reed Map, First Day.
26. Ibid.
27. Cunningham, *Shiloh and the Western Campaign,* 86
28. *OR,* vol. 10, pt. 1:27.
29. Smith, "Forgotten Inhabitants of Shiloh," 36–55.
30. Ibid., 41–42.
31. Ibid.
32. *OR,* vol. 10, pt. 2:50–51. See Carl R. Schenker Jr., "Who Failed to Fortify Pittsburg Landing?" *North and South Magazine* 13, no. 1 (May 2011): 46–53 for more on the entrenchment debate.

33. Reed Map, First Day; Johnston, "Albert Sidney Johnston at Shiloh," 551.

34. Park historian Stacy Allen has put forth an intriguing theory that the Confederate high command, in failing to understand the battlefield's geography, purposefully deployed the Southern army facing more east than north because they thought the Union line of battle faced west instead of south and that Pittsburg Landing was due east of them rather than northeast. See Stacy D. Allen, "Shiloh! The Campaign and First Day's Battle," *Blue and Gray* 14 (Winter 1997): 49. While interesting, the evidence is sketchy, and a much more simple and logical explanation can be had in examining the road layout. The vast majority of Civil War units deployed perpendicular to the road on which they advanced. The Corinth Road, where the Confederate army deployed, ran east-northeastward but took a huge turn to the north a few hundred yards forward. Had the Confederate army deployed farther forward, they no doubt would have deployed facing more north than east.

35. *OR,* vol. 10, pt. 1:581; Gentsch, "Geographic Analysis of the Battle of Shiloh," 55.

36. Reed Map, First Day.

37. *OR,* vol. 10, pt. 1:549; Genstch, "Geographic Analysis of the Battle of Shiloh," 67. For more on the action in this sector, see Alexander Mendoza, "A Terrible Baptism by Fire: David Stuart's Defense of the Union Left," in *Shiloh Campaign,* ed. Woodworth, 29–54.

38. Reed, *Battle of Shiloh,* 16.

39. Cunningham, *Shiloh and the Western Campaign,* 219–46.

40. *OR,* vol. 10, pt. 1:115–19; Gentsch, "Geographic Analysis of the Battle of Shiloh," 63, 67.

41. *OR,* vol. 10, pt. 1:203–4.

42. Ibid., 466; Gentsch, "Geographic Analysis of the Battle of Shiloh," 63.

43. *OR,* vol. 10, pt. 1:279.

44. Ibid., 480, 534; Gentsch, "Geographic Analysis of the Battle of Shiloh," 26.

45. *OR,* vol. 10, pt. 1:521, 528, 550.

46. Ibid.

47. Reed Map, Second Day, 1900, Series 6, Box 2, SNMP.

48. Smith, *Untold Story of Shiloh,* 13–15; Sword, *Shiloh,* 274, 320, 310, 447; Charles P. Roland, *Albert Sidney Johnston: Soldier of Three Republics* (Austin: Univ. of Texas Press, 1964), 348–49, 351; Charles P. Roland, *Jefferson Davis's Greatest General: Albert Sidney Johnston* (Abilene, TX: McWhiney Foundation, 2000), 82.

49. Smith, *Untold Story of Shiloh,* 18; Daniel, *Shiloh,* 207–14, 228–30, 235–37, 255–56.

50. Smith, *Untold Story of Shiloh,* 12–13; McDonough, *Shiloh,* 104, 133, 143, 150, 167. For an examination of the Hornet's Nest in history and memory, see Smith, "Anatomy of an Icon," 55–76.
51. Smith, "Why Lew Was Late," 30–37; Grady McWhiney, "General Beauregard's 'Complete Victory' at Shiloh," in *Shiloh Campaign,* ed. Woodworth, 110–22; Daniel, *Shiloh,* 219.
52. For a modern military staff ride guide by the army, see Jeffrey J. Gudmens, *Staff Ride Handbook for the Battle of Shiloh, 6–7 April 1862* (Fort Leavenworth, KS: Combat Studies Institute Press, 2005).
53. For more on Shiloh's preservation, see Timothy B. Smith, *This Great Battlefield of Shiloh: History, Memory, and the Establishment of a Civil War National Military Park* (Knoxville: Univ. of Tennessee Press, 2004).
54. For the Civil War Trust's animated maps, see http://www.civilwar.org/maps/.

## 2. To Conquer or Perish

1. Alfred Roman, *The Military Operations of General Beauregard in the War Between the States, 1861 to 1865: Including a Brief Personal Sketch of His Services in the War with Mexico, 1846–8,* 2 vols. (New York: Harper and Bros., 1883), 1:278; Johnston, *Life of Gen. Albert Sidney Johnston,* 568–70.
2. Johnston, *Life of Gen. Albert Sidney Johnston,* 569, 583–84, 613; *OR,* vol. 10, pt. 1:396; Allen, "Shiloh!," 39; Stephen D. Engle, "'Thank God, He Has Rescued His Character': Albert Sidney Johnston, Southern Hamlet of the Confederacy," in *Leaders of the Lost Cause: New Perspectives on the Confederate High Command,* ed. Gary W. Gallagher and Joseph T. Glatthaar (Mechanicsburg, PA: Stackpole Books, 2004), 152–53. After transferring to Virginia from the Western Theater, John Pope had criticized the eastern Federals in relation to his western soldiers. He also offended Robert E. Lee by issuing hard war orders to seize enemy property and kill captured guerillas. Of course, Pope went on to receive a thrashing from Lee's hand at Second Manassas. Joseph Hooker also let his mouth blunder into a bad situation, saying the nation needed a dictator and brashly stating, "May God have mercy on General Lee, for I will have none." Hooker went on to be soundly defeated by Lee at Chancellorsville. James M. McPherson, *Battle Cry of Freedom: The Civil War Era* (New York: Oxford Univ. Press, 1988), 501, 524, 584–85, 639.
3. For Johnston, see Roland, *Albert Sidney Johnston.*
4. Johnston, *Life of Gen. Albert Sidney Johnston,* 496. For Beauregard, see T. Harry Williams, *P. G. T. Beauregard: Napoleon in Gray* (Baton Rouge: Louisiana State Univ. Press, 1954), 125.

5. Roland, *Albert Sidney Johnston,* 326; Johnston, *Life of Gen. Albert Sidney Johnston,* 496, 716.
6. Johnston, *Life of Gen. Albert Sidney Johnston,* 582.
7. *OR,* vol. 10, pt. 1:403; J. B. Ulmer, "A Glimpse of Albert Sidney Johnston Through the Smoke of Shiloh," *Southwestern Historical Quarterly* 10 (4): 285–96; Johnston, *Life of Gen. Albert Sidney Johnston,* 589.
8. *OR,* vol. 10, pt. 1:403.
9. Ibid., 401; Johnston, *Life of Gen. Albert Sidney Johnston,* 594, 598.
10. *OR,* vol. 10, pt. 1:454.
11. Ibid., 407, 414–15; Reed, *Battle of Shiloh,* 81.
12. *OR,* vol. 10, pt. 1:427; Marshall Wingfield, *General A. P. Stewart: His Life and Letters* (Memphis: West Tennessee Historical Society, 1954), 55.
13. *OR,* vol. 10, pt. 1:427; Reed, *Battle of Shiloh,* 73; Ulmer, "Glimpse of Albert Sidney Johnston," 285–96.
14. *OR,* vol. 10, pt. 1:404, 569; Johnston, *Life of Gen. Albert Sidney Johnston,* 597, 608.
15. Johnston, *Life of Gen. Albert Sidney Johnston,* 597; *OR,* vol. 10, pt. 1:404, 532, 549.
16. Johnston, *Life of Gen. Albert Sidney Johnston,* 608.
17. Ibid., 612.
18. Ibid., 615.
19. D. W. Reed to Basil W. Duke, July 20, 1906, Series 1, Box 13, Folder 140, SNMP.
20. *OR,* vol. 10, pt. 1:404; Johnston, *Life of Gen. Albert Sidney Johnston,* 608, 611.
21. *OR,* vol. 10, pt. 1:621, 624; Johnston, *Life of Gen. Albert Sidney Johnston,* 611–13.
22. Johnston, *Life of Gen. Albert Sidney Johnston,* 611–13; *OR,* vol. 10, pt. 1:621, 624.
23. Johnston, *Life of Gen. Albert Sidney Johnston,* 566, 569.
24. Ibid., 613–14, 718.
25. Isham G. Harris to William Preston, Apr. 6, 1862, 1, 13, 140, SNMP; Johnston, *Life of Gen. Albert Sidney Johnston,* 614.
26. Johnston, *Life of Gen. Albert Sidney Johnston,* 614; Harris to Preston, Apr. 6, 1862, 1, 13, 140.
27. Johnston, *Life of Gen. Albert Sidney Johnston,* 614–15; William Preston Diary, Apr. 6, 1862, SNMP; Harris to Preston, Apr. 6, 1862, 1, 13, 140.
28. Johnston, *Life of Gen. Albert Sidney Johnston,* 614–15, 699.

## 3. Anatomy of an Icon

1. David W. Reed, *Campaigns and Battles of the Twelfth Regiment Iowa Veteran Volunteer Infantry: From Organization, September, 1861, to Muster-Out, January 20, 1866* (n.p.: n.p., 1903), 48–50, 53, 250.
2. Reed, *Battle of Shiloh.*
3. Ibid., 15.
4. Daniel, *Shiloh,* 197.
5. Reed, *Battle of Shiloh,* 16.
6. *OR,* vol. 10, pt. 1:404.
7. Ibid.
8. Ibid., 151, 153, 291. For more about the vegetation of the area, see Ray H. Mattison, "The Vegetative Cover of the Hornet's Nest Area During the Battle of Shiloh," Vertical Files, SNMP.
9. Reed, *Battle of Shiloh,* 70.
10. *OR,* vol. 10, pt. 1:438.
11. Reed, *Battle of Shiloh,* 84–85; *OR,* vol. 10, pt. 1:151, 438, 453. For the claim of a second Stephens assault, see Shiloh National Military Park Troop Position Tablet 337.
12. *OR,* vol. 10, pt. 1:438–39.
13. Ibid., 178, 279.
14. Ibid., 428.
15. Reed, *The Battle of Shiloh,* 17.
16. *OR,* vol. 10, pt. 1:428
17. Ibid., 466; Reed, *Battle of Shiloh,* 45.
18. *OR,* vol. 10, pt. 1:408.
19. Ibid., 574; Reed, *Battle of Shiloh,* 70, 73.
20. *OR,* vol. 10, pt. 1:165–66, 278.
21. Ibid., 151, 153, 480, 488, 491.
22. Reed, *Battle of Shiloh,* 70.
23. *OR,* vol. 10, pt. 1:149, 574.
24. Ibid., 162–64.
25. Ibid., 162–64, 498; Reed, *Battle of Shiloh,* 18.
26. Reed, *Battle of Shiloh,* 18–19, 50; *OR,* vol. 10, pt. 1:149.
27. Reed, *Battle of Shiloh,* 19, 61.
28. *OR,* vol. 10, pt. 1:179.

29. Ibid., 279.

30. Reed, *Battle of Shiloh,* 50; Tony Horwitz, *Confederates in the Attic: Dispatches from the Unfinished Civil War* (New York: Vintage Books, 1998), 177–79.

31. *OR,* vol. 10, pt. 1:101, 395, 489.

32. E. B. Whitman to J. L. Donelson, Apr. 29, 1866, E 576, Box 53, RG 92, NARA.

33. Allen, "Shiloh!," 47.

34. Ulysses S. Grant, *Personal Memoirs of U.S. Grant,* 2 vols. (New York: Charles L. Webster, 1885–86), 201.

35. Carol Reardon, *Pickett's Charge in History and Memory* (Chapel Hill: Univ. of North Carolina Press, 1997).

36. See George B. Davis, et al., *The Official Military Atlas of the Civil War* (Washington DC: Government Printing Office, 1891–95), plates 10, 12, 13, and 14 for various contemporary maps of the battlefield of Shiloh.

37. Leon J. Fremaux, "Map of the Battlefield of Shiloh, April 6 & 7, 1862," Geography and Map Division, Library of Congress; William T. Ross to "Lizzie," Oct. 31, 1864, William T. Roass Letter, Vertical Files, SNMP; *OR,* 24, 2: 393. See various Fremaux maps on file at Shiloh National Military Park and in *The Official Military Atlas of the Civil War* for variations of his maps.

38. Johnston, *Life of Gen. Albert Sidney Johnston,* 604; Manning F. Force, *From Fort Henry to Corinth* (New York: Charles Scribner's Sons, 1881), 142, 144; Roman, *Military Operations of General Beauregard*; Grant, *Personal Memoirs of U.S. Grant*; William K. Kay, "The Sunken Road," 4, Vertical Files, SNMP.

39. David G. Martin, *The Shiloh Campaign, March–April, 1862* (New York: Fairfax Press, 1987), 105; David Nevin, *The Road to Shiloh: Early Battles in the West* (Alexandria, VA: Time-Life Books, 1983), 130–35; "First Reunion of Iowa Hornet's Nest Brigade, October 12–13, 1887," 12, Series 3, Box 4, Folder 216, SNMP; *Manual of the Panorama of the Battle of Shiloh* (Chicago: A. T. Andreas, 1885), 5, 14; Buell, "Shiloh Reviewed," 504–5, 510–11; Thure de Thulstrup, *Battle of Shiloh,* lithograph, L. Prang and Company, 1888; Kay, "Sunken Road," 5.

40. "First Reunion of Iowa Hornet's Nest Brigade, October 12–13, 1887," 30.

41. Reed, *Campaigns and Battles,* 1. For Reed's participation at the Hornet's Nest Brigade reunions, see "First Reunion of Iowa Hornet's Nest Brigade, October 12–13, 1887" and "Third Reunion of Iowa Hornet's Nest Brigade, August 21–22, 1895," both in Series 3, Box 4, Folder 216, SNMP.

42. Smith, *This Great Battlefield of Shiloh*; Timothy B. Smith, "David Wilson Reed: The Father of Shiloh National Military Park," *Annals of Iowa* 62, no. 3 (Summer 2003): 333–59.

43. Smith, *This Great Battlefield of Shiloh*; "Historians and the Battle of Shiloh: One Hundred and Forty Years of Controversy," *Tennessee Historical Quarterly* 63, no. 4 (Winter 2003): 338–39.

44. Reed, *Battle of Shiloh,* 18–20.

45. Reed, *Campaigns and Battles,* 54, 61.

46. Smith, *This Great Battlefield of Shiloh,* 126–27.

47. Smith, "*Shiloh: Portrait of a Battle:* Fifty Years Later," 147–61; McDonough, *Shiloh.* The movie also influenced a young historian writing about the battle—James Lee McDonough, whose first academic book on the battle, *Shiloh: In Hell Before Night,* became the academic standard for decades. Apparently McDonough was also heavily influenced by an internal National Park Service study by Donald F. Dosch titled "The Hornet's Nest at Shiloh," which can be found in the Shiloh National Military Park Vertical Files.

## 4. A Case Study in Civil War Memory

1. Cunningham, *Shiloh and the Western Campaign,* 303.

2. For the growing body of work devoted to memory, see Michael Kammen, *Mystic Chords of Memory: The Transformation of Tradition in American Culture* (New York: Vintage Books, 1991); John Bodnar, *Remaking America: Public Memory, Commemoration, and Patriotism in the Twentieth Century* (Princeton: Princeton Univ. Press, 1992); G. Kurt Piehler, *Remembering War the American Way* (Washington DC: Smithsonian Institution Press, 1995); David Blight, *Race and Reunion: The Civil War in American Memory* (Cambridge: Harvard Univ. Press, 2001); John R. Neff, *Honoring the Civil War Dead: Commemoration and the Problem of Reconciliation* (Lawrence: Univ. Press of Kansas, 2005); William A. Blair, *Cities of the Dead: Contesting the Memory of the Civil War in the South, 1865–1914* (Chapel Hill: Univ. of North Carolina Press, 2003); Alice Fahs and Joan Waugh, eds., *The Memory of the Civil War in American Culture* (Chapel Hill: Univ. of North Carolina Press, 2004).

3. Ezra J. Warner, *Generals in Blue: Lives of the Union Commanders* (Baton Rouge: Louisiana State Univ. Press, 1964), 385–86; Toby G. Bates, "'Without Doubt, History Will Do the Gallant Hero Justice': Benjamin Mayberry Prentiss and the Failure of American History" (master's thesis, Univ. of Mississippi, 2002).

4. Warner, *Generals in Blue,* 386.

5. Ibid., 386.

6. *Shiloh: Portrait of a Battle* (Shiloh, TN: Shiloh National Military Park, 1954); Thulstrup, *Battle of Shiloh*; Smith, "History in the Making," 149–61.

7. Bruce Catton, *Grant Moves South: 1861–1863* (Boston: Little, Brown, 1960), 233–36; Williams, *P. G. T. Beauregard,* 140; John F. Marszalek, *Sherman: A Soldier's Passion for Order* (New York: Free Press, 1993), 179; Brooks D. Simpson, *Ulysses S. Grant: Triumph over Adversity, 1822–1865* (Boston: Houghton Mifflin, 2000), 132; William S. McFeely, *Grant: A Biography* (New York: W. W. Norton, 1981), 113; James M. McPherson, *Battle Cry of Freedom: The Civil War*

*Era* (New York: Oxford Univ. Press, 1988), 410; Thomas L. Connelly, *Army of the Heartland: The Army of Tennessee, 1861–1862* (Baton Rouge: Louisiana State Univ. Press, 1967), 165–66; Allan Nevins, *The War for the Union: War Becomes Revolution, 1862–1863* (New York: Charles Scribner's Sons, 1960), 85; Shelby Foote, *The Civil War: A Narrative,* 3 vols. (New York: Random House, 1958–74), 1: 340–41; William C. Davis, *Breckinridge: Statesman, Soldier, Symbol* (Baton Rouge: Louisiana State Univ. Press, 1974), 309; Herman Hattaway and Archer Jones, *How the North Won: A Military History of the Civil War* (Urbana: Univ. of Illinois Press, 1983), 168–69; Roland, *Albert Sidney Johnston,* 335–36; Nathaniel Cheairs Hughes Jr., *General William J. Hardee: Old Reliable* (Baton Rouge: Louisiana State Univ. Press, 1965), 107–8; Grady McWhiney, *Braxton Bragg and Confederate Defeat,* vol. 1, *Field Command* (New York: Columbia Univ. Press, 1969), 242; Herman Hattaway, *Shades of Blue and Gray* (Columbia: Univ. of Missouri Press, 1997), 70. While there is little doubt that Prentiss is viewed by most as a hero and by some as the most critical officer on the field of Shiloh, one young graduate student has curiously argued that Prentiss never received his fair due. Bates's "Without Doubt" is an attempt to resurrect Prentiss as a great general, arguing that history has not been fair to him. The author argues that Prentiss was doomed to obscurity because of initial unfavorable newspaper accounts. What Bates claims as the truth about Prentiss, that he won the day for the Union at Shiloh, came to the surface too late to make any difference; Prentiss was already doomed, he argues. Bates clearly believes that Prentiss was the hero of Shiloh. "Prentiss's actions on April 6 enabled the Union to avoid possible defeat and claim victory the following day," he argues. In reality, the above historians centering on Prentiss's role is clear enough evidence that Bates's argument is invalid. I argue that the two schools of thought above, the incorrect newspapers and the current thinking of Prentiss as the hero, are both in error. Bates, "Without Doubt," vi.

8. Shiloh National Military Park Tablet 435; *Shiloh: Portrait of a Battle.* While technically correct, the quote nevertheless causes viewers to assume that Prentiss had sent out the patrol.
9. Cunningham, *Shiloh and the Western Campaign,* 153–54.
10. *OR,* vol. 10, pt. 1:279.
11. Smith, *This Great Battlefield of Shiloh,* 85–87. For an example of the passionate arguments over surprise, see Grant, "Battle of Shiloh," 465–86; Buell, "Shiloh Reviewed," 487–536.
12. Shiloh National Military Park Monument 20.
13. Reed, *Battle of Shiloh,* 96, placed the total number of men fit for duty (minus the 15th and 16th Iowa and the 23rd Missouri) at 5,403; Reed, *Battle of Shiloh,* 59, states that the arrival of the 575 men of the 23rd Missouri "gave him [Prentiss] about 1,000 men," which means his original number on the Hornet's Nest line was fewer than 500.

14. *OR,* vol. 10, pt. 1:278. McDonough, *Shiloh,* 143, stated that at no time were there more than 4,300 men in the Hornet's Nest. A quantitative study by Shiloh historian Stacy Allen, "Hornet's Nest: Federal Line," Vertical Files, SNMP, stated there were 8,852 total Federals in the Hornet's Nest, but only actually 6,742 on the front line, which totaled twenty-five hundred feet in length. OR, 10, pt. 1:290–91; Reed, *Battle of Shiloh,* 96.

15. Reed, *Battle of Shiloh,* 91, 96. Five regiments lost 75 percent of those captured in the Hornet's Nest. These were the 8th Iowa, 12th Iowa, 14th Iowa, and 58th Illinois, all of Wallace's Division, and the 23rd Missouri, which arrived at the Hornet's Nest straight from the landing. The 23rd Missouri, while technically a part of Prentiss's division, had not served under him before arriving at the Sunken Road and could just as well have been a regiment of any other division. If the 23rd Missouri is taken out, Wallace's four regiments still provided 56 percent of the captured men.

16. Warner, *Generals in Blue,* 7–8.

17. William T. Sherman, *Memoirs of General W. T. Sherman: Written by Himself,* 2 vols. (New York: D. Appleton, 1875), 1:205–30.

18. Johnston, *Life of Gen. Albert Sidney Johnston,* 604, 620; Roman, *Military Operations of General Beauregard* 1:298.

19. Force, *From Fort Henry to Corinth,* 146, 159.

20. Buell, "Shiloh Reviewed," 505–6.

21. Grant, "Battle of Shiloh," 472–73.

22. *OR,* vol. 10, pt. 1:277–78.

23. "Gen. Prentiss at Washington," *Washington Herald,* Oct. 20, 1862; "Gen. Prentiss at the Board of Trade," *Chicago Tribune,* Oct. 21, 1862; "The Captivity of Gen. Prentiss," *Quincy Whig,* Nov. 1, 1862.

24. "Captivity of Gen. Prentiss"; "When Prentiss Surrendered at Shiloh," *Chicago Tribune,* Apr. 20, 1881; "Another Letter from Gen. Prentiss," *Chicago Tribune,* Apr. 22, 1881; Bates, "Without Doubt," 106.

25. "The Surprise at Shiloh," *Chicago Tribune,* Jan. 14, 1882.

26. Martin, *Shiloh Campaign,* 105; Nevin, *Road to Shiloh,* 130–35; "First Reunion of Iowa Hornet's Nest Brigade, October 12–13, 1887," 12; *Manual of the Panorama of the Battle of Shiloh,* 5, 14; Buell, "Shiloh Reviewed," 504–5, 510–11; Thulstrup, *Battle of Shiloh*; Kay, "Sunken Road," 5; "Battle of Shiloh," *Chicago Daily Tribune,* Aug. 15, 1885.

27. For a history of Shiloh National Military Park, see Smith, *This Great Battlefield of Shiloh.*

28. Shiloh National Military Park Tablet Z5. For Reed, see Smith, *Untold Story of Shiloh,* 139–55.

29. Reed, *Battle of Shiloh,* 18–20, 59; Reed, *Campaigns and Battles,* 53, 54, 61.

30. "Hero of Shiloh Passes Away," *Washington Post,* Feb. 9, 1901; *Journal of the House of Representatives of the 41st General Assembly of the State of Missouri,* 1901 (Jefferson City, MO: Tribune Printing, 1901), 287. Ironically, the Missouri legislature resolution misspelled his name as "Prentis."

31. DeLong Rice, *The Story of Shiloh* (Jackson, TN: McCowat-Mercer, 1924), 10, 13, 41, 43; Otto Eisenschiml, *The Story of Shiloh* (Chicago: Chicago Civil War Roundtable, 1946), 33–34.

32. For an assortment of Shiloh National Military Park brochures through the years, see Shiloh: Donnelson Leaflets, Vertical Files, SNMP; *Shiloh: Portrait of a Battle.*

33. Sword, *Shiloh,* 377–78.

## 5. Rewriting History

1. *OR,* vol. 10, pt. 1: 169. For Wallace, see Gail Stephens, *Shadow of Shiloh: Major General Lew Wallace in the Civil War* (Indianapolis: Indiana Historical Society Press, 2010).

2. Grant, "Battle of Shiloh," 468.

3. *OR,* vol. 10, pt. 1:170, 175, 180–81; Grant, "Battle of Shiloh," 468–69; Stacy D. Allen, "If He Had Less Rank: Lewis Wallace," in *Grant's Lieutenants: From Cairo to Vicksburg,* ed. Steven E. Woodworth (Lawrence: Univ. Press of Kansas, 2001), 73–74. It is significant that long before April 6, Wallace had determined the Shunpike to be his main route of advance and that the only movement made via the River Road was by Grant's cavalry from Pittsburg Landing, not Wallace's cavalry from Crump's Landing; Wallace's cavalry never traveled the eastern route all the way to Pittsburg Landing.

4. *OR,* vol. 10, pt. 1:170.

5. Ibid., 178, 185; Allen, "If He Had Less Rank," 74.

6. Lew Wallace to James Grant Wilson, Nov. 6, 1896, William P. Palmer Collection, Western Reserve Historical Society, Cleveland, OH; *OR,* vol. 10, pt. 1:170, 185; Robert U. Johnson and Clarence C. Buel, "The March of Lew Wallace's Division to Shiloh," in *Battles and Leaders of the Civil War,* ed. Johnson and Buel, 1:607. The various accounts of the participants concerning Baxter and the writing of the order are very confusing. Almost everyone involved had a different story.

7. *OR,* vol. 10, pt. 1:175; Grant, "Battle of Shiloh," 469.

8. *OR,* vol. 10, pt. 1:170, 175.

9. Ibid., 179, 185. Apparently, there was another cavalry officer also sent to Wallace, who stayed with the general on the march.

10. *OR,* vol. 10, pt. 1:176, 179–80; Lewis Wallace, *Lew Wallace: An Autobiography,* 2 vols. (New York: Harper and Brothers, 1906), 1:467.
11. *OR,* vol. 10, pt. 1:176.
12. Atwell Thompson to Cornelius Cadle, Aug. 2, 1895, Third Division File, SNMP.
13. *OR,* vol. 10, pt. 1:180–82, 187, 199.
14. *OR,* vol. 10, pt. 1:187–88; Johnson and Buel, "March of Lew Wallace's Division," 610. There is some evidence, however, that Wallace's mere presence in the vicinity offered some psychological help to Grant's army. Grant continually used the looming approach of Wallace's division as a means of supporting and encouraging his own troops.
15. Johnson and Buel, "March of Lew Wallace's Division," 607–10; Wallace, *Lew Wallace.* For background on the history of Shiloh National Military Park, see Smith, *This Great Battlefield of Shiloh.*
16. Lew Wallace to George W. Davis, Dec. 9, 1895, Third Division File, SNMP.
17. Shiloh National Military Park Commission Daily Events, Nov. 20, 51, SNMP; Thompson to Cadle, Aug. 2, 1895.
18. Shiloh National Military Park Commission Daily Events, Nov. 20, 50–51.
19. Joseph W. Rich, "General Lew. Wallace at Shiloh: How He Was Convinced of an Error After Forty Years," *Iowa Journal of History and Politics* 18, no. 2 (Apr. 1920): 301–8; Shiloh National Military Park Commission Daily Events, Nov. 20, 51–52.
20. Shiloh National Military Park Commission Daily Events, Nov. 21–22, 54–55, SNMP.
21. Cornelius Cadle to Lew Wallace, Mar. 3, 1902, and Lew Wallace to Cornelius Cadle, Mar. 8, 1902, both in Series 1, Box 18, Folder 253, SNMP; Joseph W. Rich, "The Battle of Shiloh," *Iowa Journal of History and Politics* 7, no. 4 (Oct. 1909): 503–81; Rich, "General Lew," 302.
22. Lew Wallace to James Grant Wilson, Nov. 6, 1896.

## 6. Secession at Shiloh

1. James L. Power, *Proceedings of the Mississippi State Convention, Held January 7th to 26th, A.D. 1861. Including the Ordinances, as Finally Adopted, Important Speeches, and a List of Members, Showing the Postoffice, Profession, Nativity, Politics, Age, Religious Preference, and Social Relations of Each* (Jackson, MS: Power and Cadwallader, 1861), 13.
2. Pauline Maier, *American Scripture: Making of the Declaration of Independence* (New York: Knopf, 1997), 152–53.

3. "Warren P. Anderson," *Jackson Weekly Mississippian,* Sept. 25, 1861; Estate of Warren P. Anderson, Deceased, Case 1823, Chancery Court Files, Hinds County Courthouse, 2nd Judicial District, Raymond, MS.
4. Francis Marion Rogers, Compiled Service Records, 14th Mississippi Infantry, NARA.
5. For Shiloh, see the standard literature on the battle, including McDonough, *Shiloh*; Cunningham, *Shiloh and the Western Campaign*; Sword, *Shiloh*; Daniel, *Shiloh*; and Reed, *Battle of Shiloh.*
6. Samuel Benton, Compiled Service Records, 9th Mississippi Infantry, NARA.
7. McPherson, *Battle Cry of Freedom,* 318.
8. John J. Thornton, Compiled Service Records, 6th Mississippi Infantry, NARA; Timothy B. Smith, *Mississippi in the Civil War: The Home Front* (Jackson: Univ. Press of Mississippi, 2010), 19.
9. *OR,* vol. 10, pt. 1:581.
10. H. Grady Howell, *Going to Meet the Yankees: A History of the "Bloody Sixth" Mississippi Infantry, C.S.A.* (Jackson: Chickasaw Bayou Press, 1981), 86–87.
11. *OR,* vol. 10, pt. 1:469.
12. James R. Chalmers, Compiled Service Records, 9th Mississippi Infantry, and General Officers, NARA; Ezra J. Warner, *Generals in Gray: Lives of the Confederate Commanders* (Baton Rouge: Louisiana State Univ. Press, 1959), 46; Hamilton Mayson, Compiled Service Records, 7th Mississippi Infantry, NARA; John B. Herring, Compiled Service Records, 5th Mississippi Infantry, NARA; Daniel H. Parker, Compiled Service Records, 7th Mississippi Infantry, NARA; *Journal of the State Convention and Ordinances and Resolutions Adopted in January, 1861, with an Appendix* (Jackson, MS: E. Barksdale, 1861), 16.
13. *OR,* vol. 10, pt. 1:548–49.
14. William F. Brantley, Compiled Service Records, 15th Mississippi Infantry, NARA; Warner, *Generals in Gray,* 32–33; Francis M. Aldridge, Compiled Service Records, 15th Mississippi Infantry, NARA; Hamilton Mayson, Compiled Service Records; Edward F. McGehee, Compiled Service Records, 2nd Confederate Infantry, NARA; Thomas D. Lewers, Compiled Service Records, Wirt Adams Mississippi Cavalry, NARA.
15. *OR,* vol. 10, pt. 1:621–22.
16. *OR,* vol. 10, pt. 1:622; Ben Wynne, *A Hard Trip: A History of the 15th Mississippi Infantry, CSA* (Macon, GA: Mercer Univ. Press, 2003), 76–77; Francis M. Aldridge, Compiled Service Records.
17. *OR,* vol. 10, pt. 1:550–51.
18. McDonough, *Shiloh,* 184–95.
19. *OR,* vol. 10, pt. 1:551–52.

20. Cunningham, *Shiloh and the Western Campaign,* 379–96.

21. John J. Thornton, Compiled Service Records; Edward F. McGehee, Compiled Service Records; Warner, *Generals in Gray,* 32–33; Bruce S. Allardice, *Confederate Colonels: A Biographical Register* (Columbia: Univ. of Missouri Press, 2008), 372. Aldridge is buried in present-day Grenada County, a postwar creation.

22. *OR,* vol. 10, pt. 1:468; John B. Herring, Compiled Service Record; Thomas D. Lewers, Compiled Service Records; Hamilton Mayson, Compiled Service Records; Daniel H. Parker, Compiled Service Records.

23. Francis M. Aldridge, Compiled Service Records.

## 7. The Forgotten Inhabitants of Shiloh

1. Richard E. Wood, "History of General Albert Sidney Johnston's Last Bivouac Site," 1997, author's copy courtesy of the Wood family.

2. Ibid.

3. Paul D. Welch, *Archeology at Shiloh Indian Mounds, 1899–1999* (Tuscaloosa: Univ. of Alabama Press, 2006), 1–2, 255, 258, 265; Smith, *This Great Battlefield of Shiloh,* 2; Haywood S. Harrell to Herb Harper, July 21, 1998, Vertical Files, SNMP.

4. Frank H. H. Roberts Field Notebook, National Anthropological Archives, National Museum of Natural History, Smithsonian Institution (hereafter cited as Roberts Field Notebook); "List of Tools Loaned to CWA by Shiloh National Military Park," n.d., ser. 2, Box 19, Folder 309, SNMP; Moreau Chambers, "Historical Reports: Indian Mounds—Shiloh," Vertical Files, SNMP; Moreau B. Chambers Field Notebook, National Anthropological Archives, National Museum of Natural History, Smithsonian Institution (hereafter cited as Chambers Field Notebook); "Tennessee: The Shiloh Mound Group, Hardin County," excerpt from the *Annual Report of the Board of Regents of the Smithsonian Institution, 1934* (Washington, D.C.: Smithsonian Institution, 1935), 394–98; Frank H. H. Roberts Jr., "Indian Mounds on Shiloh Battlefield," in *Explorations and Fieldwork of the Smithsonian Institution in 1934* (Washington DC: Smithsonian Institution, 1935), 65–68; Welch, *Archeology at Shiloh Indian Mounds,* 1–2, 22, 116, 252–55.

5. Welch, *Archeology at Shiloh Indian Mounds,*1–2, 257.

6. Ibid., 1, 255, 266; P. M. Harbert, *Early History of Hardin County, Tennessee* (Memphis: Tri-State Printing & Binding, 1968), 42–43; Charles E. Shedd, *A History of Shiloh National Military Park, Tennessee* (Washington, D.C.: Government Printing Office, 1954), 6, 8–9.

7. "Chain of Title," W. C. Meeks Land Acquisition Folder, Series 1, Box 22, Folder 312, SNMP; "Chain of Title," J. W. Sowell land, Series 1, Box 22,

Folder 326, SNMP; "Chain of Title," Seay Field land, Series 1, Box 21, Folder 298, SNMP; "Chain of Title," Tillman land, Series 1, Box 22, Folder 327, SNMP; "Chain of Title," School land, Series 1, Box 22, Folder 330, SNMP; "Chain of Title," Rowsey land, Series 1, Box 22, Folder 322, SNMP; "Chain of Title," Fraley Field land, Series 1, Box 21, Folder 290, SNMP; "Chain of Title," Cloud land, Series 1, Box 20, Folder 283, SNMP; "Chain of Title," Thomas Maxwell land, Series 1, Box 22, Folder 309, SNMP; "Chain of Title," Duncan land, Series 1, Box 21, Folder 295, SNMP; "Chain of Title," Cantrell land, Series 1, Box 20, Folder 278, SNMP.

8. "Chain of Title," School land; "Pittsburg Landing Name Explained," *Memphis Commercial Appeal,* May 3, 1952; Ronnie Fullwood, *Shiloh: House of Peace: The Church That Named the Battle* (Selmer, TN: G. and P. Printing Services, 2003), 13, 19, 22–23; B. G. Brazelton, *A History of Hardin County* (Nashville: Cumberland Presbyterian Publishing House, 1885), 35; Shedd, *History of Shiloh National Military Park,* 6; Mary E. Stricklin, "Shiloh Church," Shiloh Church—Vertical File, SNMP; "Shiloh School Property Deed," Shiloh Church—Vertical File, SNMP; "How Bloody Shiloh Got Its Name," *Memphis Press Scimitar* clipping, n.d., Shiloh Church—Vertical File, SNMP.

9. Shedd, *History of Shiloh National Military Park,* 8; Smith, *This Great Battlefield of Shiloh,* 4.

10. Bureau of the Census, Federal Manuscript Census, Population Schedule, 1860, Hardin County, Tennessee; John Paul Howell to Ronnie Brewington, Sept. 26, 1990, Rhea and Howell Family—Vertical File, SNMP.

11. Bureau of the Census, Population Schedule, 1860, Hardin County, Tennessee; "Thomas Walker," Land Owners at the Battle of Shiloh—Vertical File, SNMP.

12. "Bill of Sale," Rhea and Howell Family—Vertical File, SNMP; Charles Marshall, "Miscellaneous Incidents of the Civil War," 1–2, Historical Reports: Research Reports on Army Units in the Army of the Tennessee—Vertical File, SNMP; Bureau of the Census, Federal Manuscript Census, Slave Schedule, 1860, Hardin County, Tennessee.

13. Bureau of the Census, Federal Manuscript Census, Agricultural and Manufacturing Schedule, 1860, Hardin County, Tennessee.

14. Bureau of the Census, Populations Schedule, 1860, Hardin County, Tennessee.

15. Bureau of the Census, Agricultural and Manufacturing Schedule, 1860, Hardin County, Tennessee; "List of Houses on Shiloh Battlefield Mentioned in Reports," n.d., Series 1, Box 39, Folder 631, SNMP.

16. Brazelton, *History of Hardin County,* 67; Bureau of the Census, Population Schedule, 1860, Hardin County, Tennessee; Edith Tillman to James Sasser, Feb. 10, 1992, Tillman Cemetery—Vertical File, SNMP.

17. Smith, *This Great Battlefield of Shiloh,* 5.

18. Timothy B. Smith, "'Gallant and Invaluable Service': The United States Navy at the Battle of Shiloh," *West Tennessee Historical Society Papers* 58 (2004): 18–36.

19. "List of Houses on Shiloh Battlefield Mentioned in Reports."

20. Leroy Guthrie to M. Crowder and Family, Apr. 4, 1862, 18th Missouri File, SNMP; Duane Helweg, *Lone Survivor at Shiloh* (San Angelo, TX: Rimrock Writings, 2008), 44.

21. Marshall, "Miscellaneous Incidents of the Civil War," 1–2; "Personal Interview with Mr. Aleck McDaniel," July 22, 1938, in Mancil A. Milligan, *Seeing Shiloh 1862 and Today* (Indianapolis: Jobbers Publishing, 1940); Gaye Grainger Stokes, "The Bell Family at Shiloh," author's copy courtesy of Larry DeBerry, 2.

22. Larry DeBerry, interview with author, June 16, 2007; Duane Helweg, "My Wicker Family History: Shiloh Remembered," author's copy courtesy of Duane Helweg, 5. See also Helweg, *Lone Survivor at Shiloh.*

23. Marshall, "Miscellaneous Incidents of the Civil War," 1–2.

24. "The Fall of Shiloh Church," *Cincinnati Daily Times,* June 13, 1862; "The Fall of Shiloh Church," *Sacramento Daily Union,* July 29, 1862; Howell to Brewington, Sept. 26, 1990.

25. "Post Return of U.S. Troops Stationed at Pittsburg Landing," July 20, 1862, in "Returns from Military Posts, 1800–1916," Microfilm 617, Roll 1532, NARA; Marshall, "Miscellaneous Incidents of the Civil War," 1–2.

26. Smith, *Untold Story of Shiloh,* 85–86.

27. Stokes, "Bell Family at Shiloh," 2; Helweg, "My Wicker Family History," 19; "The Shiloh Log Church House," Shiloh Church—Vertical File, SNMP.

28. "A Visit to the Battle-Field of Shiloh—Appalling Picture," *Oxford Falcon,* May 24, 1866; "Shocking Condition of the Confederate Dead at Shiloh," *Talladega Reporter and Watchtower,* Jan. 2, 1878.

29. For the continual discovery of soldiers on the field, see Jesse H. Curtis Statement, Feb. 19, 1898, and John W. Shaw to J. W. Scully, Feb. 21, 1898, both in Series 4, Box 1, Folder 2, SNMP; R. H. Baily to Quartermaster General, Feb. 7, 1934, Series 4, Box 15, Folder 191, SNMP; "Resting Place," *Raleigh News and Observer,* May 27, 1979, in "Request for Permission for Interment of Two Confederate Soldiers on the Shiloh National Military Park," SNMP; Otis H. Jones, "Building Shiloh Park," 10, 13–14, Vertical Files, SNMP; *Report of the Proceedings of the Society of the Army of the Tennessee at the Twenty-Fifth Meeting held at Chicago, Ills. September 12th and 13th, 1893* (Cincinnati: F. W. Freeman, 1893), 25:8, 60–61. The two Confederate soldiers found in 1977 were later buried in front of one of the Confederate burial trenches in the park.

30. "Post Return of U.S. Troops Stationed at Pittsburg Landing," May and December 1867, in "Returns from Military Posts, 1800–1916," Microfilm 617, Roll 1532, NARA; "Return of the Twenty-fifth Regiment of Infantry," May

1867 and January 1868, in "Returns from Regular Army Infantry Regiments, June 1821–December 1916, Twenty-fifth Infantry Regiment, January 1867–December 1873," Microfilm 665, Roll 254, NARA; Timothy B. Smith, "'The Handsomest Cemetery in the South': Shiloh National Cemetery," *West Tennessee Historical Society Papers* 56 (2002): 1–16. This 25th United States Infantry was made up of white men, not to be confused with the African American 25th United States Infantry, which would be created in an army reorganization in 1869.

31. War Department memo, Jan. 6, 1869, Office of the Quartermaster General—General Correspondence File, Box 2116, Folder 601.1, RG 92, NARA; Chain of Title and Final Decree, Mar. 1869, Series 4, Box 1, Folder 9, SNMP; Shedd, *History of Shiloh National Military Park,* 67.
32. For a history of the park, see Smith, *This Great Battlefield of Shiloh.*
33. "Preliminary Map: Battlefield of Shiloh," Dec. 1, 1895, Series 7, Drawer 1, Folder 7, SNMP; Daniel, *Shiloh,* 143.
34. S. M. Rogers to Atwell Thompson, July 31, 1895, Series 1, Box 37, Folder 619, SNMP; Jones, "Building Shiloh Park," 7–9; Shiloh National Military Park Commission Daily Events, Feb. 10, 1902, 85, 113, SNMP.
35. Shiloh National Military Park Commission Daily Events, May 30, 1904, and May 30, 1907, 194, 249, SNMP; Atwell Thompson to D. W. Reed, Jan. 5, 1903, Series 1, Box 23, Folder 344, SNMP; "Hazel Donnell Sowell," author's copy courtesy of Larry DeBerry; Shedd, *History of Shiloh National Military Park,* 33, 38; Jones, "Building Shiloh Park," 8–9.
36. "Boundary Description: By Metes and Bounds," n.d., Series 1, Box 40, Folder 644, SNMP; W. C. Meeks Land Acquisition Folder, Series 1, Box 22, Folder 312, SNMP.
37. "Boundary Description: By Metes and Bounds"; *Congressional Record,* 53rd Cong., 3rd sess., 27, 1:19; "Accounts Paid from Rentals Received from July 1, 1911 to August 26, 1913," copy in author's possession; "Hazel Donnell Sowell"; War Department, *Annual Report of the Secretary of War, 1907* (Washington, DC: Government Printing Office, 1907), 332; War Department, *Annual Report of the Secretary of War, 1908* (Washington, DC: Government Printing Office, 1908), 178; Jones, "Building Shiloh Park," 7; Marshall Lee Jones memoir, May 11, 1976, author's copy courtesy of Larry DeBerry.
38. "Accounts Paid from Rentals Received from July 1, 1911 to August 26, 1913"; D. W. Reed to Robert F. Looney, July 14, 1899, Robert F. Looney Collection, Folder 76, Memphis–Shelby County Public Library; Welch, *Archaeology at Shiloh Indian Mounds,* 111; F. A. Large to Atwell Thompson, Jan. 20, 1899, Series 1, Box 38, Folder 626, SNMP; Atwell Thompson to D. W. Reed, May 25, 1898, Series 1, Box 38, Folder 625, SNMP; Shiloh National Military Park Commission Daily Events, Nov. 21, 1900, and June 1, 1901, 8, 31, SNMP.

39. Cornelius Cadle to Secretary of War, June 26, 1899, E 712, Box 2, RG 92, NARA; Cornelius Cadle to D. W. Reed, Jan. 3, 1901, Series 1, Box 38, Folder 627, SNMP; Atwell Thompson to Cornelius Cadle, Feb. 23, 1897, Series 1, Box 38, Folder 623, SNMP; Cornelius Cadle to D. W. Reed, Jan. 23, 1899, Series 1, Box 38, Folder 626, SNMP; Atwell Thompson to D. W. Reed, June 23, 1899, Series 1, Box 25, Folder 368, SNMP.
40. "Memories, Memories—1913," author's copy courtesy of Larry DeBerry, 1–2.
41. Chambers Field Notebook; Welch, *Archeology at Shiloh Indian Mounds,* 95.

## 8. A Case Study in Change

1. R. E. Gatewood to Quartermaster, Oct. 29, 1929, Letters Sent—Volume 8, Series 4, Artifact Cabinet 6, SNMP.
2. David M. Kennedy, *Freedom from Fear: The American People in Depression and War, 1929–1945* (New York: Oxford Univ. Press, 1999), 37–39. For West Tennessee's lack of attention to the stock market crash, see the October and November 1929 issues of the local newspaper, the *Savannah Courier.*
3. For the New Deal, see William E. Leuchtenburg, *Franklin D. Roosevelt and the New Deal* (New York: Harper and Row, 1963).
4. For Shiloh's history, see Smith, *This Great Battlefield of Shiloh.*
5. Ibid., 122, 126.
6. Ibid., 126–27.
7. Ibid.
8. Leuchtenburg, *Franklin D. Roosevelt and the New Deal,* 164–65.
9. *Shiloh: General Management Plan: Development Concept Plan* (Washington, DC: National Park Service, 1981), 32.
10. "Some Blame Dam for High Erosion Rate," *Nashville Tennessean,* 1998, copy in Shiloh National Military Park Scrapbook, SNMP.
11. Shedd, *History of Shiloh National Military Park,* 52.
12. Leuchtenburg, *Franklin D. Roosevelt and the New Deal,* 120–23.
13. Lewis M. Anderson to "All C.W.A. Foremen," Jan. 30, 1934 and Lewis M. Anderson to "All Foremen Working on Civil Works Program," Jan. 29, 1934, both in Box 8, RG 79, NARA–Southeast Region, Atlanta.
14. Welch, *Archeology at Shiloh Indian Mounds,* 2.
15. Ibid., 95; Robert A. Livingston to Arno Cammerer, Jan. 18, 1934, Series 2, Box 19, Folder 309, SNMP.
16. Roberts Field Notebook; "List of Tools Loaned to CWA by Shiloh National Military Park."

17. Chambers, "Historical Reports: Indian Mounds—Shiloh"; Chambers Field Notebook; "Tennessee: The Shiloh Mound Group, Hardin County," 394–98; Welch, *Archeology at Shiloh Indian Mounds,* 95–96, 100, 102.

18. Chambers Field Notebook; Welch, *Archeology at Shiloh Indian Mounds,* 95.

19. Roberts, "Indian Mounds on Shiloh Battlefield," 65–68.

20. Ibid.; A. E. Demaray to Robert A. Livingston, Jan. 20, 1934, Series 2, Box 19, Folder 309, SNMP.

21. W. W. Luckett to Verne E. Chatelain, Nov. 18, 1935; "Research Studies, Shiloh National Military Park," n.d.; Charles S. Dunn to Branch Spalding, Nov. 22, 1937; and "Research Studies Made During the CWA Period, Shiloh National Military Park," n.d., all in "Historical Reports," Vertical Files, SNMP; Trustees M.E. Church to R. A. Livingston, Feb. 3, 1934, Box 8, RG 79, NARA–Southeast Region, Atlanta.

22. Leuchtenburg, *Franklin D. Roosevelt and the New Deal,* 133–34.

23. Robert A. Livingston to Verne A. Chatelain, Dec. 12, 1933, Series 2, Box 20, Folder 328, SNMP.

24. Shedd, *History of Shiloh National Military Park,* 46; Robert W. Andrews to Kenneth B. Simmons, Feb. 7, 1935, Series 2, Box 11, Folder 207, SNMP; Blueprints, "Entrance Stations," Series 8, Map Drawer 11, Folder 91, SNMP.

25. "Progress Report," Nov. 3, 1934, and "Final Analysis Report," July 11, 1935, both in Series 2, Box 23, Folder 387, SNMP; Blueprints, "Employee Residence #3, #4, #5, and #6," Series 8, Map Drawer 11, Folders 87–90, SNMP.

26. "Progress Report," Nov. 3 and 23, 1934, and Jan. 2, 1935, and "Final Analysis Report," July 11, 1935, all in Series 2, Box 23, Folder 387, SNMP; Blueprints, "Administration Building," Series 8, Map Drawer 11, Folder 86, SNMP.

27. "Specifications for Constructing the Concessions Building and Oil Storage Building, Shiloh National Military Park, Shiloh, Tennessee," Series 2, Box 16, Folder 260, SNMP; Blueprints, "Concessions Building," Series 8, Map Drawer 11, Folder 98, SNMP.

28. Leuchtenburg, *Franklin D. Roosevelt and the New Deal,* 174; John C. Paige, *The Civilian Conservation Corps and the National Park Service, 1933–1942: An Administrative History* (Washington, DC: National Park Service, 1985), 97. Much of the following discussion of the CCC at Shiloh is based on Timothy B. Smith, "Black Soldiers and the CCC at Shiloh National Military Park," *CRM: The Journal of Heritage Stewardship* 3, no. 2 (Summer 2006): 73–84.

29. "ECW Monthly Progress and Cost Report," Feb. 1937, E75, Box 7, RG 79, NARA; "Dedication of THC Marker for CCC Co. 2425, MP-3, Shiloh National Military Park, July 14, 1990," in Dedication Remarks for Placement of CCC Marker—July 14, 1990—Vertical File, SNMP; "Camp Inspection Report," Oct. 3, 1938, E 115, Box 199, RG 35, NARA; "2425th Company, MP-3,

Pittsburg Landing, Tennessee," in *Official Annual Civilian Conservation Corps "C" District, Fourth Corps Area—1937,* Patsy Weiler Collection, Albert Gore Research Center, Middle Tennessee State Univ. (hereafter cited as Weiler Collection). The *Official Annual* is also in the Civilian Conservation Corps (CCC) in Tennessee Collection, Tennessee State Library and Archives (hereafter cited as TSLA). See also Civilian Conservation Corps, RG 93, TSLA, for Tennessee camps. The enrollees came from Alabama, Mississippi, Florida, Georgia, North Carolina, Louisiana, Tennessee, and South Carolina.

30. Smith, *This Great Battlefield of Shiloh,* 123; "2423rd Company, MP-7, Corinth, Mississippi," in *Official Annual Civilian Conservation Corps "C" District, Fourth Corps Area—1937,* Weiler Collection; "Tennessee Camp MP-7," May 25, 1937; "Emergency Conservation Work Camp Report," Nov. 29, 1935, E 115, Box 199, RG 35, NARA; "Camp Report," July 8, 1934; "Camp Report," May 25, 1937; Toliver T. Thompson to J. S. Billups, Nov. 29, 1935, E 115, Box 199, RG 35, NARA; Jean Hager memo, May 25, 1937, E 115, Box 199, RG 35, NARA; Shedd, *History of Shiloh National Military Park,* 46. Enrollees came from Alabama, Mississippi, Georgia, Tennessee, and Florida. Later, men from New York, New Jersey, and West Virginia also joined the camp.

31. "Rated Members," Nov. 27, 1936, E 115, Box 199, RG 35, NARA; "Camp Report," July 8, 1936, E 115, Box 199, RG 35, NARA; "Forestry Personnel," Nov. 27, 1936, E 115, Box 199, RG 35, NARA; "Army Personnel," Nov. 27, 1936, E 115, Box 199, RG 35, NARA; "Camp Report," Nov. 29, 1935, E 115, Box 199, RG 35, NARA; "Fourth Enrollment Period Report, Tennessee Camp MP-3," Mar. 31, 1935, SNMP; Paige, *Administrative History,* 66. For more information on District C, Fourth Corps Area, see the Civilian Conservation Corps (CCC) in Tennessee Collection, TSLA.

32. Camp Report, July 8, 1936, Nov. 27, 1936, and May 25, 1937, all in E 115, Box 199, RG 35, NARA; T. J. McVey Construction Report, Nov. 27, 1936, E 115, Box 199, RG 35, NARA; Narrative Report of Tennessee Camp MP-7, Mar. 31, 1935, E 42, Box 28, RG 79, NARA.

33. Erosion control memo, Mar. 11, 1935, Series 2, Box 9, Folder 168, SNMP; Alex Bradford to R. A. Livingston, Mar. 31, 1935; E 42, Box 27, RG 79, NARA; Smith, *This Great Battlefield of Shiloh,* 99. For a detailed look at a particular project, see "Final Construction Report, Shiloh National Military Park, Eastern Corinth, Hamburg-Crump, and Peabody Monuments Roads, project 4A1," Series 1, Box 76, Folder 1126, SNMP. Included are maps, paperwork, and bids for the project.

34. O. E. Van Cleve to Governor Hill McAlister, July 19, 1935, and Secretary of War to Senator Kenneth McKellar, July 15, 1935, both in Hill McAlister Papers, Box 77, Folder 8, TSLA (hereafter cited as McAlister Papers); John A. Salmond, *The Civilian Conservation Corps, 1933–1942: A New Deal Case Study* (Durham, N.C.: Duke Univ. Press, 1967). The black CCC companies at Shiloh were but 2 of the nearly 150 such companies at camps nationwide.

35. Kenneth McKellar to Governor Hill McAlister, Aug. 27, 1935; Governor Hill McAlister to Kenneth McKellar, Aug. 30, 1935; John W. Hamilton to Governor Hill McAlister, Aug. 14, 1935, and Ralph Perry to John W. Hamilton, Aug. 15, 1935, all in McAlister Papers. Further research may reveal the extent to which public resistance to the presence of black CCC camps pushed the activity of the CCC to national parks.

36. "A Corinth Citizen" to President Roosevelt, June 30, 1937, E 115, Box 199, RG 35, NARA.

37. Chief National Park System Planning Section to Acting Superintendent, July 27, 1939, Series 2, Box 12, Folders 225, SNMP.

38. I. E. Smart to "Officers of the Veterans Administration at Washington DC," Apr. 13, 1936, E 115, Box 199, RG 35, NARA; J. S. Billups to J. J. McEntee, July 13, 1936, E 115, Box 199, RG 35, NARA; Charles H. Taylor to Adjutant General, Oct. 5, 1937, E 115, Box 199, RG 35, NARA. Although the CCC investigated the matter further, the results of its investigation are not documented.

39. John Hope Franklin, *From Slavery to Freedom: A History of Negro Americans,* 3rd ed. (New York: Vintage Books, 1969), 534–36; Leslie H. Fishel Jr. and Benjamin Quarles, *The Negro American: A Documentary History* (1967; reprint, Glenview, Ill.: Scott, Foresman, 1976), 448, 455, 463; James Oliver Horton and Lois E. Horton, *Hard Road to Freedom: The Story of African America* (New Brunswick, NJ: Rutgers Univ. Press, 2001), 265–67; Paige, *Administrative History,* 94.

40. See Timothy M. Davis, "Mission 66 Initiative," *CRM: The Journal of Heritage Stewardship* 1 no. 1 (fall 2003): 97–101 for more information on Mission 66.

41. Franklin, *From Slavery to Freedom,* 523–25, 534, 538; Paige, *Administrative History,* 97.

42. "Camp Report," Nov. 29, 1935, and undated report, both in E 115, Box 199, RG 35, NARA; "2423rd Company, MP-7, Corinth, Mississippi"; "Fourth Enrollment Period Report."

43. "Camp Inspection Report," May 15, 1940, E 115, Box 199, RG 35, NARA; Michael A. Capps, "Shiloh National Military Park: An Administrative History," 1993, unpublished manuscript, 43–45. For more information on the side camp, see Series 2, Box 7, Folders 112–13, SNMP. The side camp workers built the Ochs Museum at Point Park.

44. For the Bureau of Public Roads, see Record Group 30 in the National Archives. For the United States Geological Survey, see Record Group 57.

45. Robert A. Livingston to Oliver G. Taylor, May 1, 1934, Series 2, Box 20, Folder 320, SNMP; C. D. Monteith to R. W. Andrews, Sept. 28, 1934, Series 2, Box 9, Folder 178, SNMP; "Monumentation-Topo Maps," Series 7, Map Drawer 5, Folder 93, SNMP.

46. Blueprints, "Proposed Eastern Corinth, Hamburg-Crump and Peabody Monument Roads," Series 8, Map Drawer 8, Folder 43, SNMP; "Maintenance and Post Construction for Shiloh National Military Park," Series 2, Box 21, Folder 343, SNMP; "Final Construction Report—Project 4A1," Miscellaneous Files, SNMP.

47. "Maintenance and Post Construction for Shiloh National Military Park," Series 2, Box 21, Folder 343, SNMP; "Final Construction Report—Project 4A1"; Blueprints, "Proposed Hamburg-Purdy and Corinth-Headquarters Roads," Series 8, Map Drawer 8, Folder 42, SNMP.

48. "Recommendation for the Naming and Altering of Certain Names of Roads Within Shiloh National Military Park," and A. E. Demaray to Robert A. Livingston, Mar. 12, 1936, Series 2, Box 21, Folder 345, SNMP; "Final Construction Report—Project 4A1."

49. Smith, *This Great Battlefield of Shiloh,* 120–21.

50. For Livingston's approval of most projects, see the various blueprints of work with his signature, Series 8, SNMP.

51. "Hearing Before Special Committee, Senate Resolution No. 198," 9, Nov. 18–19, 1935, SNMP; James Marvin Powell, *NBH: A Biography of Nicholas Brodie Hardeman* (Nashville: Gospel Advocate, 1964), 352.

52. Robert Dean Pope, "Senatorial Baron: The Long Political Career of Kenneth D. McKellar" (Ph.D. diss., Yale Univ., 1976); "Hearing Before Special Committee, Senate Resolution No. 198," 165, 317; James W. Lantrip Jr., "Kenneth McKellar's Role in the Investigation of War Industries, 1917–1918," *West Tennessee Historical Society Papers* 55 (2001): 72–97; "Fued," *Time,* May 25, 1942; "The Facts of Life," *Time,* May 14, 1945.

53. "Hearing Before Special Committee, Senate Resolution No. 198," 1, 28–30, 72, 121; "Senators McKellar and Frazier," *Savannah Courier,* Nov. 22, 1935.

54. "Hearing Before Special Committee, Senate Resolution No. 198," 40, 133, 225–27, 230, 436.

55. "Hearing Before Special Committee, Senate Resolution No. 198," 321, 445.

56. "Livingston Resigns as Supt. Park," *Savannah Courier,* Apr. 17, 1936; Zeb McKinney email to author, Jan. 25, 2006; Smith, *This Great Battlefield of Shiloh,* 136.

## 9. History in the Making

1. The author was the ranger at the desk.

2. The author also heard these comments from the public. For a good feel of how visitors view the film, see the Shiloh National Military Park visitor register for polarized comments.

3. The only possible comparison is *Story of a Patriot,* produced and shown at Colonial Williamsburg since 1957.
4. Charles S. Dunn to Director, Mar. 13, 1937, Series 1, Box 57, Folder 884, SNMP.
5. Unidentified newspaper clipping, n.d., Series 1, Box 58, Folder 902, SNMP; John O. Cunningham, interview with author, June 14, 2005; "Major Lykes to Speak at Methodist Church Tonight," *Iuka Vidette,* Feb. 24, 1955, Series 1, Box 58, Folder 902, SNMP.
6. "Slide Index—Shiloh Portrait of a Battle," n.d., and "Narration for Shiloh Slide Lecture," Oct. 6, 1953, both in Series 1, Box 78, Folder 1144, SNMP; unidentified newspaper clipping, n.d., Series 1, Box 58, Folder 902, SNMP.
7. "Slide Index—Shiloh Portrait of a Battle" and "Narration for Shiloh Slide Lecture."
8. Paul Flowers to James W. Howell, Oct. 17, 1954, Series 1, Box 78, Folder 1144, SNMP; *Jackson Sun,* Feb. 16, 1955, Series 1, Box 58, Folder 902, SNMP; unidentified newspaper clipping, n.d., Series 1, Box 58, Folder 902, SNMP; unidentified newspaper clipping, n.d., Series 1, Box 58, Folder 902, SNMP.
9. *Jackson Sun,* Feb. 16, 1955; "Motion Picture of 'Shiloh—Portrait of a Battle,'" n.d., Series 1, Box 78, Folder 1144, SNMP; "Battlefield Will Come Alive in Shiloh Film Tomorrow," *Memphis Commercial Appeal,* Apr. 6, 1956, Series 1, Box 59, Folder 905, SNMP.
10. "Motion Picture of 'Shiloh—Portrait of a Battle.'"
11. Francis C. Shelton to Joe Winningham, Mar. 12, 1955, and Ira B. Lykes to R. A. Livingston, Feb. 17, 1955, both in Series 1, Box 78, Folder 1144, SNMP; Ira B. Lykes to Bob Guinn, Oct. 18, 1954, Series 1, Box 78, Folder 1144, SNMP. It is a tremendous testimony to Livingston that he remained involved and dedicated to Shiloh even after his resignation. He faithfully wrote each donor a thank you note on behalf of the association.
12. "Money Contributions to Shiloh Motion Picture," through May 6, 1955, Series 1, Box 78, Folder 1144, SNMP; Paul Flowers to Tennessee Historical Commission, Feb. 28, 1955, Series 1, Box 57, Folder 884, SNMP.
13. *Jackson Sun,* Feb. 16, 1955; J. Louis Adams to G. Edward Friar, Mar. 7, 1955, Series 1, Box 78, Folder 1144, SNMP.
14. Ira B. Lykes to Lou Peneguy, Dec. 31, 1958, Series 1, Box 78, Folder 1145, SNMP.
15. Ira Lykes to Herbert Kahler, n.d., and Ira B. Lykes to Ray Dame, Sept. 30, 1954, both in Series 1, Box 78, Folder 1144, SNMP; unidentified newspaper clipping, n.d., Series 1, Box 58, Folder 902, SNMP.
16. Unidentified newspaper clipping, n.d., Series 1, Box 58, Folder 902, SNMP; "Shiloh—Portrait of a Battle," Series 1, Box 78, Folder 1145, SNMP.

17. Ira B. Lykes to Paul Flowers, Oct. 7, 1955, Series 1, Box 78, Folder 1144, SNMP; "Shiloh—Portrait of a Battle," SNMP.

18. "Work Underway on Color Film of Shiloh Battle; Weapons Needed for Shooting Scenes April 4–5," *Daily Corinthian,* Mar. 17, 1955, Series 1, Box 58, Folder 902, SNMP; "Loan of Equipment for Use in Production of Shiloh Motion Picture," May 6, 1955, Series 1, Box 78, Folder 1144, SNMP; "Shiloh Lives Again in Film," *Washington Post,* Apr. 17, 1956, Series 1, Box 59, Folder 905, SNMP.

19. "Work Underway on Color Film of Shiloh Battle; Weapons Needed for Shooting Scenes April 4–5"; Clyde Tapp, interview with author, June 7, 2005; John O. Cunningham, interview with author, June 7, 2005; Henry Outlaw, interview with author, June 14, 2005.

20. "Shiloh—Portrait of a Battle," SNMP; Outlaw interview.

21. "Work Underway on Color Film of Shiloh Battle; Weapons Needed for Shooting Scenes April 4–5"; "Loan of Horses, Saddles, Teams, Wagons, and Surrey for Use in Motion Picture," Series 1, Box 78, Folder 1144, SNMP; James Lewis, interview with author, Apr. 29, 2005; Cunningham interview, June 14, 2005.

22. Wilmer W. Nichols, interview with author, June 9, 2005; Lewis interview; Bobby Nichols, interview with author, June 14, 2005; Lowell Blakney, interview with author, July 9, 2005.

23. Outlaw interview; Jimmy Cooksey, interview with author, June 4, 2005.

24. "Shiloh Park Group Gets Buffalo Meat for April Feast," *Daily Corinthian,* Mar. 7, 1955, Series 1, Box 58, Folder 902, SNMP; Lewis interview; Cunningham interview, June 7, 2005; Wilmer W. Nichols, interview; Outlaw interview.

25. "Shiloh Lives Again in Film"; James W. Howell to Superintendent, Fredericksburg National Military Park, May 13, 1955, Series 1, Box 78, Folder 1144, SNMP; James W. Howell to Gordon Draper, May 14, 1955, Series 1, Box 78, Folder 1144, SNMP; Lewis interview; "Motion Picture of 'Shiloh—Portrait of a Battle'"; "Shiloh—Portrait of a Battle," SNMP.

26. Ira Lykes to "Peoples," June 8, 1955, Series 1, Box 78, Folder 1144, SNMP.

27. Ira B. Lykes to Paul Flowers, Oct. 7, 1955, and Ira B. Lykes to Seale Johnson, Apr. 6, 1956, both in Series 1, Box 78, Folder 1144, SNMP; J. Louis Adams to John Mercier, June 21, 1956, Series 1, Box 78, Folder 1145, SNMP. For a look at the complexity of the script, see "Script—Editorial Notes and Matching Instructions for the Sound Motion Picture Documentary 'Shiloh—Portrait of a Battle,'" Nov. 15, 1955, Artifact Cabinet 1, Drawer 7, SNMP; "Battlefield Will Come Alive in Shiloh Film Tomorrow."

28. Lykes to Flowers, Oct. 7, 1955; Shipping Memorandum, Jan. 18, 1956; and James W. Holland to Ira B. Lykes, May 10, 1956; and Lykes to Flowers,

Oct. 7, 1955, all in Series 1, Box 78, Folder 1144, SNMP; "Battlefield Will Come Alive in Shiloh Film Tomorrow."

29. Lykes to Flowers, Oct. 7, 1955, and Lykes to Johnson, Apr. 6, 1956; Adams to Mercier, June 21, 1956; "Battlefield Will Come Alive in Shiloh Film Tomorrow"; Charles S. Shedd to Lloyd S. Howard, Apr. 13, 1957, B. C. Yates to Superintendent Shiloh National Military Park, Nov. 26, 1958, and Floyd B. Taylor to Leslie Houston, Apr. 22, 1957, all in Series 1, Box 78, Folder 1145, SNMP.

30. "Unit Citation," n.d., Series 1, Box 78, Folder 1146, SNMP; Conrad L. Wirth to Regional Directors, n.d., Series 1, Box 78, Folder 1144, SNMP.

31. Outlaw interview; "Shiloh Lives Again in Film"; "Shiloh—Portrait of a Battle," SNMP.

32. Acting Regional Director to Superintendent, Shiloh, Sept. 29, 1961, Series 1, Box 78, Folder 1145, SNMP. One man complained as early as 1961 that Kansas had been left off the map of the states in the introduction.

33. Edwin C. Bearss, Chief Historian Emeritus, National Park Service, interview with author, Aug. 11, 2004.

34. William C. Davis, *The Cause Lost: Myths and Realities of the Confederacy* (Lawrence: Univ. Press of Kansas, 1996), 200.

35. *OR,* vol. 10, pt. 1:277–80; "First Reunion of Iowa Hornet's Nest Brigade, October 12–13, 1887"; Reed, *Battle of Shiloh.*

36. Rice, *Story of Shiloh*; Eisenschiml, *Story of Shiloh.*

37. O. E. Cunningham, "Shiloh and the Western Campaign of 1862" (Ph.D. diss., Louisiana State Univ., 1966); Sword, *Shiloh*; McDonough, *Shiloh.*

38. Bearss interview, Aug. 11, 2004.

# Index

*Rethinking Shiloh* was designed and typeset on a Macintosh OS 10.4 computer system using InDesign software. The body text is set in 10/13 Adobe Caslon Pro and display type is set in Americana. This book was designed and typeset by Stephanie Thompson and manufactured by Thomson-Shore, Inc.